Posttraumatic Stress Disorder:
A Lifespan Developmental Perspective

Andreas Maercker
Matthias Schützwohl
Zahava Solomon
(Editors)

Posttraumatic Stress Disorder

A Lifespan Developmental Perspective

Hogrefe & Huber Publishers

Seattle · Toronto · Bern · Göttingen

Library of Congress Cataloging-in-Publication Data

Post-traumatic stress disorder : a lifespan developmental perspective /
edited by Andreas Maercker, Matthias Schützwohl, Zahava Solomon
  p. cm.
  Includes bibliographical references.
  ISBN 0-88937-187-3
1. Post-traumatic stress disorder—Age factors. I. Maercker, Andreas,
1960– . II. Schützwohl, Matthias, 1962– . III. Solomon, Zahava.
RC552.P67P665   1999   616.85'21—dc21   98-36649 CIP

Canadian Cataloguing in Publication Data

Main entry under title:
Post-traumatic stress disorder: A lifespan developmental perspective
Includes bibliographical references and index.
ISBN 0-88937-187-3
1. Post-traumatic stress disorder. 2. Life change events – Psychological aspects.
I. Maercker, Andreas, 1960– . II. Schützwohl, Matthias, 1962– . III.
Solomon, Zahava.
RC552.P67P67   1999   616.85'21   C98-931811-7

© Copyright 1999 by Hogrefe & Huber Publishers

USA:	P.O. Box 2487, Kirkland, WA 98083-2487
	Phone (425) 820-1500, Fax (425) 823-8324
CANADA:	12 Bruce Park Avenue, Toronto, Ontario M4P 2S3
	Phone (416) 482-6339
SWITZERLAND:	Länggass-Strasse 76, CH-3000 Bern 9
	Phone (031) 300-4500, Fax (031) 300-4590
GERMANY:	Rohnsweg 25, D-37085 Göttingen
	Phone (0551) 49609-0, Fax (0551) 49609-88

Printed and bound in USA
ISBN 0-88937-187-3

Publication of this volume was supported by the Public Health Research Network in Saxony (# DLR 01 EG 9410, A3).

Contents

PART III: FROM ADULTHOOD TO OLD AGE

PART IV: COPING, SOCIAL SUPPORT, MEANING, AND GROWTH

List of Contributors

George A. Bonnano, PhD
Department of Psychology
The Life Cycle Institute
The Catholic University of America
Washington, DC 20064
USA

Sigrun-Heide Filipp, PhD
University of Trier
Department of Psychology
Tarforst
D-54286 Trier
Germany

Karni Ginzburg, MA
The Bob Shapell School of Social
Work
Tel Aviv University
Ramat Aviv
Tel Aviv, 69978
Israel

Werner Greve, PhD
Criminological Research Institute of
Lower Saxony
Lützerodestr. 9
D-30161 Hanover
Germany

Daniela Hosser, Dipl. Psych.
Criminological Research Institute of
Lower Saxony
Lützerodestr. 9
D-30161 Hanover
Germany

Andreas Kruse, PhD
Department of Psychology
University of Heidelberg
Bergheimer Str. 20
D-69115 Heidelberg
Germany

Tamar Lavi, BA
The Bob Shapell School of Social
Work
Tel Aviv University
Ramat Aviv
Tel Aviv, 69978
Israel

Andreas Maercker, PhD, MD
Dresden University of Technology
Department of Psychology
D-01062 Dresden
Germany

Rolf Manz, PhD
Dresden University of Technology
Research Association Public Health
Saxony
Fiedlerstr. 27
D-01307 Dresden
Germany

Eric Schmitt, PhD
Department of Gerontology
University of Heidelberg
Bergheimer Str. 20
D-69115 Heidelberg
Germany

Matthias Schützwohl, Dipl. Psych.
Dresden University of Technology
Department of Psychology
D-01062 Dresden
Germany

Zahava Solomon, PhD
The Bob Shapell School of Social
Work
Tel Aviv University
Ramat Aviv
Tel Aviv, 69978
Israel

Crystal Park, PhD
Psychology Department
Miami University
Oxford, OH 45056
USA

Axel Perkonig, PhD
Department of Psychiatry
University of Regensburg
Universitätsstr. 84
D-93042 Regensburg
Germany

Frauke Teegen, PhD
Department of Psychology
University of Hamburg
Von-Melle-Park 5
D-20146 Hamburg
Germany

Hans-Ulrich Wittchen, PhD
Max-Planck-Institute of Psychiatry
Clinical Psychology and
Epidemiology Unit
Kraepelinstr. 2
D-80804 Munich
Germany

Introduction:
Developmental-Related Trauma Studies

Andreas Maercker, Zahava Solomon and Matthias Schützwohl

While traumatic stress often results in PTSD and other psychopathologies, there is considerable variability in response to traumatic events. Some people develop pathology, some are or seem to be unaffected, and yet others report increased maturity and depth of personality. A host of biological, psychological, and social factors have been proposed as being implicated in both the risk and course of PTSD. But the fact that traumatic events are usually sudden and unexpected and the fact that traumatization itself can bring about a range of physiological, personality, social changes together make it difficult, probably impossible, to obtain reliable information about predisposition.

Among the few variables that can be investigated independently of the trauma itself is age, or developmental phase. This volume documents our expanding knowledge of three areas: (1) trauma aftereffects related to the age at which the traumatic experience occurs, (2) continuities and discontinuities in self-concept following trauma, and (3) trauma-caused developmental changes throughout the lifespan.

Age or developmental stage has been recognized as a risk factor in traumatization ever since biblical times: "Law prohibits sending a whole list of men to battle. These are men who have recently married, planted their vineyards but not harvested their fruits" (Deuteronomy, 20: 5–8). In other words, the law proposes that at certain life stages, persons are focused on their developmental tasks and do not have the psychological energy to deal with major stressors.

Developmental phase can be regarded as one of the variables that may affect the outcome of traumatic experiences. Yet although various studies have linked the age at which the traumatic experience occurs to its aftereffects, the issue has not been thoroughly explored. Two contrasting assumptions – that trauma aftereffects are the product of pretrauma personality defects and, alternatively, that trauma largely overshadows the entire pretrauma character – have led to the relegation of age to a minor variable in most studies.

This volume attempts to redress this imbalance by looking at how developmental phase is related to coping with traumatic events. It asks how similar stressors effect people who experience them at different stages of their lives. Are children, adolescents, young adults, midlifers, and the elderly effected in the same way? Does children's limited understanding of danger accord them protection? Or do their limited coping abilities render them more vulnerable? Does adult maturity increase resilience? Or do the responsibilities of adulthood increase the burden? What happens to the elderly? Does a lifetime of accumulated experience give them the wisdom to overcome trauma? Or does the frailty of age undermine their ability to deal with it?

It is generally agreed that different developmental phases entail different tasks and pose different challenges. How does the traumatic experience affect those tasks and challenges? For example, how does it effect a young person's moral development and perception of death? And his or her ability to form and maintain intimate relationships?

Trauma usually shatters that continuity that is generally considered crucial to adult development. Traumatized persons often divide their lives between before and after the trauma. Although most studies point to a decrease in distress over time, the traumatic experience invariably leaves a deep and enduring imprint, not only in the form of ineradicable memories but in the entire personality and orientation to life. Even persons who are free of clinical symptoms have been found to suffer from a certain alienation, difficulties in intimate relationships, and a sense of foreshortened future. Their view of the world and themselves generally changes, as the trauma strikes at their assumptions of an orderly, safe, and just world, at their sense of human goodness and self-worth. At the same time, there are people who emerge from traumatic experience with an enhanced sense of strength and self-esteem. This book examines not only posttraumatic pathology, but these changes as well, both the losses and the gains.

The third issue that this volume explores is the different manifestations of prior trauma at different points of the life cycle. PTSD is notoriously chameleon. In many cases, it develops within a short time after the traumatic event; in others, years may pass before its delayed onset. Usually, after an initial period of virulence, its symptoms subside, only to flare up again, triggered by age, illness, or a stressful event, developmental life change, or chance occurrence that is reminiscent of the traumatic event.

Several chapters in this book focus on the repercussions of earlier trauma in old age. At this period of life, the increase in free time, reduction of social interaction, and the loss of meaningful occupation that come with retirement; the convergence of losses in the form of declining health and strength and the death of spouse and friends; the tendency to engage in intensive life review; and the spectre of impending death may all create particular stress. The elderly who have endured trauma are especially vulnerable to delayed onset PTSD or to exacerbation or reactivation of earlier stress reactions.

The book takes a lifespan approach. This is not a theory per se, but a way of viewing human development: as a multidimensional lifelong process characterized by an amalgam of gains and losses, vulnerability and resistance, and variability both within and among persons. It seeks to relate to persons over different phases in life, beyond their obvious individual differences. It recognizes that human development is not simply a function of biological and psychological processes, but also of social and historical changes. With respect to trauma, this means that events that occur after the traumatic experience, such as the social reception of the survivors, may also affect its outcome.

The core methodology of the lifespan approach is the longitudinal study. Unfortunately, being a preliminary effort to look at trauma from a lifespan perspective, the book has more cross-sectional and retrospective studies than longitudinal ones. It is hoped that these findings will inspire more longitudinal research.

The first two chapters introduce various aspects of lifespan developmental psychology.

In Chapter 2, Maercker outlines lifespan developmental propositions and applies them to the differential effects of traumatization in youth and old age. The first part of the chapter presents symptom trajectories of victims of persecution and crime, the second part deals with changes in occupational and social functioning in younger and older trauma victims.

In Chapter 3, Filipp presents a three-step social cognitive model of readaptation after extreme events, beginning with the construction of perceptive reality, followed by comparative processes, and ending with a re-interpretation of reality.

The next three chapters deal with the aftereffects of trauma suffered in childhood and youth.

In Chapter 4, Solomon and Lavi address the relationship between age and traumatization issue through the perspective of the impact of war on children. Most of our knowledge of the traumatic effects of war relates to adults, that is the soldiers who fight it. But the increasing involvement of children in wars makes it imperative to explore the impact of war on young people.

In Chapter 5, Teegen presents her research findings on the long-term sequelae of childhood sexual assault as well as on the factors that precipitate the symptoms and maintain them for decades after the initial traumatization.

In Chapter 6, Perkonigg and Wittchen present the findings of an epidemiological study regarding the lifetime prevalence of traumatic events in adolescence and young adulthood, as well as the age of onset, risk factors for PTSD, and the comorbidity of traumatic events and PTSD with other disorders.

Chapters 7 through 9 focus on the impact of trauma in old age.

In Chapter 7, Solomon and Ginzburg examine how the elderly respond to trauma. The first part explores the effect of this developmental stage on adjustment to current trauma, asking whether the elderly cope with and adjust to such trauma differently from younger adults. The second part explores whether prior experiences, including earlier exposure to trauma, affect persons' adjustment to aging – that is whether the aging process of trauma victims differs from that of persons who had the good fortune to have been spared earlier trauma.

In Chapter 8, Kruse and Schmitt present data showing that the perception of current life situations by Jews who survived extermination camps as young adults or were forced to flee Nazi Germany is colored by these experiences. They further show that reminiscences of the earlier trauma are intensified with age. They also investigate, the conditions that provoke recollection and the association between recollection and coping.

Chapter 9 focuses on the impact of trauma occurring in old age. In a representative survey of elderly crime victims, Hosser and Greve explore the psychological effects of criminal victimization and the moderating influences of social support and coping resources. On the basis of their findings, they argue the need for a specific geronto-victimological perspective in trauma study.

The last three chapters deal with the interplay between traumatic effects and personal coping, social support, and historical context.

In Chapter 10, Schützwohl, Maercker, and Manz show that years after their political persecution, the social support received by the former victims ameliorated the degree of traumatic hyperarousal, though, on the other hand, the social support they received was lessened by posttraumatic avoidance behavior.

In Chapter 11, Bonanno discusses one of the basic psychological assumption of trauma processing: the "working-through" hypotheses. He puts it in cross-cultural perspective and by this mean shows its limits.

In Chapter 12, Park gives a prospect on a different side of trauma aftereffects and assess the potential positive affects of trauma, conceptualized as personal growth (psychological maturity). It illustrates how — in life-span terms — there are both "gains and losses" associated with experiencing trauma.

In closing, we hope to provide an enhanced vision of human lifespan developmental processes as applied to extreme stress responses.

What remains for the future? New propositions and hypotheses should be derived, developed, and tested. More work is needed to integrate theories of development, aging, functional adaptation, and PTSD. Researchers in the PTSD field, life-span developmentalists, and gerontologists should cooperate in interdisciplinary, longitudinal research to advance our knowledge and to develop appropriate intervention programs in this area.

PART I:
INCORPORATING
LIFESPAN
PROPOSITIONS

Lifespan Psychological Aspects of Trauma and PTSD: Symptoms and Psychosocial Impairments*

Andreas Maercker

The aim of this chapter is to find clues as to what role chronological age or developmental phase plays in the process of adaptation following traumatization. The chapter's basic assumption is that a person's psychological as well as biological developmental stage has significant influence on the nature, extent, and pattern of posttraumatic stress disorder (PTSD). Developmental influences are thought to orchestrate the other known etiological factors for PTSD such as trauma severity and cognitive processing.

Two assumptions will be discussed in detail and investigated empirically: (1) that there exist specific vulnerable life stages, e. g., adolescence and old age, that are responsible for particularly severe PTSD symptoms after traumatization; (2) that traumatization leads to psychosocial disadvantages (in partnership, family, education, and professional career) depending on the developmental stage during which traumatization occurred. Thus, throughout this chapter a distinction is made between clinical PTSD symptoms and psychosocial consequences (or disadvantages) of traumatization during lifespan. The latter may not only result from trauma but can also be due to stress and changes caused by posttraumatic symptomatology. This distinction seems important with regard to some investigations where the two areas are not disentangled (see McFarlane & Yehuda, 1996).

The empirical part of the chapter is based on two trauma groups with manmade traumas: former political prisoners in the former East Germany and crime victims (Maercker & Schützwohl, 1997; Schützwohl & Maercker, 1997).

---

* The research reported in this chapter was supported by a grant from the German Federal Ministry of Education and Research (Forschungsverbund Public Health Sachsen DLR01EG9410, A3). I gratefully acknowledge the contributions and collegial support by Frank Eckhardt, Ilona Glöckner, Michael Hillmann, Jürgen Margraf, Britta Schöne, and Matthias Schützwohl. Special thanks are due to Alexandra M. Freund (Max-Planck-Institute for Human Development and Education) for her helpful comments on an earlier draft.

It is expected that both trauma groups will contribute to similar life span consequences although the crime-victim group stands for a singular trauma of short duration (Type I trauma) whereas the imprisonment group stands for a multiple longer-lasting trauma (Type II trauma; see Terr, 1989).

Contributions Toward a Developmental Lifespan Psychopathology

The assumptions put forward in this chapter reach beyond the scope of psychopathology, clinical psychology or psychiatry thereby broadening the focus to include lifespan developmental psychopathology. Lifespan developmental psychopathology is a subdiscipline of clinical as well as developmental psychology. It has so far only taken the form of theoretical approach (see Lerner, Hess, & Nitz, 1990; Maercker, 1998; Noam & Gill, 1991; see Chapter 1) which is defined as an area of research exploring psychological disorders and forms of therapy in relation to biological, psychological, and social processes of individual development. Lifespan developmental psychopathology constitutes an extension of developmental psychopathology of childhood and adolescence (Cicchetti & Cohen, 1995; Rutter & Garmezy, 1983; Rutter, 1994) and encompasses the entire lifespan from infancy to old age.

Two methodological sources are of particular relevance in this respect: first, the approach of general lifespan psychology (e. g., Baltes, 1987, 1997; Lerner, 1986) and, second, systematic longitudinal investigations of psychological disorders (e. g., Angst, 1986; Häfner, Nowotny, Löffler, an der Heiden, & Maurer, 1995; Walker, 1991; Wittchen & v. Zerssen, 1987). Both approaches are comparatively novel – they were introduced in the 1980s and 1990s and have as yet hardly been applied by the broader scientific community in clinical psychology and psychiatry.

Lifespan psychology focuses on a number of basic methodological positions that can also serve as reference points in the investigation of traumatization and posttraumatic stress disorder. Of several basic positions formulated by lifespan psychologists (see Baltes, 1987, 1997) only the most relevant to the present context will be introduced:

- *Multidimensionality.* Development is a lifelong process that encompasses biological, psychological, and social processes closely interacting with one another. The term development refers to microstructural biological changes, changes in mental performance levels, capability of experiencing, and changes in social roles.
- *Multidirectionality.* Processes of change may take place simultaneously but not necessarily uniformly. This applies to changes within and between various biological, psychological, and social spheres of development.

– *Multifunctionality*. Development subsumes positive advancements ("gains") or negative disadvancements ("losses") in the adaptive physical and psychological capacity of the organism to interact with his or her environment.

These positions were developed for the purpose of studying psychological phenomena *across all ages*, ranging from childhood into old age. In contrast to the assumption of orderly hierarchical stages specific to certain age stages (e. g., Erikson, 1959; Vaillant, 1977), multidimensionality, multidirectionality, and multifunctionality occur across all stages of the life cycle in integral areas of functioning such as occupation (Havighurst, 1972), social roles (Elder, 1974), sexual behavior (Masters & Johnson, 1970), social relations (Carstensen, 1991), personality development (Loevinger, 1976; McCrae & Costa, 1990), and use of leisure time (Neugarten, 1974). All of these areas of functioning ebb and flow across every individual's life span.

Lifespan research on mental disorders still exist only in rudiment. Systematic longitudinal investigations of psychological disorders were done primarily for the most widespread of psychological disorders: for schizophrenia (Häfner et al., 1995; Walker, 1991), for affective disorders/depression (Angst, 1986; Bronisch et al., 1987), and for anxiety disorders (Wittchen & v. Zerssen, 1987). Research objectives of these investigations are, e. g., age of onset, changes in symptom patterns, disorder-related social shifts, and spontaneous remissions over extended periods of years. Any one of these topics is also of potential interest to PTSD research.

To take schizophrenia research as an example, it has been shown that the differences in age of primary onset correspond with different developmental processes of biological systems specifically with regard to hormonal changes (Häfner et al., 1995). The difference in age of onset leads to different levels of highest educational levels achieved. Furthermore, it was also shown that individuals who get ill at an earlier age tend to develop greater extents of social deficits then do those who developed symptoms at an older age. Moreover, recent findings point to the fact that schizophrenic symptoms diminish in old age and show milder disturbances which allow for improved social (re)integration in advanced life stages.

For PTSD, there are almost no analyses of lifetime longitudinal data that could offer insights in the long-term course of PTSD. However, a conceptual framework of PTSD's longitudinal course has been proposed by McFarlane and Yehuda (1996). Rather than describing the possible symptom changes over time, this model is aimed at describing different etiological factors contributing to the precipitation and maintenance of the disorder (e. g., preevent, event, and postevent factors). It also incorporates other possible influences on traumatization in terms of a resiliency-vulnerability concept. Single factors described

are "personality," "past experience," "family history," and coping style. McFarlane and Yehuda (1996) place the trauma aftermath into the life course but do
not relate its investigation to lifespan psychological positions and findings.

Chronological Age and Developmental Phases

The variable "chronological age" is only of limited heuristic value for investigating development (Wohlwill, 1970; Schaie, 1965). Most psychiatric investigations, however, explore chronological age in terms of interval scales (with years
or decades as time units). In most cases these studies lack conclusive explanations and models regarding the causal relationships of age effects. Chronological age or the passage of time has no exploratory value in itself. Pathological
changes do not come about as a result of passage of time but rather as the
result of life events and/or psychological and biological processes that affect
these changes. Such events and processes may correlate with age in various
ways. Age has to be seen merely as cover variable or proxi for numerous
reactions that take the course of varying temporal dynamics. The influence of
biogenetic factors, for example, diminishes during the period of adult age,
whereas the importance of personal, sociopsychologically formed goal-setting
increases (Baltes, 1997).

For scientific purposes it is therefore useful to investigate lifelong processes
by means of a concept of defined developmental phases or periods rather than
by reference to the continuous age variable. The differentiation between life
stages was fertilized by the drawing up of the concept of development tasks
(Havinghurst, 1972; see detailed description below in Section 4.1). These tasks
are defined by approximately constant biological and psychosocial phenomena. Their variance in temporal appearance can, however, be accounted for.

The distinction that is currently being drawn in textbooks of developmental
psychology (e. g., Bornstein, 1992) divides the life-stages to be considered in
relevant studies into: adolescence between the ages of 13–22 years (first phase
"adolescence" 13–17, second phase "youth" 18–22), young adulthood (ranging
from 22–35), middle adulthood (35–50) and late adulthood (50–60/65). This is
followed by older age, where differentiations are made between early senescence (60/65–75) and late senescence (over 75).

So far, current studies on trauma and their psychological consequences do
not follow the distinction made in developmental psychology. Instead they
employ either numeric divisions according to decades (e. g., age-group 30–39,
40–49, etc.) or pragmatic-atheoretical divisions (e. g., "persons below 60 years
old," "persons above 60 years old"). The purpose of the latter divisions is
primarily to gain group sizes of approximately equal proportions. In part, this
lead to findings about seemingly equal age groups (e. g., "older persons"), that

can hardly be compared with one another, as age-boundaries are too differentiate ("elderly," i. e., > 50 years vs. "elderly," i. e., > 65 years).

Theories of the Effect of Age-at-Traumatization on Symptomatology

In this section, the assumption is elaborated that age at traumatization has an important impact on the probability of developing posttraumatic stress disorder *(age-differential vulnerability)*. It is hypothesized that childhood, adolescence and senescence are phases in life bearing a particularly high risk for the development of PTSD. The following discussion, however, is limited to adolescence and old age as high risk periods because my studies thus far do not encompass childhood. In this section, I focus on the nature and the extent of symptomology rather than on further psychosocial consequences of age-differential vulnerability, e. g., professional achievement and family satisfaction.

Researchers in the 1950s and 1960s pointed out successive patterns of different psychiatric disorders for different ages at traumatization (von Baeyer, Häfner, & Kisker, 1964; Bensheim, 1960; Strauss, 1957). More recently, stress theory served as background for psychological research on war and disaster aftermaths (Norris & Murell, 1988; Solomon, 1995). Based on this research, I will argue for a broader view on age-related psychological and biological changes that allows for the construction of models of traumatization effects.

The following two excerpts taken from Maercker (1998a) will exemplify subjective views reflecting a heightened vulnerability during adolescence:

A young woman who was imprisoned for political reasons at the age of 17 reports:

And then I was sentenced to 10 months in jail. I was seventeen years old at the time. And that was kind of, well you can imagine, when you come to experience something like that at such a young age; you know, my first really bad experience in life. I guess that really got to me. First, because I was really pretty green until then and then sort of got pulled out of a perfect idyll. You know I grew up in a village. Everything was normal at home. I had a really normal home, you know, always harmony. And then all of a sudden something like that happens to me. You see, I'd never had any bad experiences before or anything really negative. And that was the first one and so damn hard and really bad from the start. Well, that was basically the worst about it all.

A man who was imprisoned at the age of 20 reports:

. . . (I was put) into solitary confinement without anything, behind thick walls at just twenty years of age. And then all that began. That was the shock of my

life. . . . I had no strategy. First – talking about the first couple of weeks here – the first weeks were paralyzing. That's what it was for me anyway; I couldn't even think straight. You have to imagine I was just twenty. Hey, that's no excuse, but it gives you an idea. That – I never imagined would ever happen to me. You know I imagined I could escape (the country) – manage to get across the border with all my poems. Get them published. You see I did have plans – just in case I got lucky; not in case that things got out of hand. You see, I never thought – what do I do if I get jailed? I never wasted a thought on that idea. I was in an absolutely positive frame of mind. And then it oc- curred to me – . . . life, its all over for me, cut, over, buried alive. . . . It was in effect the forming experience of my life. . . . .

What these examples show is that victims themselves reflect a relation be- tween a certain age at traumatization and severity of trauma sequelae.

Early Studies on Successive Disorder Patterns

There are only few studies on the relationship between age of traumatization and symptomatology. Earlier psychiatric studies focused on determining a suc- cession of ages of onset (predilection ages) and their related syndromes (von Baeyer et al., 1964; Bensheim, 1960; Strauss, 1957). Psychiatrists referred to the typical consequences of traumatization through experiences in concentration camps during childhood – before the age of ten – as "autistic arrest of devel- opment" (Bensheim, 1960, p. 465). The consequences of traumatization during adolescence were labelled anxiety problems. Traumas occurring during "ma- ture adulthood" (21–51) were thought to cause reactive depressions and neur- asthenia (von Baeyer et al., 1964, p. 135 f.). Syndrome frequencies served as empirical proof of this succession of predilection ages. However, the studies suffered from methodological weaknesses. For example, it is doubtful whether diagnoses of syndromes were made independent of assumptions about the relation of predilection age and symptoms.

A different sequence was postulated by Bensheim (1960) who investigated the psychological consequences of detention in concentration camps casuisti- cally. He assumed that traumatization during childhood would lead to changes in psychomotor functioning in later life such as chronic urge to move, hysterical movement disorders as well as anxiety attacks, and antisocial behavior. Trau- matization during adolescence was assumed to lead to psychovegetative prob- lems, e. g., heart neurosis, psychosomatic illnesses. Furthermore, traumatization during early adulthood would lead to chronic anxiety states, e. g., intrusive recollections, dreams of anguish and depressive states – these descriptions come closest to current definitions of PTSD symptomology. According to

Bensheim (1960), traumatization during middle adulthood lead to typical depressive states, partly with anxious-paranoid tendencies. In support of these assumptions Bensheim (1960) provided casuistic pieces of evidence which called for further systematic examination.

Although providing interesting hypotheses about the association of age at traumatization and subsequent symptomatology, both models did not elaborate the causal mechanisms or processes underlying their postulated age sequences. For example, they made only cursory remarks on the assumed general psychological and biological maturation.

Stress Theory of Age-Specific Traumatization Effects

More recent studies on age-specific vulnerabilities are concerned with victims of catastrophes and war. They are based on classical approaches in stress-theory (e. g., Norris & Murell, 1988; Solomon, 1995; Thompson, Norris, & Hanacek, 1993). These studies are not concerned with a succession of different syndromes but instead investigate quantitative differences within the symptomatology of stress (i. e., PTSD symptoms, depressions, anxieties, physical complaints). Thompson, Norris, and Hanacek (1993) presented a number of different assumptions and explained them with reference to traumatization through natural catastrophes. These assumptions (or perspectives) are: the exposition perspective, the resource perspective, the inocculation perspective, and the burden perspective. The first two can be condensed by virtue of their common aspects, as was done by Solomon (1995, p. 143 .f).

Both the *exposition and the resource perspective* postulate that the extent of psychological trauma increases with age. More specifically, the exposition perspective proposes that traumatization at an older age leads to more severe symptomology as the victim's flexibility in coping with the trauma impact typically decreases with age. Older individuals, for example, find it harder to circumvent averse conditions such as the emergency situation immediately following trauma. The resource perspective proposes that the elderly have limited coping abilities and therefore experience a greater degree of posttraumatic symptomatology. This assumption is supported by investigations on lowered social and financial resources of the elderly (Phifer, 1990).

The *inoculation perspective,* in contrast, suggests that coping abilities increase with age as the elderly have generally been confronted with coping experiences during life crises. This hypothesis is based on Eysenck's (1983) inoculation theory, which in turn is grounded on the assumption that exposure to stressful situations earlier in life increases the resiliency toward stressful conditions later on in life. This theory is supported by a number of findings on the stress perception following natural catastrophes, where older individuals showed lower levels of stress than did younger ones (see Norris & Murell, 1988).

While the aforementioned perspectives assume a linear relationship between age and the effects of traumatization, the *burden perspective* proposes that middle-aged individuals show the greatest degrees of psychological impairment following trauma. From a social psychological viewpoint this assumption is accounted for by the greater responsibilities of middle-aged adults. They are typically entrusted with such responsibilities as child-rearing, employment, care of possessions. These responsibilities, in turn, may be more severely disturbed through traumatization than is the case with young adults and the elderly. Elder and colleagues (Elder, Shanahan, & Clipp, 1994) published considerations similar to the burden-perspective with regard to their study on war aftermath.

Data by Thompson et al. (1993) on tornado victims aged 18 to "over 60" support the burden perspective. The middle-aged group (or rather individuals in their middle and late adulthood; 40–59 years) showed the highest stress levels at different points of measurement up to two years following the catastrophe. It is questionable, however, to what extent the study's result can be generalized for trauma and PTSD research for at least three reasons. First, the age groups were divided atheoretically (see above). The second – and probably more relevant reason – is the use of undifferentiated symptom measures. No distinction was made between the PTSD symptom categories intrusion, avoidance, and hyperarousal, emphasizing mainly the distress ratings. Third, it is also doubtful whether these assumed causal relationships can be applied to manmade or longer-lasting trauma, such as political imprisonment.

Some support for the burden hypothesis, however, comes from the investigation on veterans of war by Elder et al. (1994). The authors showed that soldiers who were drafted during middle adulthood (33–41 years) showed higher degrees of incurred psychological impairment than did recruits older than 20 years of age. Unfortunately, interesting comparison groups of even older or younger traumatized war-veterans were not evaluated.

Psychological and Physiological Approaches of Age-Specific Vulnerabilities

A third theoretical approach attempts to explain age-specific vulnerabilities for posttraumatic stress disorder on the basis of bio-psycho-social changes across the lifespan. This approach differentiates between the individual PTSD symptom categories (intrusion, avoidance, and hyperarousal). The approach assumes:

– biological changes constitute the basis from which result

- altered cognitive processes in the realm of information processing. These are accompanied by
- changes of self-image and relevant coping abilities.

Overall, these changes result in heightened vulnerability towards traumatization occurring during adolescence and older age.

Biological Changes

Two processes that are of relevance to the concept of vulnerability with regard to trauma will be outlined: neurofunctional frontality and regulation of arousal. A detailed discussion of the complexity of biological changes in the process of maturation during childhood and adolescence as well as its differentiation at an older age are beyond this chapter (see Birren et al., 1992).

Neurofunctional frontality can be defined as a brain-organic prerequisite for goal-oriented cognitive and behavioral activities (Vreeling, 1993). One of its most essential features is the discrimination between relevant and irrelevant stimuli, a prerequisite for inhibition of cognitive interference. During the process of phylogenetic evolution the frontal cortex has reached its maximum capacity in human beings. During ontogenetic development, the frontal cortex is the last brain region to develop. Its circumference develops rapidly from birth until the age of two, and less afterwards until the age of seven. It is fully developed only by the beginning of young adult age (approx. 20–22 years of age) (Luria, 1973). Indications of a beginning involution of the frontal cortex can be observed regularly during late adult age (fifth and sixth decade); particularly a reduction of circumference, volume, and cell density (Fuster, 1989). Neurobiologists have summarized their findings by stating that the brain region that was ontologically the latest to have developed is also the first one to regress (see Dempster, 1992).

Allocation and regulation of arousal is a biological function, localized in the ascending reticular activating system (ARAS) in Diencephalon and Thalamus. Again the brain section in charge is biologically fully developed at around the age of 20. One can therefore assume a different arousal regulation during adolescence than during middle adulthood. Following middle adulthood, the arousal regulation during later adult age and old age undergoes changes for which certain process parameters have repeatedly been described (Prinz, Dustman, & Emmerson, 1990; Woodruff, 1985). During dormancy, the excitation level of the elderly is generally characterized by underarousal (Woodruff, 1985). When, on the other hand, confronted with sensory stimuli, the elderly are characterized by overexcitability, which is manifested in both, the height of amplitudes of excitation and extended amplitude duration (Prince et al., 1990). In other words, the excitation-regression takes place at a slower pace.

In summary, one may assume that when confronted with traumatic stimuli, the elderly develop more severe reactions in terms of, both, their extent and their duration (stimulus persistence), whereby more posttraumatic overexcitation becomes clinically observable. There are, in fact, published reports substantiating this hypothesis. In a descriptive study Goenijan et al. (1994) found that "older individuals" (i. e., over 55) showed higher hyperarousal levels one and a half years after an earthquake had taken place than did "younger individuals" (i. e., 18–53). However, this age-difference was not found for the PTSD categories of intrusion and avoidance.

Cognitive Changes

On the second level of explanation, cognitive changes across the human lifespan are to be discussed. A phenomenon closely related with frontality is that of *cognitive inhibition*, i. e., the inhibition of information for a number of cognitive processes that is irrelevant to a given situation (Dempster, 1992).

It is believed that cognitive inhibition-mechanisms are directed by the frontal lobe, the brain section responsible for goal-directed action. The efficiency of cognitive inhibition can be demonstrated experimentally by means of several paradigms. Old people, for instance, seem to be more susceptible to proactive interference, as can be tested with the Stroop Test (Dempster, 1992; but see Graf & Uttl, 1995). Weakened cognitive inhibition-processes could otherwise lead to a flooding of the working memory with intrusive traumatic elements of memory, e. g., visual, auditive memories – in other words, the intrusion symptoms would be intensified. There is still a lively discussion in the cognitive aging research on the inhibition processes and its possible implications (see Hasher & Zachs, 1988).

Self-Concept and Coping Changes

On a third level, self-concept and coping changes can be discussed along with their influence on age-specific trauma-symptoms (see Cole & Putnam, 1992; Jackson, 1982; Laufer, 1988). In general, the role of altered self-concepts and coping processes following traumatization has been subject to numerous investigations (e. g., Aldwin, 1993; Horowitz, 1986; Solomon, Mikulincer, & Avitzur, 1988; Valentiner, Foa, Riggs, & Gershuny, 1996). During adolescence the *differentiation of self-concept* (its elaboration and extension) is of central importance (see Harter, 1993). Under normal circumstances the adolescent's self-concept becomes multifaceted which allows for the adoption of multiple roles (Döbert & Nunner-Winkler, 1984; see Freund, 1995). Adolescents practice explorative behavior in order to test the borders of their self-control, while the majority of them manages to keep these tests within adaptive bounds. In doing so, a great number of different coping processes can be tested. Traumatization during adolescence can inhibit the process of self-concept differentiation (Janoff-Bulman, 1995) and can cause the individual's repertoire of coping-processes to "freeze" at a poorly developed state. At the same time trauma can impair the differentiation of emotional regulation because of changes of the individual's self-image (see Horowitz, 1986).

There is a great number of descriptive findings from research on coping that relate to the subject of old age and that in part lack a uniform taxonomy, methodological foundation and further far reaching validization (Strack & Feifel, 1996; see Filipp, this volume). In more general terms these studies suggest there is *no tendency towards uniform coping-strategies in old age*, i. e., interindividual differences in coping-behavior remain stable. Individuals who age well (or "successful") have a consistently broad spectrum of coping strategies at their disposal (Weisman, 1984). By the same token, there seems to be a tendency towards *increased emotion-centered coping* when aging is accompanied by health difficulties (Folkman, Lazarus, Pimley, & Novacek, 1987). In these cases avoidance strategies reign most prominently: Old people, for example, have a tendency to keep out of conflict situations and act as if nothing had happened (see Staudinger et al., 1997). The increased use of emotion-centered coping styles were also supported by Labouvie-Vief, Hakim-Larson, and Hobart (1987), who found that older people employ various defense strategies. These can take the form of intentional repression, denial, or reaction formation such as distracting occupation with bodily functions). In contrast to these observations Blanchard-Fields and Camp (1990) found that while in comparison with younger individuals, the elderly view emotionally stressful situations more readily as nonproblematic. These do not have to be interpreted as expressions of defense or avoidance. An overview of the coping literature suggests that the elderly can intentionally draw on increasingly more avoidance strategies the older they get, while at the same time interindividual differences during old age can in fact become greater (and so can the statistical variance).

Summary

How can the theoretical and empirical findings of the three strands of research outlined so far be summarized? Poor preconditions exist for adaptation following traumatic impact during adolescence consequent to a need for psychological differentiation (maturation) and a reduced repertoire of available coping abilities during this period of the lifespan. This might be due to adolescents being in a state of psychological and physiological instability (Marcia, 1980).

At the other end of the lifespan, elderly too appear to show greater vulnerability to traumatization than do young and middle aged adults. The aging-process is based on biological changes leading to reduced cognitive inhibition of stimulation and unstable arousal via reduction of frontality.

Studies on Age at Traumatization and PTSD Symptoms

A number of hypotheses can be derived from the above: Individuals who were traumatized during adolescence or old age should exhibit a greater extent of posttraumatic stress symptoms. Furthermore, increases in symptomatology are expected specifically with regard to the PTSD symptoms groups (intrusion, avoidance, and hyperarousal) and not for other forms of psychopathology. These hypotheses are tested in two samples, an ex-political prisoner sample and a crime victim sample. Among the group of former political prisoners only the increased vulnerability to traumatization during adolescence can be examined because the age of traumatization of this sample ranged only from adolescence to middle age (17–55 years). Consequently, old age as the other phase of increased vulnerability to trauma has to be ignored – this part of the assumption is investigated in the crime victim sample.

Former Political Prisoners in East Germany

Victims who were imprisoned and tortured for political reasons have already been investigated in several countries (Bauer et al., 1993; Basoglu et al., 1994; Kuch & Cox, 1992; Maercker & Schützwohl, 1997). High incidences of PTSD and other psychiatric disorders were found in the majority of these studies. The study carried out in Dresden between 1994 and 1997 had the goal of recording the psychological well-being of former political prisoners from the German Democratic Republic (GDR) (Maercker & Schützwohl, 1997). In the former GDR's totalitarian system, up to 200,000 individuals were imprisoned for political reasons between 1949 and 1989 (Fricke 1986; Werkentin, 1995).

Sample and Methods. The sample investigated consisted of a nonclinical population of 146 individuals who were recruited through the media. Participants had been subject to prosecution for a variety of reasons: (1) because of active political opposition towards the GDR (e. g., social-democrats, students, collaborators of Western espionage services), (2) adherence to a social class discriminated against by the political leadership of the GDR (entrepreneurs, clergymen, private farmers), (3) politically nonactive individuals who had spoken against their superiors, (4) and increasingly so during the 1980s, politically nonactive GDR citizens eager to emigrate to the West. (The same sample is also subject to analyses in Chapter 10, Schützwohl et al.).

The average duration of imprisonment in the sample was around three years (M = 38 months; SD = 43 months). The former prisoners had suffered multiple traumatic events, e. g., death threats, physical maltreatment, witnessed torture or violent deaths, darkroom confinement (see Maercker & Schützwohl, 1997, for a detailed description). Eighty-five percent of those investigated were male. The mean age of participants at the time of the study was 54 years (SD = 12 years, range 27–82). With regard to socioeconomic antecedents and first career moves, the sample represents a balanced societal average ranging from unskilled workers to academics and entrepreneurs.

For methodological reasons it is important to note that a considerable number of years had passed since the time at which the trauma had occurred. On average 23 years (SD = 18, range 5–38) had elapsed since the time of imprisonment. Diagnoses regarding posttraumatic stress disorders were made by the use of a structured diagnostic interview (Margraf, Schneider, & Ehlers, 1991; German version of Anxiety Disorders Interview Schedule-R, ADIS-R, DiNardo & Barlow, 1988). The structured diagnostic interview allows for the acquisition of current and lifetime diagnoses. Participants were also required to fill in the Impact of Event Scale–Revised (IES-R) with subscales on intrusion, avoidance, and hyperarousal (Weiss & Marmar, 1996, modification of IES: Horowitz, Wilner, & Alvarez, 1979). Thirty percent of the participants of this study were diagnosed with current PTSD and 60% of the sample showed PTSD-lifetime diagnoses (Maercker & Schützwohl, 1997).

Age-related subdivision of the sample into trauma age groups. The former political prisoners group were divided into three age groups depending on the individual's age at traumatization (beginnings). It resulted in a group of participants who were imprisoned during adolescence (16–21 years; N = 57), at young adulthood (22–35 years; N = 64), and in middle adulthood (36–55 years; N = 20). The three trauma age groups differed with regard to current age at the time investigation ($F(2, 142) = 9.1, p < .001$) and gender proportion ($\chi^2 (2, N = 146) = 7.5, p < .05$). The groups, however, did not differ with regard to the stressor criteria of duration of imprisonment ($F(2, 142) = 0.9$, n. s.) and imprisonment conditions (i. e., number of maltreatment measures; $F(2, 142) = 1.4$, n. s.). It was therefore decided to investigate the above mentioned assumptions by controlling for current age and gender proportion.*

---

* When comparing the current frequency of diagnoses by crosstables one has to renounce controlling age and sex variables. In crosstable analysis, current PTSD diagnoses showed a V-shaped frequency distribution: adolescents 37%, young adults 21%, middle aged adults 36% for which only the difference between adolescents and young adults was significant ($\chi^2 (2, N = 140) = 9.9, p < .01$).

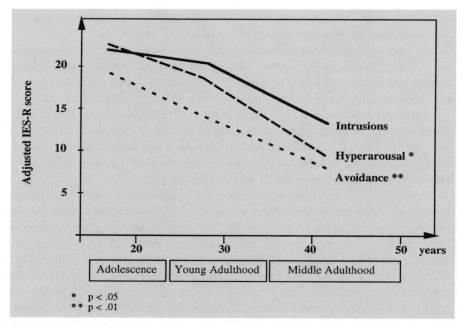

Figure 1. Means of the three IES-R subscales in three trauma age groups (adjusted for current age and sex).

Findings. In analyzing the PTSD symptom scores of the IES-R the covariables were included using a multi-variate repeated measures design (the three IES-R subscores Intrusion, Hyperarousal, Avoidance as repeated measures). A main effect was found for trauma age groups ($F(9, 396) = 2.05, p < .05$) where those undergoing trauma during adolescence showed the highest values followed by those detained during young and middle adulthood (see Figure 1).

Statistical post hoc examinations revealed significant differences for avoidance and hyperarousal, but not for intrusion symptoms. In extension of the analyses' focus, univariate analyses of (co-)variance were performed on other symptom measures: depression (BDI, Beck, 1978), anxiety symptoms (BAI, Beck et al., 1988), and general psychopathology (SCL-90 global symptom index, see Derogatis, 1977) where current age and sex served as covariables. None of these results reached significance with regard to the effect of the trauma age group. However, looking at diagnoses for affective disorders (dysthymic and major depressive syndrome) by means of the structured clinical interview a different pattern was found. Participants who had been detained during young adulthood (22–35 years) were most frequently diagnosed as being depressed (26%), compared to 16% participants traumatized in adolescence, and 5% traumatized in middle adulthood (χ^2 (2; $N = 140$) = 5.9, $p < .05$).

Overall, results show that the PTSD symptoms of hyperarousal and avoidance occur less frequently in those traumatized during adolescence and middle adulthood. Before these result will be discussed in more detail, they will be compared with findings from a study on crime victims including older people.

Crime Victims

The effects of crime are both pervasive and persistent. PTSD symptoms occur regularly in the aftermath of victimization (e. g., Kilpatrick et al., 1989; Davis & Breslau, 1994; Resnick et al., 1993; Schützwohl & Maercker, 1997). Although most studies on crime victims concentrated on sexual assaults, I will present results of a study on a sample of nonsexual assault crimes. The participants in this study had incurred simple or severe physical injury usually in the context of robbery.

Sample and Methods. Twenty-seven individuals volunteered to participate in the study by contacting the victims-aids-organization "White Ring." The sample did not constitute a clinical sample. Forty-four percent were women. The mean age was 45 years of age (SD = 17, range 20–82). On average, the interviews took place 28 months following the crime. Again, the structured diagnostic interview (German ADIS-R version) and the IES-R were used. Based on the diagnostic interviewer-ratings, sum scores were computed adding the 17 single PTSD symptoms across symptoms group. The DSM-IV criteria for posttraumatic stress disorder were met by 27% of the crime victims. At the time of the study 12 crime victims still suffered from physical aftereffects. Because of the small number of participants, the age variable was analyzed continuously, i. e., it was not divided into traumatization age groups.

Findings. The crime victims' chronological age at traumatization was positively correlated with the sum score of ADIS-R-interviewer ratings as well as the IES-R subscales of intrusion and hyperarousal ($r > .30$). Only the avoidance subscale showed a different pattern. Because of the small sample size, only the correlation between diagnostic sum scores and age reached significance ($r = .41$, $p < .05$) as did those between IES-R-intrusion values and age ($r = .43$. $p < .05$). It can therefore be concluded that the higher the participants' age the more posttraumatic stress symptoms were found and the more frequently self-reported intrusions indicated were.

In a second step, it was tested which kind of nonlinear regression might best describe the variables' relationship beyond that of a linear linear approach of correlations. For the diagnostic sum score, the cubic regression equation (turned S-curve) accounted for the highest amount of variance ($R^2 = .34$ $F(1$,

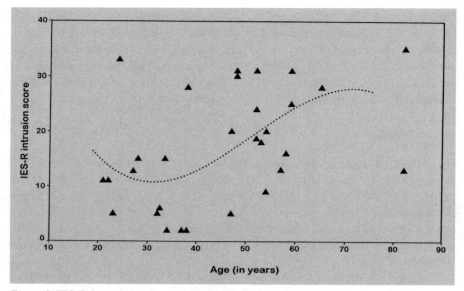

Figure 2. IES-R intrusion values of crime victims (N = 30) with cubic regression curve on chronological age.

24) = 4.10, $p < .05$). The bottom of the S-curve lay between age 25–30 and the peak around age 60. For IES-R-Intrusions the cubic equation, too, showed the highest amount of explained variance with $R^2 = .32$ ($F(1, 24) = 4.01, p < .05$) (see Figure 2).

For the hyperarousal scale the linear regression equation reached the most favourable model of fit with $R^2 = .13$ ($F(1, 26) = 4.09, p = .05$). Once again, an age trend pattern was observed with regard to posttraumatic-stress-symptoms, this time, however, with the exception of avoidance symptoms. The avoidance scale did not reach significant results in any of the tested equations.

Answered and Unanswered Questions

The findings in two groups of victims depict pieces of evidence for a two-peaked vulnerability curve for PTSD symptoms. Thus, the findings support the theoretically guided assumption of higher vulnerabilities in adolescents and subjects beyond young adulthood. The two samples, however, showed differences which need to be taken into consideration. For example, it was expected that the age-related vulnerability would appear specifically with regard to intrusions and hyperarousal. As far as intrusion symptoms of former political prisoners were concerned, no age trend could be found whereas in the crime victims group intrusion showed the expected age trend.

Precipitation and maintenance of intrusive symptoms may vary in persons who underwent multiple trauma (like political prisoners) in contrast to those who had experienced only a single traumatic event (like crime victims). The difference could be explained, for instance, on the basis of the mere quantity of various traumatic events that intrude the victim's memory (either sponta- neously or as a result of stimuli or reminders triggering of flashbacks). No age trend pattern could be observed, however, in crime victims with a single trau- ma that bears a lower risk of triggering memories. When comparing the means the IES-R intrusion subscale with values reported in the literature (Horowitz, Field, & Classen, 1993) the political prisoners sample showed somewhat higher values than other trauma groups whereas the crime victims' mean values ap- peared comparatively lower. Another interpretation is that the age-sensitive avoidance symptom score in crime victims is indicative of the fact that phobic symptoms that often develop in response to a single trauma follow a different age trend than do other posttraumatic stress-symptoms.

The most unequivocal results were obtained with regard to the adolescent group and the old age group. Both group scores were highest on measures of increased posttraumatic hyperarousal. As far as the increased vulnerability in old age is concerned these results are in accordance with those of another study that found heightened posttraumatic arousal in late adult age or early old age when compared to an age group of young and middle aged adults (Goenijan et al., 1994).

Overall these results can be considered further proof of assumptions made on the basis of reviews of literature on biological, cognitive and self-image and changes of coping styles. It was hypothesized that decreased frontality and a decrease in cognitive inhibition during adolescence and increased age leads to a proneness to intrusion and hyperarousal. The fact that the age-related peak for values of intrusion and hyperarousal symptoms clusters around the age of 60 may suggest that the above mentioned biological and cognitive changes already form clinically relevant consequences in this age range.

As far as literature on traumatization in adolescence is concerned, I am not aware of any existing study on PTSD in adolescents that deals specifically with differences between age groups. The findings by Harmless (1990) that suggest an increased trauma related vulnerability in adolescence referred to the crite- ria of general social adjustment (Social Adjustment Scale). Other investiga- tions on traumatized adolescents did not include any age comparison groups (Mghir, Freed, Raskin, & Katon, 1995; Sack et al., 1994).

Two minor points of interest remain to be discussed beyond these findings: First, no age trend was found in the sample of former prisoners on measures that were not specifically aimed at PTSD symptomology, such as measures of depression, anxiety, and general psychopathology. These results emphasize the

necessity for concise statements to be made on the nature of psychopathological measures. Considering the multidimensionality and multidirectionality of
psychological processes during lifespan specific assumptions seem indispens-
able. Evidence supporting the inoculation perspective (Thompson et al., 1993),
for example, according to which middle adulthood is characterized by greater
resiliency against stress, appears to apply to general stress measures (e. g., items
like "How often during the past month have you felt confident about your
ability to solve your problems") as well as ratings of general psychopathology
but not to specific PTSD symptoms.

Second, in the group of former prisoners an increase in the frequency of
depressive disorders (dysthymic and major depressive syndrome) was observed among those who were traumatized during early adulthood. This is in
accordance with earlier psychiatric findings of Bensheim (1960) and Baeyer
et al. (1964), who found a preponderance of depressive disorders among individuals who were traumatized when they were older than twenty years of age.
As these findings were preempted by Bensheim's as well as Baeyer et al.'s
(1964) assumption of varying predilection ages for different psychiatric disorders further research in this area is required.

Traumas do not only result in psychiatric symptoms, however, but also affect
victims in terms of their social, professional and private lives. These aspects
will be discussed in the following section.

Psychosocial Consequences of Traumatization During Lifespan

The study of psychosocial consequences of trauma is the main topic of the
following section. Psychosocial consequences can be defined as changes in
different areas of life relevant for preservation of one's subsistence. These
include, for example, features in the areas of professional life and the family
(see Elder, Pavalko, & Clipp, 1993). In Section 2, I already pointed to the fact
that marital and family problems, unemployment and suicide have been known
as serious long-term consequences of traumatization and posttraumatic stress
disorders (see Hendin & Haas, 1991; Jordan et al., 1992; Pavalko & Elder,
1990). This section's major focus is on trauma induced changes in the areas of
education, profession, relationship, and the family.

The following excerpt of an interview that was carried out with a participant
of the Dresden study exemplifies subjectively perceived psychosocial changes
with regard to attitudes towards love and relationships (see Maercker, 1998a):

> *... One of the things that struck me most about my life was the fact that I*
> *always had different women. As I really loved my wife I figured that it had*
> *to do with the fact that I'd spent the most precious time of any man's life*

behind bars. After all, I'd spent seven years in prison. It was the time of my youth, you see, from age twenty to twenty seven. When others made their forming experiences I too made forming experiences but really in quite a different way . . .

How can pathways of life-long changes in social attitudes and achievements be conceptualized?

Theoretical Perspectives on Psychosocial Impairments

From a psychological point of view there are several theoretical perspectives offering possible explanations for the development of psychosocial consequences of trauma: (a) development-related complications, (b) disorder-related complications as well as (c) combined developmental- and disorder-related complications. All three perspectives share the assumption that individual factors are responsible for the development of psychosocial consequences of trauma. An explanatory approach based on a sociological perspective, in contrast, places the emphasis on (d) external societal constraints that affect the psychosocial aftereffects of trauma. These perspectives shall be described in more detail below.

a) *Development related complications*: According to this perspective psychosocial aftereffects of trauma result from impairments incurred during a developmental phase in life. This perspective was proposed for instance by Cole and Putnam, 1992 (see also Laufer, 1988) on the basis of Erikson's (1959) psychodynamic developmental theory and theories of developmental tasks by Havinghurst (1972) and Neugarten (1968). Jackson (1982) coined the term of *developmental arrest* to describe a condition whereby the afflicted individual persevers at the developmental stage during which s/he had been traumatized. From this perspective any traumatization during adolescence is related to certain complications later on in life (e. g., difficulty in establishing stable erotic relationships during subsequent life stages).

Erikson's model (1959, 1982) postulates the existence of a primary developmental conflict for each age phase such as the conflict between the individual's search of identity and role confusion during adolescence. There are a number of publications in the literature on PTSD that make reference to Erikson's theory of development (e. g., Harmless, 1990; Jackson, 1982; Laufer, 1988). Harmless (1990) compared two groups of former soldiers who had fought in the Vietnam war during adolescence (17–19) or during young adulthood (21–28). Harmless predicted that soldiers who had been adolescents at the time they were traumatized would show a preponderance of disorders typical of stage five where the conflict of "identity vs. role confusion" prevails.

Results of Harmless' (1990) study showed that soldiers who had been deployed during adolescence were significantly more often involved in criminal acts and law suits later on in life, than were those combat veterans who had been soldiers during young adulthood (45% vs. 11%). Moreover, those who had been traumatized during adolescence had changed their workplaces significantly more often later on in life and had been dismissed from their jobs significantly more frequently. With regard to interpersonal relationships, former adolescent soldiers were found to have poorer skills in talking to their partners about intimate problems even though they showed a greater interest in having intimate relationships than the older soldiers. Harmless (1990) concluded that these findings were proof of the hypothesis that the psychosocial aftereffects of trauma were dependent on stages of the individual's development.

These findings, however, can only in part be viewed as proof of a development-related psychological mediation of psychosocial complications. Furthermore, Harmless' study is not suited as confirmation of the Eriksonian model since the areas of intimacy, profession and social relations showed unspecific impairment in former adolescent soldiers that cannot be unequivocally described by the notion of identity versus role confusion. Rather, these results

Table 1. Overview of formulations of developmental phases, developmental tasks, and its impairments or disorders from adolescence to adulthood.

Age or developmental stage	Extension	Contents of Developmental Tasks	Problems, Impairments
Adolescence/ Transition into adulthood	17–22 years	· identity elaboration · experiences if intimacy and peer relationships · decision of professional education	· general vulnerability · unstable relationships · primary career problems (youth unemployment)
Early adulthood	22–35 years	· longer lasting relationships (marriage) · founding a family · professional career: first steps	· relationship (marriage) problems · career problems
Middle adulthood/ "Midlife" transition	35–50 years	· professional zenith *or* · reorientation in career, relationship, and hobbies · assisting one's children in their development and supporting their growing independence	· subjective perceived failure in job, relationship, and family · dropout from professional life, e. g., unemployment, early retirement) · "empty nest" syndrome

substantiate the assumption that individuals who were traumatized during adolescence are at an increased risk of developing a greater number of unspecific psychosocial deficits.

The second concept of sequential psychosocial developmental processes are the theories of developmental tasks (Havighurst, 1972; Neugarten, 1968). These are based on the idea that the different age groups are characterized by certain psychosocial patterns. One can assume that psychosocial patterns are affected by traumas in such a way that disorders develop. Table 1 shows important psychosocial developmental tasks arranged according to age phases (see Levinson, 1978; Vaillant, 1977).

The concept of developmental tasks have turned out an important theoretical frame for the lifespan developmental psychology, e. g., with regard to the clarification of a number of age differential effects (see Oerter & Montada, 1995).

There are hardly any empirical studies on the concept of developmental tasks in PTSD research. A study by Yeheskel (1995) made reference to this concept. Yeheskel (1995) interviewed Holocaust survivors in Israel (1) with regard to the fulfillment of developmental tasks at the ages of 6 years (childhood), 15 years (youth), 24 years (adolescence), and 44 years (middle adulthood), (2) with regard to current close personal relationships, and (3) with regard to current engagements in "purposeful major activities." The dependent variable was the current state of health which was measured using the sense of coherence questionnaire (Antonovsky, 1987). Results showed that only the presence of purposeful major activities was correlated with health status, whereas the fulfillment of developmental tasks did not reach the level of significance when correlated with the current state of health. The study is mentioned here despite its methodological weaknesses (e. g., operationalizing of developmental tasks or the dependent variable), as there are no other studies that have dealt with the assumed association between psychosocial indicators, traumatization and developmental phases.

b) *Disorder-related complications:* According to this second theoretical perspective the occurrence of psychosocial changes following trauma is mediated by the development of posttraumatic stress disorders and their accompanying psychological impairments. These, in turn, also affect a variety of spheres of life such as education, family, and professional life. This perspective has so far not been explicitly formulated. Rather, it was merely an implicit basic assumption in a number of studies dealing with trauma sequelae, especially in those reporting on Vietnam veterans (Boman, 1990; Byrant & Harvey, 1995; Hendin & Haas, 1991; Jordan et al., 1992).

An investigation of a large group of American Vietnam veterans (McCarren et al., 1995) showed that combat veterans with a diagnosis of PTSD had higher divorce-rates as well as unemployment rates, and had less often acquired higher educational levels or professional status. There was a stronger relationship between PTSD diagnoses and psychosocial impairments than there was between trauma or stressor intensity and psychosocial sequelae. Conversely, Boman (1990) suggested in his review of various studies on psychosocial variables that traumatization, diagnoses of PTSD and negative psychosocial aftereffects are by no means unequivocal concepts and that they have little predictive value.

On the level of possible psychological mechanisms one might want to consider a number of PTSD symptoms that might have detrimental effects on psychosocial functioning. For instance, posttraumatic difficulties to concentrate could have a negative effect on work performance and thereby lead to a higher frequency of work related problems including unemployment. Likewise, the posttraumatic symptom of estrangement feelings may be related to family and marriage problems, eventually resulting in higher divorce rates. Thus far, however, these specific pathways have not been empirically investigated. It also remains questionable whether the above mentioned causal relationships are powerful enough to be verified by means of a field trail.

(c) *Combined development- and disorder-related complications:* A third theoretical perspective is based on the underlying assumption that disorder specific as well as psychogenetic impairments need to be considered in explanations of trauma sequelae. So far, there are no explications of such a combined explanatory approach in the literature. It could be hypothesized, however, that it is only the combination of a developmental impairment and the presence of posttraumatic stress disorder that result in psychosocial problems.

The developmental stage of adolescence during which the risk of developing PTSD is increased could bring about far greater degrees of psychosocial impairments than is the case during later life stages when the risk of developing PTSD is lower. I am currently not aware of any existing empirical literature dealing with these possible relationships.

(d) *External societal constraints (sociological perspective):* In the literature on trauma sequelae it has been argued that external factors considerably determine the extent of psychosocial consequences (e. g., Agger & Jensen, 1990; Fontana & Rosenheck, 1994; Herman, 1992). Here, the term societal constraints refers to experiences of discrimination, marginalization, cultural deprival, prejudice or repression of individuals following traumatic experiences. Victims of sexual assault, for example, have often been faced with the dilemma of having to fear possible marginalization and stigmatization by their social environment when disclosing their traumatic experiences (see Herman, 1992). Similarly, as Fontana and Rosenheck (1994) showed in their study, public opinion in the USA led to relatively greater degrees of posttraumatic complications in Vietnam veterans than was found in soldiers who had fought in World War II or the Korean War.

External societal constraints were especially obvious for political prisoners in the former East German state (GDR). Following their release from prison they were exposed to a number of repressive measures that were especially directed against educational and career aspects of life (see Müller, 1997; Werkentin, 1995). The GDR's regime did everything to impede their victims' professional developments following incarceration, thereby depriving them of all possibilities of reaching influential professional and social positions. With regard to the investigated sample of former political prisoners, any study dealing with the factors responsible for psychosocial consequences needs to take these relationships into consideration.

Education, Carrier, and Divorce Rates in Trauma Victims: Data from the Ex-Political Prisoners Study in Dresden

The following three assumptions were investigated within the former political prisoners group:

1) *Existence of impairments:* It has been assumed that the trauma group would show a greater number of psychosocial impairments or changes in the areas of education, professional life and the family when compared with a nontraumatized control group.

2) *Pattern of impairments:* Different psychosocial consequences should be related with one another. These relations were believed to be relatively weak, as a multidirectionality of developmental processes is assumed (see above Section 1). At the same time, one can presume that negative psychosocial consequences do not exist in isolation from one another. This means that professional impairments correlate for instance with discriminatory factors regarding education and family problems.

3) *Prediction of impairments:* The various psychosocial impairments are more closely related to the presence of a PTSD diagnosis than they are with development related impairments. This assumption is based on the fact that a close causal pathway can be established between PTSD symptoms and unemployment or family problems (e. g., by taking into consideration such factors as difficulties concentrating and estrangement feelings). In contrast, an explanation based on development-related complications is possible only when the additional explanatory variable of age related increases in vul-

nerability is considered. In this context the possibility of a combined (i. e., interactive) influence through disorder-related and development-related factors was also explored. The variable of external influence on the above mentioned relationships will be controlled for by looking at whether the former prisoners had lived in East or West Germany upon their release from prison. It is assumed that those who had remained in East Germany experienced less favorable psychosocial consequences than those who had moved to West Germany because of the politically repressive environment for ex-prisoners in the East.

Selection of Psychosocial Indicators

Indicators of psychosocial functioning that are of particular relevance to the problem of trauma sequelae and are often investigated, are unemployment (Byrant & Harvey, 1995; Kulka et al., 1990; McCarren et al., 1995) and marital or family relationship (Elder, Shanahan, & Clipp, 1994, Laufer & Gallups, 1985). The study on ex-political prisoners also considered educational development following traumatization as a psychosocial indicator. The domain of professional life was investigated with regard to unemployment and career direction. In order to determine the role of family-related indicators of psychosocial functioning the occurrence of divorce was investigated (current and lifetime rates).*

Findings

Existence of impairments: In order to prove the first assumption, the traumatized ex-prisoners group and the nontraumatized age- and sex-matched control group were compared (see Maercker & Schützwohl, 1997 for detailed description of comparison group). As Table 2 shows, both groups differed sig-

---

* The psychosocial variables investigated were derived from two questionnaires: a sociodemographic questionnaire and the Biographical and Life-Event Questionnaire (Maercker, 1994). The variable "educational qualification" was measured using an ordinal scale ranging from "1" (secondary school) to "5" (university degree). For subsequent analyses the variable "low educational qualification" was created which allows for categorical (yes/no) allocations to be made according to the lowest educational level achieved. Information on career direction was gathered using questions of self-assessment ("All in all, which of the following adjectives best describe the course of your professional career?: a predominantly rising career = +1; approximately constant = 0; predominantly on the decline = –1"). The categorical variable of "negative career direction" includes only those individuals who had described their career as having been "predominantly declining." With regard to unemployment a differentiation was made between current unemployment and any unemployment (experienced) in life. The item "unemployment, ever" inquired whether there had ever been a period of unemployment that had lasted more than three months. The control variable "East vs. West German residency following release from prison" differentiated categorically between East and West Germany domiciles.

Table 2. Indicators of life time psychosocial development: Comparison between trauma-tized former prisoners and comparison group.

	Former prisoners	Comparison subjects	Tests
Highest educational level (1–5)	2.53 ± 1.44[1]	3.47 ± 1.64[1]	$F(1,240) = 18.85$***
Career direction (–1 – +1)	0.00 ± 0.82[1]	0.31 ± 0.73[1]	$F(1,146) = 4.77$*
Unemployment, current	22.5%	16.0%	$\chi^2(1,187) = 1.26$
Unemployment, ever[2]	36.1%	29.3%	$\chi^2(1,147) = 1.12$
Divorce, current	24.3%	14.7%	$\chi^2(1,187) = 1.90$
Divorce(s), ever[3]	34.3 %	22.1%	$\chi^2(1,147) = 3.89$*

*$p < .05$, ***$p < .001$
[1]Mean ± SD, [2]extended over 3 months, [3]one or more than one

nificantly with regard to educational qualification, career direction and life-time divorce rate. The group of former prisoners had achieved lower educa-tional qualifications and had average career directions of "zero" as well as a higher divorce rate.

In order to control for the external societal factor (i. e., "East vs. West Ger-man residency following release from prison"), the variables from Table 2 were additionally compared between the East versus West residents groups. Those who had emigrated to the West did not differ significantly from those who had remained in East Germany with regard to educational qualifications, unem-ployment rates, or divorce rates. Only with regard to career direction did those former prisoners who had emigrated to West Germany achieve higher values than did the East Germans ($M_{West} = .36$, $M_{East} = -.17$; $F(1, 126) = 8.53$; $p < .01$).

These results seem to confirm similar findings in other trauma victim groups (Byrant & Harvey, 1995; Elder, Pavalko, & Clipp, 1994; McCarren et al., 1995; Pavalko & Elder, 1990) even if the specific historical circumstances of the man-made traumatization by political persecution is taken into account. The unexpected finding that unemployment rates in both groups did not differ significantly, may be due to a regionally and historically specific external bias, i. e., the high unemployment rates in East Germany in the 1990s following German reunification that has been affecting members of all educational back-grounds and personal fates.

Pattern of impairments: The second assumption was tested by interrelating the psychosocial variables of the various indicator domains. Unexpectedly, only one interarea correlation was significant (at the low level of $r = .19$, $p < .05$): the relationship between low educational qualification and negative ca-reer direction. This result did not change when correlations were calculated separately for prisoners who had remained in the East and those who had been able to move to West Germany following their release from prison.

Thus, the second assumption of an association of psychosocial life tracks should be rejected. The multidirectionality of various psychosocial areas of functioning and life (see Baltes, 1987) became obvious to a greater extent than previously assumed. The fact that unemployment and divorce rates were not associated with each other, points to the fact that core psychosocial areas seem to be unrelated even in trauma victims.

Predictors of impairments: In order to test the third assumption on predictors of impairments statistical logit models were calculated. The logit model estimates are based on odds ratio-calculations and an approximate correspondence to the value of explained variance (R^2) provided by the value of concentration (Magidson, 1981).

Four separate logit-models were applied which comprised the predictor variables of PTSD-diagnosis (lifetime), age at imprisonment group (adolescents, young adults vs. middle-aged adults) and the control variable "East vs. West German residency following release from prison." The odds ratios resulting from the analyses are summarized in Table 3.

The figures in the upper sections of Table 3 represent odds ratio values. These odds ratio values are to be read as follows: individuals with a life time PTSD diagnosis are 2.97 times as likely to achieve only a low educational level (i. e., approx. three-fold risk) as those who never classified as suffering from PTSD.*

Only the variable of negative career direction is explained by significant odds-ratios of all included predictors. This led to a relatively satisfactory value of association which approximates 17 percent of explained variance for the equation. In contrast, the logit-equation with the worst goodness-of-fit value ($p = .29$) was the model for the divorce variable where the predictors made no significant contribution.

Thus, the investigation of the third assumption led to mixed patterns of findings. One reason is possibly the lack of significant correlations of the psychosocial variables (see above). Each of the four psychosocial variables was explained on the basis of a different predictor combination. However, the theoretically preferred assumption that the presence of a PTSD diagnosis was significantly related with negative psychosocial effects could be confirmed with regard to 2–3 indicators (educational qualification, career direction, and – almost significantly – divorce rate). This result supports the theoretical perspective of disorder-related complications, according to which psychosocial

---

*   In an additional step of testing the interaction hypothesis between developmental and disorder related complications, several interaction terms of "age groups × PTSD diagnosis" were calculated and introduced into the four models. In none of the models did this result in a goodness-of-fit improvement.

Table 3. Odds ratios, goodness-of-fit, and measures of association of various predictors of psychosocial indicators (figures between 0 and 1 indicate a higher risk for the first mentioned group).

Models:	(1) Low educational qualification	(2) Negative career direction	(3) Unemployment, ever	(4) Divorce, ever
Predictors:				
PTSD diagnosis, Lifetime	2.97*	3.52*	1.17	2.08+
Adolescents vs. young adults	.90	2.94*	3.94*	1.54
Young vs. middle-aged adults	1.49	0.02*	0.25	0.71
West vs. East residency after release	2.27+	5.70*	1.03	$-^a$
Goodness-of-fit[b]	$\chi^2 = 6.65$; $p = .51$	$\chi^2 = 3.68$; $p = .82$	$\chi^2 = 3.89$; $p = .79$	$\chi^2 = 8.56$; $p = .29$
Association measure[c]	.09	.17	.07	.05

*Significant (95% confidence interval oversteps 1.0)
+Tendentially significant (95% confidence interval > 0.9)
[a]Not included in equation
[b]p-values > .50 indicate sufficient model fit (optimal: $p > .75$)
[c]Concentration, approximates explained variance R^2

changes following trauma are predominantly determined by the extent of the disorder (see Bryant & Harvey, 1995). In the present study the three psychosocial variables affected by the presence of PTSD were the ones also shown to be negatively affected in the trauma vs. control group comparison. (The generally found high rate of unemployment may also subsume the effect of a PTSD diagnosis).

The Multiplicity of Relevant Perspectives

The finding of mainly disorder-related complications of life track indicators appears to be in contrast to the perspective of development-related complications (Harmless, 1990; Jackson, 1982; Laufer, 1988). Yet, indications for development-related impairments also appeared in the presented data.

Development-related impairments – notably among those who were traumatized during adolescence – were found with regard to negative career direction and the rate of unemployment. This suggests that, once impaired by trauma, initial developmental tasks that are relevant to professional life may lead to persistent negative professional consequences. A development-related increase of the rate of divorce later on in life was not found. This contradicts Harmless' (1990) findings, which indicated that individuals who had been traumatized as adolescents typically suffered from multiple relationship problems that conflicted with their desire to live with a partner. Here the study of other psychosocial indicator variables would be helpful in gaining a deeper understanding of the interactions involved.

In addition, the analyses also explored ways in which external societal influences impact on trauma sequelae. It was hypothesized that the persisting repressive conditions in East Germany had a negative impact on psychosocial indicators. The analyses confirmed this contention only with regard to the variable of career direction and basically also with regard to that of educational qualification. These two variables are characterized by a high societal determination.

There are, of course, a number of points regarding these analyses that need to be considered with caution. Primarily, one could point to the very basic question of whether a cross-sectional set of retrospectively collected data constitutes appropriate material for an investigation of the research questions involved. Only correlative, not causal explanations can be provided. Low educational qualification, for example, may not only be the result of a PTSD diagnosis but conversely may as well be its precondition. Moreover, part of the data were information pertaining to the past. This highlights the problem of memory stability (see Bradburn, Rips, & Shevell, 1987). Data consisting of factual, autobiographical information (e. g., divorce: yes/no) are likely to be less strongly affected by retrospective falsification than are memories of past psychological states (Jenkins, Hurst, & Rose, 1979). One could argue that the relatively high degree of explained variance for the variable of career direction may merely reflect a retrospective falsification bias. Information about career development is likely to be influenced by subjective self-assessment and self-evaluation.

Further studies on psychosocial consequences of trauma should also include time- and sequence-related information, e. g., the question of whether trauma during adolescence results in a retardation, disrupture, or the ending of education. Likewise, it should be explored whether the incidence of divorce before trauma results in an increased risk of developing PTSD as well as further divorces following trauma. Further detailed research in this area is necessary.

Conclusions

What lessons could be drawn from the studies presented? First, two risk groups for trauma effects are clearly identified: adolescents and elderly. Second, the methodology of PTSD research deserves attention: At the beginning of this chapter the suggestion was made that propositions of lifespan psychology could provide a useful tool for the investigation and interpretation of findings in the field of traumatization and PTSD. The three propositions mentioned were those of *multidimensionality*, *multidirectionality*, and *multifunctionality*. In conclusion, these propositions will be discussed in view of to the results obtained.

The *multidimensionality* proposition emphasizes differences between the biological, psychological, and social level of lifespan development. This proposition was taken into account in the present chapter by differentiating between psychological symptoms of PTSD (intrusion, hyperarousal, avoidance) on the one hand and impaired psychosocial areas of functioning or areas of life (education, profession, relationship/family) on the other. This differentiation reflects various degrees of determination by bio-genetic processes, societal constraints, and individual resources. Thus, one aspect of this study's findings deserves mentioning: While the analyses of the PTSD symptoms explained a relatively high amount of variance (up to 34%), the analyses performed on data regarding psychosocial changes explained a far smaller proportion of variance (up to 17%). This may mean that psychosocial changes in different live areas are in fact co-determined by a great number of additional factors that have been taken into consideration for further lifespan studies in the field.

The *multidirectionality* of lifespan-related findings is reflected by the fact that even though developmental processes change simultaneously, they do not change uniformly. Evidence for this assumption is provided by both analyses: The PTSD symptoms show age trends of differing degrees of significance. It appears that posttraumatic symptoms of hyperarousal are clearly dependent on the age at which traumatization occurred (see Goenjian et al., 1994). This may possibly account for the close relationship between symptoms of hyperarousal and biological functions as well as the somatic maturation processes associated with it. The aspect of multidirectionality was reflected in the analysis of psychosocial variables in low or missing relationships between the various indicators of functioning. This finding may possibly bear positive implications in as far as those trauma victims experiencing various forms of adversity during their educational career may not necessarily have to suffer from professional and marital problems as well.

The *multifunctionality* of a lifelong development that encompasses loss as well as gain remained uncommented in the present analyses. Yet, one of the more important findings of research in the area of trauma sequelae is the fact that the overall negative phenomena of trauma can in fact bear merits that emerge as a result of living through stress and suffering. Such possible positive consequences of trauma as "personal growth" have been highlighted by Antonovsky (1987), Frankl (1963), Maercker (1992), Tedeschi and Calhoun

(1995), and Park (see Chapter 12). The results obtained by the study of personal growth in the group of political prisoners will be published elsewhere (Maercker & Park, 1998). In conclusion, the investigation on trauma sequelae during lifespan should tend to pay attention to both theses qualities of losses and gains.

A more complete picture of trauma sequelae during lifespan also has implications for the conceptualization of therapeutic approaches (see Maercker, 1997). The fact that an individual's age at the time of traumatization constitutes a potentially relevant risk factor – especially adolescence and old age – is of immediate clinical relevance. Treatments of trauma sequelae need to address psychological disturbances on the symptom level as well as to offer assistance in overcoming the concomitant psychosocial impairments. Furthermore, beyond the scope of this chapter's analyses, therapeutic approaches should help trauma survivors to restore their interrupted pathways of life. A lifespan developmental perspective may offer therapists additional means for adequate and effective treatments of the patients' needs.

References

Agger, I., & Jensen, S.B. (1990). Testimony as ritual and evidence in psychotherapy for political refugees. *Journal of Traumatic Stress, 3*, 115–130.

Aldwin, C.M. (1993). Coping with traumatic stress. *PTSD Research Quarterly, 4*, 1–7.

Aldwin. C.M. (1994). *Stress, coping, and development.* New York: Guilford.

Angst, J. (1986). *The course of major depression, atypical bipolar disorder, and bipolar disorder.* Berlin: Springer-Verlag.

Antonovsky, A. (1987). *Unraveling the mystery of health.* San Francisco: Jossey-Bass.

Baeyer, W. v., Häfner, H., & Kisker, P.K. (1964). *Psychiatrie der Verfolgten* (Psychiatry of the persecuted). Berlin: Springer-Verlag.

Baltes, P.B. (1987). Theoretical propositions of life-span psychology: On the dynamics between growth and decline. *Developmental Psychology, 23*, 611–626.

Baltes, P.B. (1997). On the incomplete architecture of human ontogeny. *American Psychologist, 52*, 366–380.

Basoglu, M., Paker, M., Paker, Ö., Özmen, E., Marks, I., Incesu, C., Sahin, D., & Sarimurat, N. (1994). Psychological effects of torture: A comparison of tortured with nontortured political activists in Turkey. *American Journal of Psychiatry, 151*, 76–81.

Bauer, M., Priebe, S., Häring, B., & Adamczak, K. (1993). Long-term sequelae of political imprisonment in East Germany. *Journal of Nervous and Mental Disease, 181*, 257–263.

Beck, A.T. (1978). *The depression inventory.* Philadelphia: Center for Cognitive Therapy.

Beck, A.T., Epstein, N., Brown, G., & Steer, R.A. (1988). An inventory for measuring clinical anxiety: Psychometric properties. *Journal of Consulting and Clinical Psychology, 56*, 893–897.

Bensheim, H. (1960). Die KZ-Neurose rassisch Verfolgter. Ein Beitrag zur Psychopathologie der Neurosen [The KZ neurosis. A contribution to the psychopathology of neuroses]. *Nervenarzt, 31,* 462–469.

Birren, J.E., Sloane, R.B., Cohen, G.D. et al. (Eds.) (1992). *Handbook of mental health and aging.* San Diego: Academic Press.

Blanchard-Fields, F., & Camp, C.J. (1990). Affect, individual differences, and real world problem solving across the adult life span. In T.M. Hess (Ed.), *Aging and cognition: Knowledge organization and utilization.* Amsterdam: Elsevier.

Boman, B. (1990). Are all Vietnam veterans like John Rambo? In M.E. Wolf & A.D. Mosnaim (Eds.), *Posttraumatic stress disorder.* Washington: American Psychiatric Press.

Bornstein, M.H. (1992). *Developmental psychology.* Hillsdale: Erlbaum.

Bradburn, N.M., Rips, L.J., & Shevell, S.K. (1987). Answering autobiographical questions: The impact of memory and inference on surveys. *Science, 236,* 157–161.

Bronisch, T., Cording-Trömmel, C., Krieg, J.C., Hecht, & Wittchen, H.U. (1988). Verlauf und outcome depressiver Erkrankungen: Eine vergleichende Analyse [Course and outcome of affective disorders: A comparison study]. In H.U. Wittchen & D. v. Zerssen (Eds.), *Verläufe behandelter und unbehandelter Depressionen und Angststörungen.* [Courses of treated and untreated depressive and anxiety disorders]. Heidelberg: Springer-Verlag.

Bryant, R.A., & Harvey, A.G. (1995). Posttraumatic stress in volunteer firefighters: Predictors of distress. *Journal of Nervous and Mental Disease, 183,* 267–271.

Carstensen, L.L. (1988). The emerging field of behavioral gerontology. *Behavior Therapy, 19,* 259–281.

Carstensen, L.L. (1991). Selectivity theory: Social activity in life-span context. In K.W. Schaie (Ed.), *Annual review of gerontology and geriatrics, 11.* New York: Springer-Verlag.

Cicchetti, D., & Cohen, D.J. (Eds.) (1995). *Developmental Psychopathology. Vol. 2: Risk, disorder, and adaption.* New York: Wiley.

Cole, P.M., & Putnam, F.W. (1992). Effect of incest of self and social functioning: A developmental psychopathology perspective. *Journal of Consulting and Clinical Psychology, 60,* 174–184.

Davis, G.C., & Breslau, N. (1994). Post-traumatic stress disorder in victims of civilian trauma and criminal violence. In D.A. Tomb (Ed.), *The Psychiatric Clinics of North America, 8,* 289–300.

Dempster, F.N. (1992). The rise and fall of the inhibitory mechanism: Toward a unified theory of cognitive development and aging. *Developmental Review, 12,* 45–75.

Derogatis, L.R. (1977). *SCL-90-R. Administration, scoring and procedures manual-I for the R(evised) Version.* Baltimore: John Hopkins University School of Medicine.

Döbert, R., & Nunner-Winkler, G. (1984). Die Bewältigung von Selbstmordimpulsen im Jugendalter. Motiv-Verstehen als Dimension der Ich-Entwicklung [Regulation of suicidal impulses in adolescence. Motive comprehension as dimension of ego-development]. In W. Edelstein & J. Habermas (Eds.), *Perspektivität und Interpretation* [Perspectivity and interpretation]. Frankfurt a.M.: Suhrkamp.

Elder, G.H. (1974). *Children of the great depression.* Chicago: University of Chicago Press.

Elder, G.H. Jr., Pavalko, E.K., & Clipp, E.C. (1993). *Working with archival data: Studying lives.* Newbury Park, CA: Sage.

Elder, G.H., Shanaham, M.J., & Clipp, E.C. (1994). When war comes to men's lives: Life-course patterns in family, work, and health. *Psychology and Aging, 9,* 5–16.

Erikson, E.H. (1959). *Identity and the life cycle.* New York: International Universities Press.

Erikson, E.H. (1982). *The life cycle completed.* New York: Norton.

Eysenck, H.J. (1983). Stress, disease, and personality: The inoculation effect. In C.L. Cooper (Ed.), *Stress research.* New York: Wiley.

Folkman, S., Lazarus, R.S., Pimley, S., & Novacek, J. (1987). Age differences in stress and coping procedures. *Psychology and Aging, 2,* 171–184.

Fontana, A., & Rosenheck, R. (1994). Traumatic war stress and psychiatric symptoms among World War II, Korean, and Vietnam War veterans. *Psychology and Aging, 9,* 27–33

Frankl, V. (1963). *Man's search for meaning.* New York: Washingtons Square Press.

Freund, A. (1995). *Die Selbstdefinition alter Menschen* [Self-definition of the elderly]. Berlin: edition sigma (Studien und Berichte des Max-Planck-Instituts für Bildungsforschung, Bd. 61.

Fricke, K.W. (1986). *Zur Menschen- und Grundrechtssituation politischer Gefangener in der DDR* [Human rights situation of political prisoners in the GDR]. Köln: Verlag Wissenschaft und Politik.

Fuster, J.M. (1989). *The prefrontal cortex* (2nd ed.). New York: Raven.

Goenjian, A.K., Najarian, L.M., Pynoos, R.S., Steinberg, A.M., Manoukian, G., Tavosian, A., & Fairbanks, L.A. Posttraumatic stress disorder in elderly and younger adults after the 1988 earthquake in Armenia. *American Journal of Psychiatry, 151,* 895–901.

Graf, P., & Uttl, B. (1995). Component processes of memory: Changes across the adult life-span. *Schweizerische Zeitschrift für Psychologie, 54,* 113–130.

Haberman, S.J. (1982). Analysis of dispersion of multinominal responses. *Journal of the American Statistical Association, 77,* 568–580.

Häfner, H., Nowotny, B., Löffler, W., an der Heiden, W., & Maurer, K. (1995). When and how does schizophrenia produce social deficits? *Eur. Arch. Psychiatry Clin. Neurosci., 246,* 17–28.

Harmless, A. (1990). Developmental impact of combat exposure: comparison of adolescent and adult Vietnam veterans. *Smith College Studies in Social Work, 60,* 185–195.

Harter, S. (1993). Visions of the self: Beyond the me in the mirror. In J.E. Jacobs (Eds.), *Nebraska Symposium on Motivation, 1992: Developmental perspectives on motivation.* Lincoln: University of Nebraska Press.

Hasher, L., & Zacks, R.T. (1988). Working memory, comprehension, and aging: A review and a new view. *The Psychology of Learning and Motivation, 22,* 193–224.

Havighurst, R. (1972). *Developmental tasks and education* (3rd ed.). New York: Basic Books.

Hendin, H., & Haas, A.P. (1991). Suicide and guilt as manifestations of PTSD in Vietnam combat veterans. *American Journal of Psychiatry, 148,* 586–591.

Herman, J.L. (1992). *Trauma and recovery.* New York: Basic Books.

Horowitz, M.J. (1986). *Stress response syndromes* (2nd ed.). Northvale, NJ: Aronson.

Horowitz, M.J., Field, N.P., & Classen, C.C. (1993). Stress response syndromes and their treatment. In L. Goldberger & S. Bresnitz (Eds.), *Handbook of stress.* New York: Free Press.

Horowitz, M.J., Wilner, N., & Alvarez, W. (1979). Impact of event scale: A measure of subjective distress. *Psychosomatic Medicine, 41,* 207–218.

Jackson, H.C. (19829. Moral nihilism: Developmental arrest as a sequela to combat stress. In S.C. Feinstein, J.G. Looney, A.Z. Schwarzberg & A.D. Sovosky (Eds.), *Adolescent psychiatry, Vol. 10.* Chicago: University of Chicago Press.

Janoff-Bulman, R. (1995). Victims of violence. In G.S. Everly Jr. & J.M. Lating (Eds.), *Psychotraumatology*. New York: Plenum Press.

Jenkins, C.D., Hurst, M.W., & Rose, R.M. (1979). Life changes. Do people really remember? *Archives of General Psychiatry, 36,* 379–384.

Jordan, B.K., Marmar, C.R., Fairbank, J.A., Schlenger, W.E., Kulka, R.A., Hough, R.L., & Weiss, D.S. (1992). Problems in families of male Vietnam veterans with posttraumatic stress disorder. *Journal of Consulting and Clinical Psychology, 60,* 916–926.

Kilpatrick, D.G., Saunders, B.E., Amick-McMullan, A., Best, C.L., Veronen, L.J., & Resnick, H.S. (1989). Victim and crime factors associated with the development of crime-related posttraumatic stress disorder. *Behavior Therapy, 20,* 199–214.

Kuch, K., & Cox, B.J. (1992). Symptoms of PTSD in 124 survivors of the Holocaust. *American Journal of Psychiatry, 149,* 337–340.

Kulka, R., Schlenger, W., Fairbank, J.A., Hough, R., Jordan, K., Marmar, C., & Weiss, D. (1990). *Trauma and Vietnam war generation: Findings from the National Vietnam Veterans readjustment study.* New York: Brunner/Mazel.

Labouvie-Vief, G., Hakim-Larson, J., & Bobart, C.J. (1987). Age, ego level, and the lifespan development of coping and defense processes. *Psychology and Aging, 2,* 286–293.

Laufer, R.S., & Gallops, M.S. (1985). Life-course effects of Vietnam combat and abusive violence: Marital patterns. *Journal of Marriage and the Family, 47,* 839–853.

Laufer, R.S. (1988). The serial self. War trauma, identity, and adult development. In J.P. Wilson, Z. Harel & B. Kahana (Eds.), *Human adaption to extreme stress. From the Holocaust to Vietnam.* New York: Plenum.

Lerner, R.M. (1986). *Concepts and theories of human development.* New York: Random House.

Lerner, R.M., Hess, L.E., & Nitz, K. (1990). A developmental perspective of psychopathology. In M. Hersen & C.G. Last (Eds.), *Handbook of child and adult psychopathology. A longitudinal perspective.* New York: Pergamon.

Levinson, D.J. (1978). *The seasons of a man's life.* New York: Ballantine Books.

Loevinger, J. (1976). *Ego development: Conceptions and theories.* San Francisco: Jossey-Bass.

Luria, A.R. (1973). *The working brain: An introduction for neuropsychology.* New York: Basic Books.

Maercker, A. (1992). Weisheit im Alter [Wisdom in old age]. *Münchner Medizinische Wochenschrift, 134,* 518–522.

Maercker, A. (1998). Höheres Lebensalter, Bewertungsprozesse und Anpassungsstörungen [Old age, appraisal processes, and adjustment disorders]. *Zeitschrift für Klinische Psychologie, 27,* 144–146.

Maercker, A. (Ed.) (1997). *Therapie der posttraumatischen Belastungsstörungen* [Treatment of posttraumatic stress disorder]. Berlin: Springer-Verlag.

Maercker, A., Bonanno, G.A., Horowitz, M.J., & Znoj, H.J. (1998). Prediction of complicated grief by positive and negative themes in narratives. *Journal of Clinical Psychology, 54,* 1–20.

Maercker, A., & Schützwohl, M. (1997). Psychological long-term effects of political imprisonment: A group comparison study. *Social Psychiatry and Psychiatric Epidemiology, 32,* 434–442.

Magidson, J. (1981). Qualitative variance, entropy, and correlation ratios for nominal dependent variables. *Social Science Research, 10,* 177–194.

Marcia, J.E. (1980) Identity in adolescence. In J. Adelson (Ed.), *Handbook of adolescence*. New York: Wiley.

Margraf, J., Schneider, S., & Ehlers, A. (1991). *DIPS. Diagnostisches Interview bei psychischen Störungen.* Berlin: Springer-Verlag.

Masters, W.H.& Johnson, V.E. (1970). *Human sexual inadequacy*. Boston: Little Brown.

McCarren, M., Janes, G.R., Goldberg, J., Eisen, S.A., True, W.R., & Henderson, W.G. (1995). A twin study of the association of posttraumatic stress disorder and combat exposure with long-term socioeconomic status in Vietnam veterans. *Journal of Traumatic Stress, 8*, 111–124.

McCrae, R.R., & Costa, P.T., Jr. (1990). *Personality in adulthood*. New York: Guilford.

McFarlane, A.C., & Yehuda, R. (1996). Resilience, vulnerability, and the course of posttraumatic reactions. In B.A. van der Kolk, A.C. McFarlane & L. Weisaeth (Eds.), *Traumatic stress*. New York: Guilford.

Mghir, R., Freed, W., Raskin, A., & Katon, W. (1995). Depression and posttraumatic stress disorder among a community sample of adolescent and young adult Afghan refugees. *Journal of Nervous and Mental Disease, 183*, 24–30.

Müller, H.D. (1998). Haftbedingungen für politische Häftlinge in der DDR (Imprisonment conditions for political prisoners in the GDR). In A. Stephan (Ed.), *Die Vergangenheit läßt uns nicht los ...* [The past won't let loose of us ...]. Magdeburg: Bundeszentrale für politische Bildung.

Neugarten, B.L. (1968). *Middle age and aging*. Chicago: University of Chicago Press.

Noam, G.G., & Dill, D.L. (1991). Adult development and symptomatology. *Psychiatry, 54*, 208–217.

Norris, F., & Murell, S. (1988). Prior experience as a moderator of disaster impact on anxiety symptoms in older adults. *American Journal of Community Psychology, 16*, 665–683.

Pavalko, E.K., & Elder, G.H. (1990). World War II and divorce: A life-course perspective. *American Journal of Sociology, 95*, 1213–1234.

Phifer, J.(1990). Psychological distress and somatic symptoms after natural disaster: Differential vulnerability among older adults. *Psychology and Aging, 5*, 412–420.

Prinz, P.R., Dustman, R.E., & Emmerson, R. (1990). Electrophysiology and aging. In J.E. Birren & K.W. Schaie (Eds.), *Handbook of the psychology of aging*. San Diego: Academic Press.

Resnick, H.S., Kilpatrick, D.G., Dansky, B.S., Saunders, B.E., & Best, C.L. (1993). Prevalence of civilian trauma and posttraumatic stress disorder in a representative sample of women. *Journal of Consulting and Clinical Psychology, 61*, 984–991.

Rutter, M., & Garmezy, N. (1983). Developmental psychopathology. In E.M. Hetherington (Ed.), *Handbook of child psychology. Socialization, personality, and development* (4th ed.). New York: Wiley.

Rutter, M. (1994). Continuities, transitions, and turning points in development. In M. Rutter & D. Hay (Eds.), *Development through life*. Oxford: Blackwell.

Sack, W.H., McSharry, S., Clarke, G.N., Kinney, R., Seeley, J., & Lewinsohn, P. (1994). The Khmer adolescent project. *Journal of Nervous and Mental Disease, 182*, 387–395.

Schützwohl, M., & Maercker, A. (1997). Posttraumatische Belastungsreaktionen nach kriminellen Gewaltdelikten [Posttraumatic stress reactions following criminal victimization]. *Zeitschrift für Klinische Psychologie, 26*, 258–268.

Solomon, Z. (1995). Holocaust survivors in the Gulf War. In Z. Solomon, *Coping with war-induced stress*. New York: Plenum Press.

Solomon, Z., Mikulincer, M., & Avitzur, E. (1988). Coping, locus of control, social support, and combat-related posttraumatic, stress disorder: A prospective study. *Journal of Personality and Social Psychology, 55*, 279–285.

Staudinger, U.M., Freund, A.M., & Smith, J. (1997). *Differential coping patterns in old age.* Berlin: Max-Planck-Institute for Human Development and Education (unpublished manuscript).

Strack, S., & Feifel, H. (1996). Age differences, coping, and the adult life span. In M. Zeidler & N.S. Endler (Eds.), *Handbook of coping.* New York: Wiley.

Strauss, H. (1957). Besonderheiten der nichtpsychotischen Störungen bei Opfern der nationalsozialistischen Verfolgung und ihre Bedeutung bei der Begutachtung [Features of non-psychotic disords in victims of Nazi persecution and its importance for medical certification]. *Nervenarzt, 28*, 344–352.

Tedeschi, R.G., & Calhoun, L.G. (1995). *Trauma and transformation.* London: Sage.

Terr, L.G. (1989). Treating psychic trauma in children, *Journal of Traumatic Stress, 2*, 3–20.

Thompson, M.P., Norris, F.H., & Hanacek, B. (1993). Age differences in the psychological consequences of Hurricane Hugo. *Psychology and Aging, 8*, 606–616.

Vaillant, G.E. (1977). *Adaptation to life.* Boston: Little, Brown.

Valentiner, D.P., Foa, E.B., Riggs, D.S., & Gershuny, B.S. (1996). Coping strategies and posttraumatic stress disorder in female victims of sexual and nonsexual assaults. *Journal of Abnormal Psychology, 105*, 455–458.

Vreeling, F.W. (1993). *Primitive reflexes in healthy adults and neurological patients.* University of Maastricht: Dept. of Health Sciences.

Walker, L.E. (1991). Post-traumatic stress disorder in women: Diagnosis and treatment of battered women syndrome. *Psychotherapy, 28*, 21–29.

Weisman, A.D. (1984*). Coping capacity: On the extent of being mortal.* New York: Human Sciences Press.

Werkentin, F. (1995). *Politische Strafjustiz in der Ära Ulbricht* [Political justice in the Ulbricht era]. Berlin: Ch. Links.

Wittchen, H.-U., & von Zerssen, D. (1987). *Verläufe behandelter und unbehandelter Depressionen und Angststörungen* [Courses of treated and untreated depressions and anxiety disorders]. Berlin: Springer-Verlag.

Woodruff, D. (1985). Arousal, sleep, and aging. In J.E. Birren & K.W. Schaie (Eds.), *Handbook of the psychology of aging* (pp. 261–295). New York: Van Nostrand Reinhold.

Yeheskel, A. (1995). The intimate environment and the sense of coherence among holocaust survivors. *Social Work in Health Care, 20*, 25–36.

A Three-Stage Model of Coping with Loss and Trauma: Lessons from Patients Suffering from Severe and Chronic Disease

Sigrun-Heide Filipp

Critical Life Events as Producers of Change

Critical life events, characterized by threat, adversity, loss or trauma, are inevitable parts of most people's lives; losses in life include not only separations and departures from those we love, but also losses of dreams and of unrealistic optimism, losses of illusions of invulnerability, of freedom, of power, of safety, or of living in a meaningful world. Sometimes – to quote from a book on "Necessary losses" by Judith Viorst (1986) – the most traumatic loss is that of our own younger selves. These various experiences and events in people's lives have always attracted the scientific curiosity of researchers. Three markedly different perspectives have been adopted within this tradition (for an overview, Montada, Filipp, & Lerner, 1992).

First, within lifespan developmental psychology, the concept of significant life events has been proposed for many years as one of the organizing explanatory principles for adult developmental change (Baltes, 1979). On the one hand, systems of influences that regulate the nature of life-span development have been distinguished according to the (now more prominent) view that the timing of events within the individual life-span, rather than their very nature, might be the crucial variable in understanding their impact. On the other hand, the concept of life events as producers of change has gained a rather positive connotation in that "change" has frequently been associated with "growth" (Lerner & Gignac, 1992). Such propositions can be traced back to the work of Erikson (1959) and others who have conceptualized personality growth as occurring through life transitions or changes and the resolution of developmental crises. Similarly, Antonovsky (1979) proposed that researchers need to reorient their investigations in the direction of salutogenesis. This view implies that the process of coping with life changes, as long as they do not overwhelm the individual's resources for coping with them, may actually result in heightened feelings of competence and an improved sense of well-being. Given the fact that the concept of significant life events includes normative role transitions as well as loss and trauma, representing an overwhelmingly broad category of possible experiences, it is not too surprising that changes associated with major life events imply both risk and opportunities for growth; indeed, change in itself might constitute an ultimate prerequisite for growth.

Second, within the traditional "stress and coping paradigm," changes brought about by significant life events have always been equated with the stress generated by the necessity to adjust to altered life circumstances; the amount of readjustment being directly indicative of the amount of stress. As reflected in the early work of Holmes and Rahe (1967) and others, change in itself has been given a negative connotation despite the particular nature of the change-producing event. Here, all changes have been conceived as confronting the organism with demands for adaptation and as deviations from the equilibrium. According to such a view borrowed from homeostatic conceptions, the organism is viewed as vulnerable to the negative effects of stress. Hence, life change is considered to be a risk factor for various forms of pathology, such as coronary heart disease (see for an overview Rahe, 1988) or depression (Brown & Harris, 1989). More recently, a rather differentiated perspective has been adopted by elaborating either those particular features that turn life changes into especially "stressful" experiences (like uncontrollability, unexpectedness, or extremely negative affectivity) or by investigating more carefully the personal and social conditions under which life changes exert their particularly detrimental effect on individual's health and emotional well-being.

Third, some life events take on a particular nature by carrying along with them the trauma of victimization, as may be observed in victims of crime, of natural disasters, of serious accidents, of rape, or of life-threatening disease (for an overview, Davidson & Foa, 1993). Changes in life brought about by experiences of this kind certainly cannot be described simply in terms of "stress" or of deviations from equilibrium. Rather, the trauma of victimization may best be understood in terms of the intense challenge posed to these victims' basic assumptions about themselves and the world they live in (Janoff-Bulman & Schwartzberg, 1991). Life in the aftermath of victimization will never be the same as before; nor will these people be the same. Victims of life crises will have to revise their internal models of their selves and the world. However, as will be argued and illustrated with some of our empirical data, this is a painful and long-lasting process that cannot always be accomplished successfully. On the other hand, as we all know, loss and trauma do not lead inevitably to despair and feelings of victimization. Some people, even in the aftermath of severe loss, can maintain a sense of fulfillment, gratitude, and meaningfulness, whereas others continue to live their lives preoccupied with feelings of injustice, bitterness, and self-pity. Thus, one of the most challenging tasks facing researchers in this field is to find out more about what makes the difference between these two groups of people – an issue that is usually referred to as the issue of "coping research."

Modeling the Process of Coping with Loss and Trauma

One might start here with a quotation from an article published some years ago by Taylor (1984). When asked to review the state of the art in coping research, she wrote:

> Were one to seek a body of psychological literature that is a model of conceptual clarity and organization, the coping literature would be the last place to look. Indeed, it is hard to think of a literature that is in worse shape. Were it an area in its research infancy, empirical promise alone might be sufficient to accept this state temporarily; early research generates a sense of optimism that organizational and conceptual confusion will shortly be resolved empirically. Unfortunately, the coping literature is not in its infancy. It somewhat resembles a three-car garage filled to the rafters with junk, and clearing it up is such a formidable task that, understandably, few have been willing to undertake it (p. 2313).

Many years later one is tempted to agree with this conclusion. The coping literature is either filled with attempts to dichotomize modes of coping in rather static terms (e. g., monitoring vs. blunting; Miller, 1992) or to enumerate the various modes of coping in a theoretically rather ambiguous manner (e. g., Muthny, 1989).

Coping, in its most general meaning, represents nothing other, according to our view, than all (not necessarily successful; see Filipp & Klauer, 1991) attempts to gradually transform an objective reality comprised of "bad news," that is, losses, threats, or trauma, into a subjective reality, in which victims can continue to live in relative peace. This seems, at first glance, to resemble attempts to bring "what is" and "what ought to be" into better alignment – a notion that the concept of coping shares with many approaches in which the reduction of discrepancies are the core issue. Throughout the relevant research there is considerable consensus, despite differences in conceptualization and naming, that bringing "is" and "ought" into better alignment can be accomplished through two fundamental avenues: either to change circumstances and to bring them into line with one's wants and needs, that is "changing the world," or to change one's beliefs, lower one's aspirations, or replace one's unattainable goals, that is "changing the self" (see Rothbaum, Weisz, & Snyder, 1982).

Certainly, active attempts to change the world – often referred to also as "problem-focused coping" – may be a common and adaptive response to many stressful situations in life (Lazarus & Folkman, 1984). And in line with the proposition of the "primacy of primary control," recently introduced by Heck-hausen and Schulz (1995), one could expect that people start out to shape "what is" to fit their particular aspirations, needs, and potentials. However, such attempts to change the world are certainly of little use in coping with loss and trauma as, for example, in coping with the diagnosis of cancer or with the unexpected and early loss of one's spouse. Rather, the major coping task faced by these individuals is to reconcile themselves to a situation that cannot be changed and over which they have little, if any, control. They obviously need to change their expectations and conceptions of "what ought to be" in their lives. They will have to alter their aspirations, goals, and personal beliefs, and disengage from unattainable goals, as described by Klinger (1975) and others (see Martin & Tesser, 1989); they will have to change standards according to which they evaluate their selves, and they will be forced to rearrange their conceptions of what constitutes "a good life" – all in all, modes of dealing with loss and trauma that should result in considerable reductions of the discrepancy between "is" and "ought."

However, a control view on coping ("changing the world") as well as the conception of "changing the self" in order to reduce discrepancies, as just briefly described, presupposes that individuals are indeed aware of these discrepancies between "is" and "ought" and look at the reality, they have to live in, in a fairly undistorted manner. But, as we all know, this is by no means the rule. In addition, there is a strong appreciation within the literature that objective reality is sometimes so ambiguous and complex ("What did the doctor say?") that individuals have considerable power to define and shape reality through their constructs and appraisals.

Accordingly, as will be argued here, we do need to know more than these two main avenues in order to understand the process of how victims of life crises gradually come to terms with their lot and to take the large interindividual differences more seriously into account. Thus, the position taken here is that coping with loss and trauma can best be understood in terms of how victims of life crises are going to process, step by step, extremely "bad news" from the world. Such a notion has long and convincingly been promoted by Horowitz (1982); and despite some profound criticism of stage-like conceptions of the coping process, for example, of the problems involved in subjecting these models to a rigorous empirical test (Wortman & Silver, 1992), we consider such an "information-processing view" of coping to be an extremely useful and theoretically promising approach (see also Foa & Kozak, 1986). Transformation of objective reality into one's subjective reality includes the individual's selective attention to and construals of what happened to him or her, ruminations on whether and how what happened could have been avoided, appraisals of one's resources for dealing with or overcoming what happened, comparisons of one's own current life with that of others or with hypothetically worse worlds, and all the many other types of "intrapsychic" modes of coping (Lazarus & Folkman, 1984) that are to be observed in victims of life crises as are to some extent reported in the literature.

In this chapter, we shall address some of the steps through which victims of life crises are seen to construe their subjective realities* by referring to three fundamental processes, not necessarily conceived of being sequential in nature: first, *attentive processes* that contribute to the construction of an individual's *"perceptive reality,"* mainly considered here in terms of selectively attending to "bad news" and, thus, defending positive illusions; second, *comparative processes* that help to shape perceptive reality toward a reality that victims of life crises can gradually tolerate, accept, and live in; and third, *interpretative processes* that help to construe an *"interpretative reality,"* mainly through ruminative thinking and related attempts to ascribe subjective meaning to what currently makes up one's perceptive reality. Thus, rather than referring to coping as either changing the world or changing the self, we want to highlight the process through which victims of life crises struggle towards re-establishing "a better world to live in," as is also conveyed through the notion of "reality negotiation" (Snyder, 1989). Due to the fact that our own research has mainly focused on the process of coping with the onset of severe and life-threatening disease, we shall primarily refer to studies that were related to that type of loss and trauma**.

Construing "Perceptive Reality" by Defending Positive Illusions

Despite the long-standing dominant view in psychology that accurate perception of reality is a hallmark of mental health, and despite the idea claimed by

---

* We borrow this ingenious notion from Watzlawick (1976) and appreciate it for reflecting most clearly what is crucial to the transformation of "objective reality" into a "subjective reality."

** Most of our research to which is referred through this chapter has been supported by a Grant from German Research Association (Fi 346/1–3; 346/2–3) as well as from the German Federal Ministry of Research and Technology. Extremely helpful contributions to this chapter have been made by Dr. Dieter Ferring (University of Trier) and Dr. Thomas Klauer (University of Rostock) whom I wish to thank. In addition, assistance by cand. psych. Anna Sequeira is appreciated.

many prominent authors that "mature" coping lies in attempts to come into touch with reality (see Haan, 1977), one can easily argue that life cannot be lived easily, particularly in the aftermath of victimization, without a set of (possibly shared) illusions and self-deceptions as so nicely and ingeniously described in the work of Taylor and her coworkers (Taylor & Brown, 1988; Brown, 1991). Self-enhancing illusions are ubiquitous in healthy, well-adjusted people; almost all of us believe, to some degree, in personal invulnerability; many of us also believe, at least somehow, in personal immortality; and those among us, who have been close to patients suffering from life-threatening disease, have not infrequently come to the insight that all our striving and productivity stems from a single powerful psychological force, the denial of death. These "illusions" are integrated in a system of beliefs (i. e., our assumptive worlds; see above) many of which may never be challenged or examined (elsewhere called "primitive" beliefs; Rockeach, 1968), whereas other beliefs are forged out of the "bad events" of our lives.

Loss and trauma do not just disrupt plans, hopes, and options for the future in those being exposed to it; loss and trauma particularly challenge positive illusions that individuals hold about themselves and the world in which they live. Any dispute as to whether or not defending positive illusions in the face of loss and trauma as can be observed in, for example, patients suffering from life-threatening disease, is inferior to more mature and reality-based coping efforts appears to be fruitless, since many victims of life crises need to live "as if" and to use "as if" as a workable strategy in their real worlds (Snyder, 1989).

Of course, it is also well known from studies of other types of stressful events that, on the other hand, illusions and self-deceptions can be maladaptive and can exert a heavy toll (e. g., in coping with loss of job and unemployment; see Frese, 1992). The core issue within coping research, accordingly, has always been to know what kinds and degrees of illusionary thinking are damaging, what kinds are constructive and under what conditions. Usually it is argued that the costs and benefits of defending positive illusions (and of other denial-like processes; see Lazarus, 1983) depend on whether or not a given type of stressful experience must be encountered again and again and whether or not direct action, that would otherwise be highly adaptive, is suppressed. In particular, if circumstances are truly resistant toward change, it is highly "realistic" to attempt to let go of any commitments that have been destroyed, rather than to continue to fight for their recovery (Janoff-Bulman & Brickman, 1982).

Moreover, it is widely assumed that strategies to defend and maintain positive illusions are of importance particularly to patients suffering from severe disease like cancer because these strategies ultimately contribute to *hope*. Hope, by definition and despite various metaphors that are linked to it (e. g., "hope as a bridge" or "hope as a protected area"; see Snyder, Irving, & Anderson, 1991), implies goal-setting and future-referenced events that are wished for, that have positive affect and have some subjective probability of occurrence. Clinicians often emphasize that many cancer patients do not hope exclusively for recovery, extended survival, or a return to previous ways of life. Rather, hope is considered to constitute a kind of "world view" in patients that may guide them safely through the dark side of their lives. Accordingly, hope is often seen to be a prerequisite for successful coping – even more, in the words of Weisman (1979) – *hoping is coping*, and its crucial importance with regard to the "giving up – given up" cycle has been outlined over many decades. In fact, there is a long tradition of considering hope and the quality of survival as mutually related factors. Thus there are good reasons to use the hope versus hopelessness construct in studying emotional well-being and adaptation in severely ill patients, in particular, because hope, in turn, is also seen to be steady enough to withstand reality (Snyder et al., 1991). Our own longitudinal observations of patients suffering from cancer provide impressive illustrative of this latter point (see for further details Filipp, 1992).

Within the time span of this study, a subsample of $n = 56$ (out of a total of $N = 332$) patients had died from cancer, but for each patient within this subsample a complete data set was available with assessments of coping, emotional well-being, and hopelessness at four waves of measurement during the first year of the study. Based on these data sets, a follow-back perspective could be adopted by tracing back the course of their coping with and adapting to cancer in patients nearing their death. In addition, it was of crucial interest to see whether and how these terminal cancer patients differed in their course of coping and emotional adjustment from patients who were still alive after the fourth measurement wave. Accordingly, the sample of decedents was matched for comparison purposes with the sample of survivors with respect to age, gender, and medical variables (as obtained from their physicians at the time of study onset). Subsequent analyses proved that these two samples did not differ in respect to age, gender, and even some medical variables (e. g., tumor site, multimorbidity). Matching efforts were unsuccessful for other medical variables, indicating that the group of deceased, in fact, was in an advanced stage of cancer from the very beginning of the study (e. g., tumor size, relapse, physician's prognosis at t1). Within the present line of reasoning, the crucial issue is changes in hopelessness (as measured by a German Version of the Beck-Scale; Krampen, 1979) over the time span of 1 year that can be observed in both subsamples.

As Figure 1 shows, a dramatic increase in hopelessness characterizes the sample of patients who subsequently died. This increase may be considered to reflect the breakdown of all coping mechanisms that might have, up till then, helped these patients to defend positive illusions and to maintain hope. This

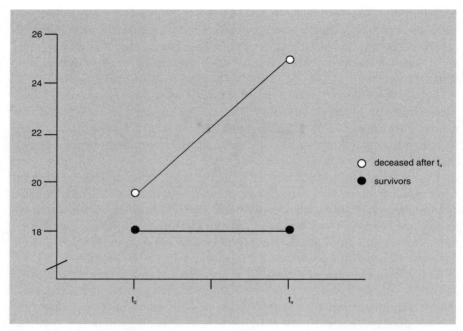

Figure 1. Levels of hopelessness in two samples of cancer patients (survivors and deceased) at two waves of measurement.

conclusion can be drawn rather confidently, because these patients, though in an advanced stage of their disease from the very beginning of the study (as mentioned above), did *not* differ from the group of survivors in level of hopelessness at earlier waves of measurement (here: at t2). Lessons from these patients teach us that hope indeed did withstand reality, even for a considerable amount of time. Yet, what about the increasing loss of hope to be observed later? Can we consider the increase in hopelessness as being reflective of the fact that most patients in that subsample no longer adhered to "false hopes"? Had they reached the final stage of "acceptance," or is hopelessness in these patients indicative of nothing other than despair and "*depressive* realism" (Alloy & Abramson, 1988; italics added)? Certainly, these questions are of fundamental importance for both practitioners in the medical setting and coping researchers. Yet we have, if any, only very provisional answers (Filipp, 1992).

Thus, there is an impressive array of findings in support of the notion of people's capacity to defend positive illusions as an adaptive mode of dealing with their fate. In other words, many strategies employed by victims of life crises are powerful and effective in reducing the threat imposed on their selves and they help them to operate on the basis of an "unrealistic optimism," "illusion of invulnerability," or even "illusion of immortality." However, the adaptive value of coping by primarily defending positive illusions often can be observed only in the short run (as illustrated above), and it is equally well documented that, over the course of time, positive illusions have to give way to threatening information that cannot either remain unattended or easily be altered in meaning.

In addition, to be selectively inattentive implies, by definition, that a person must have some awareness of threatening information in order to know where not to look (sometimes referred to as the "paradox of denial"). From this perspective, the various modes of coping that are so loosely assumed elsewhere under "emotion-focused" coping might be much better thought of as attempts to actively negotiate or construe one's own perceptive reality rather than simply as a distortion of it. This certainly necessitates the capacity for attention control (see for an overview Uleman & Bargh, 1989). However, the "luxury of mental control" is frequently lost when people encounter severe threat: "Small stresses occupy our minds with worry and distract us from the things we would like to think about; large stresses wrest our attention away repeatedly, sometimes chronically, and leave us wondering if we can control our minds at all" (Wegner, 1988, p. 683). In fact, previous work has pointed to a tendency among those who have undergone major negative life changes to experience involuntary, intrusive, and distressing ruminations (i. e., thoughts, memories, and/or mental images related to the event; e. g., Silver, Wortman, & Klos, 1982). One might conclude from these observations that ruminative thinking might be a necessary step in processing "bad news from the world," presumably of particular value in the construction of one's "interpretative reality." Before we address the issue of ruminative thinking (see below), special attention will be given to yet another way of construing "perceptive realities," namely through selective (i. e., palliative) comparison processes within which victims of life crises might evaluate their lot by adopting various different frames of reference.

Shaping "Perceptive Reality" Through Palliative Comparisons

After victims have become fully aware of "what is" in terms of their perceptive realities, a further important step in the coping process, may be attempting to construct a better "reality to live in" through presumably palliative (i. e., selective) comparison processes. Despite the fact that modern coping literature is filled with theoretical accounts and empirical examples of palliative comparisons with others (i. e., social comparisons) or with hypothetically worse worlds, as also evidenced in "counterfactual thinking" (Davis & Lehman,

1995), we shall argue here that *temporal comparisons* might be used in a palliative manner as well. In addition, we shall briefly refer to how victims of loss and trauma might make use of their past in a more general sense.

Social Comparisons in Coping with Loss and Trauma

Many approaches toward a better understanding of how victims of life crises ultimately come to terms with their lot (or with what they now have accepted as their new reality) have highlighted the role of (selective) comparison processes (e. g., Taylor & Lobel, 1989). These processes might be seen as an effective means to ultimately shape the interpretative reality towards a reality in which individuals can continue to live in the aftermath of victimization. In particular, *social* comparison activity has been recognized as an important aspect of coping efforts. Originally, Wills (1981) has suggested that threats to self-esteem would encourage individuals to engage in selective downward comparisons (i. e., with less advantaged others) in order to improve the way they feel about themselves. In the meantime, downward comparisons have been considered, more generally, as a useful strategy in coping with threat, loss, and trauma. Results from various studies have highlighted that, under these conditions of life, individuals are especially inclined to compare themselves selectively with others who are worse off (see Taylor & Lobel, 1989). Despite some confusions and also contradictory evidence with regard to how social comparisons are used in response to loss and trauma and with regard to their presumed adaptive value (see for an overview Buunk, 1994), the notion of selective (i. e., self-enhancing and/or palliative) comparisons as addressed from "Neo-social comparison theory" (Wills & Suls, 1991) is highly prominent in the literature. Moreover, yet another way of engaging in social comparisons has been reported, namely, that victims of life crises (e. g., rape victims) do not just use social comparison information that lies at hand; rather, they often also tend to *actively generate* comparison information by construing "false consensus" (i. e., overestimate the proportion of others with a similar fate) in order to avoid or reduce negative feelings of uniqueness (Goethals, Messick, & Allison, 1991).

In the aftermath of traumatization individuals might not only selectively use or generate social comparison information; in addition, one can assume that comparisons are also made within a temporal frame of reference, for example, by comparing "what one has" with "what one had earlier." Thus, one might ask under what conditions social and temporal comparison processes complement, substitute, or supersede each other in creating and preserving subjective well-being in victims of life crises (Filipp & Ferring, in press).

Temporal Comparisons in Coping with Loss and Trauma

At first glance, in the aftermath of victimization, temporal comparisons are highly likely to result in extremely negative evaluations of the present, because they might make victims fully aware of what has been lost. However, it shall be argued here that temporally based comparisons might be equated with potentially adaptive responses as well. In more general terms we shall outline that the understanding of the coping process will be substantially enlarged by taking a more careful look at how victims related their past and present in their construals and appraisals of what has happened to them.

The Role of the Past in Coping with Loss and Trauma

An individual's prior history of life events and the way he or she makes use of the past might become observable in victims of life crises in several ways. First, victims might dwell on their past experiences and this can, though must not, be done in a highly explicit and thoughtful manner (as illustrated by "instrumental reminiscence"; Wong & Watt, 1991). In fact, for those psychologists who study reminiscence in old age, this idea is by no means new. In this respect, autobiographical knowledge derived from one's past is seen to be employed in order to maintain a coherent sense of self, to integrate and comprehend information related to the present, to solve current problems, and to guide planning for future actions (for a renewed interest in autobiographical memory, see Webster & Cappeliez, 1993). For example, Staudinger, Freund, Linden, and Maas (1996), based on data from the Berlin Aging Study, have highlighted the role of dwelling on the past in elderly people's coping: at the level of means, their sample, when presented a fairly comprehensive list of altogether 13 modes of coping, reported this coping mode as being most characteristic of their ways to deal with current problems in life. For researchers coming from the coping domain, however, life review, reminiscence, or autobiographical memories are rather novel and unfamiliar concepts.

The role of prior exposure to critical life events may be highlighted not only by investigating individual's autobiographical reflections and temporal comparisons (see below), but also, more generally, by asking what people might have learned from prior exposures to critical life events. The core issue is whether the successful resolution of critical events in earlier stages of life contributes to a heightened resilience or, in contrast, to a heightened vulnerability to maladaptive coping with critical events in later years. There is evidence in favor of both assumptions.

Prior experiences have been reported to operate as a risk factor in coping with later events. The widespread assumption is that the accumulation of var-

ious critical events within a given period of time (rather than the mere exposure) represents a serious threat to the individual's resource-deficit balance in
coping with a present event (Holmes & Rahe, 1967). More specifically, taking
the sample case of victimization by physical attacks as an illustration, Janoff-
Bulman (1979) has been able to show that repeated exposure to a given event
does make a difference. Women who had been exposed to such an experience
a second time, tended to blame themselves for being victimized by attributing
the attack to stable internal factors (i. e., characterological self-blame), which,
in turn, impeded resolution of the crisis and facilitated intrusive thoughts. On
the contrary, in the case of a single experience, behavioral self-blame was much
more likely to occur and to facilitate the victim's posttrauma recovery.

On the other hand, recollections of the past might also be considered adaptive. They can provide people with a particular time in their lives that they may
use palliatively as a frame of reference in considering their present. What has
been introduced elsewhere as the general "comparison standard effect of
memories" (see Clark & Collins, 1993) can be demonstrated nicely here with
reference to a finding reported by Elder (Elder & Caspi, 1988). Based on the
sample of the Berkeley Growth Study that he had followed up many years
later, Elder observed that for those men who had experienced particularly
stressful years in their childhood (due to economic constraints within the
Great Depression), there was a long-term positive impact in terms of higher
levels in life-satisfaction in their middle age. This transformation of experience
was presumably less due to having learned particular coping responses; rather,
one can assume that modest standards for evaluating one's life evolving during
that time have made it easier to perceive relative gratifications in later years.
More recently, Aldwin, Sutton, and Lachman (1996) reported from three studies, in which community samples of various ages were enrolled as subjects, that
a majority of their subjects reported drawing upon prior experiences, though
not necessarily upon a similar episode, in coping with a recent problem and
that perceptions of current mastery obviously were bolstered by earlier successful coping episodes.

In general, the likelihood that successful coping with a present crisis depends
greatly upon the individual's history of prior events, in particular upon his or
her (perceived) successes and failures in confronting previous life events. This
means that how individuals handle a current crisis might be a direct reflection
of how they have handled crises in their past. Those who successfully resolved
problems or crises in previous stages may have achieved a lasting solution to
present crises, because the subjective achievements derived from previous solutions are seen as the building blocks for present and future solutions. When
a crisis is resolved, the individual may emerge from his or her engagements
with a new skill, with self-confidence, or other enabling self-attitudes that are

added to his or her repertoire of coping responses. Crucial to this line of rea-soning is the idea that personal memories of past coping episodes and self-per-ceptions of one's coping abilities derived from the past (also to be named as "coping efficacy") seem to play a buffering role in the coping process in that they provide people with a particular sense of coping competence (Aldwin et al., 1996). Although there are some related theoretical concepts that come fairly close to such a notion (e. g., learned resourcefulness, hopefulness, sense of mastery, internal control beliefs), it is still unclear how these various con-cepts might be related to an individual's history of stress and coping and ac-count for variations in coping with loss and trauma. Whether or not reliance on autobiographical knowledge and past experiences might be adaptive cer-tainly needs a closer consideration.

Propositions from Temporal Comparison Theory

Finally, the role of the past may be highlighted in yet a different manner which can be illustrated by outlining some propositions borrowed from temporal comparison theory, originally proposed by Albert (1977). Core issues within temporal comparison theory are related to two fundamental questions: When do people compare their present selves with past selves, and what are the (intended or unintended) consequences of such comparisons? Until now, re-search has hardly ever focused on the functional role of temporal comparisons in coping with loss and trauma. This notion has gained attention for years, primarily again in gerontology, where some authors have claimed that tempo-ral comparison information is particularly salient in the elderly (Suls & Mullen, 1982). In addition, a few studies have dealt with perceptions of change in terms of appraisals of "naturally occurring change." Here, research has often focused on "implicit theories of stability and change" (Ross, 1989), that is, on subjects' beliefs about developmental changes across the life span and their very nature in terms of gains and losses (see also Heckhausen, Dixon, & Baltes, 1989).

Other research has examined how people perceive their own personality functioning over major phases of their adult lives. For example, Ryff (1982) has investigated perceptions of improved or worsened functioning over time within various age groups. Subjects had to explicitly compare themselves as they are at present with how they were at an earlier age on a variety of attri-butes (e. g., autonomy, purpose in life, positive relations with others). One finding from this research was that younger subjects perceived improvement on almost all aspects of psychological functioning; whereas past assessments within the older group were generally closer to their present assessments, thereby indicating an attempt to construe temporal consistencies and mainte-nance of prior levels of functioning. This latter finding points to the *consistency*

motive as being highly dominant within the elderly and to the elderly's need
to perceive similarity across the life span as a resource in coping with the
decrements of old age. These considerations might be applied equally to individuals who have to cope with victimization, and temporal comparison theory
can be fruitfully used as a conceptual tool in studying how people cope with
loss and trauma. Here, obviously, are the crossroads at which temporal comparison theory meets *self-consistency theory*.

Although the need for positive self-regard and self-enhancing motives have
dominated the literature on self-conceptions for decades, there are strong theoretical arguments and a considerable amount of empirical evidence in favor
of the need for self-consistency (see for an overview Swann, 1983). Many authors insist that self-conceptions are highly enduring and stable over time;
some even suggest that trying to change persons' conceptions of themselves is
rather like fighting windmills. In line with this reasoning, Swann and Hill (1982)
have referred to practitioners of brain-washing techniques in prisoner-of-war
camps who have typically failed to create lasting changes in the self-conceptions of their captives despite their ability to exert nearly complete control
over these victims' physical and psychological environments. Thus, it is not too
surprising that longitudinal investigations have revealed that self-conceptions
remain stable over considerable periods of time (Filipp & Klauer, 1986), and
that most people proved to regard self-confirmatory feedback as more diagnostic than disconfirmatory feedback.

Accordingly, fairly consistent conclusions can be derived from the studies of
these various "self-verification processes" contributing to self-consistency (see
for an overview Swann, 1983). People strive to display signs and symbols of
who they are, selectively affiliate with partners whose appraisals confirm their
self-conceptions, are inclined to present themselves in ways that elicit self-confirmatory reactions from their social environment, and, in general, are "seeing"
(i. e., selectively attending to, selectively encoding and retrieving, as well as
selectively interpreting) more self-confirmatory evidence than actually exists.
Obviously there are strong arguments in favor of the individual's need for
self-consistency despite experimental evidence from laboratory studies also
pointing to the malleability of self-conceptions under certain conditions. These
arguments relate to the notion that people's self-conceptions are an important
means through which they predict and control their world; threatening their
self-conceptions should, accordingly, threaten their perceptions of control.

Individuals are not obsessed with self-evaluation and self-verification, particularly when objective evidence and/or social evidence provides them with
a sense of self-identity and when this evidence is readily available. However,
self-verification activities may become intensified in times of crisis in which a
tremendous incoherence between past and present is created, and thus they

may differ from the rather automatic, nonreflective activities that characterize routine self-verification. Interestingly enough, almost an identical proposition has been made within temporal comparison theory. In fact, temporal comparison theory has proposed that these comparisons are more likely to occur during times of rapid change, and that they might be even more likely when the affective quality of the present is extremely negative. Thus, the tremendous changes that are brought about in victims' lives by their experiences of loss and trauma are considered to make their past more salient than is the case in times of "smooth functioning."

Forced temporal comparisons in these hard times might lead individuals to recognize that they have been, in fact, undergoing considerable change (i. e., discrepancies between the current self and retrospective perceptions of the self); given their need to maintain a sense of self-continuity and self-consistency, this need is then seen to form the explicit motivational base for temporal comparisons (along with the need to predict what lies ahead might, in these cases, as a second motivational basis for temporal comparisons). Accordingly, temporal comparison theory proposes that there will be a strong tendency to change the past self to make it appear closer and more similar to the present. Furthermore, victims of life crises might attempt to find something that is constant by analytically distinguishing their "fundamental self" from the different changes that other facets of their selves have been undergoing. Thus, a heightened tendency to engage in temporal comparisons is conceived of as a means of coping with a dramatically altered life change by either minimizing or "cognitively separating" the change that has been brought about.

However, discrepancies between past and present selves cannot always be reduced and consistency cannot always be inferred from or construed by temporal comparisons; in these cases, the construction of *positive* changes is then likely to occur. Accordingly, temporal comparisons that present (subjective) evidence of maturation, progress, or growth should then be favored, quite consistent with research on self-enhancing processes, over those comparisons that present evidence of decay or decline. In this sense, temporal comparisons are related conceptually and functionally to other modes of coping with loss and trauma in which defending positive illusions is the core issue. In fact, it is widely argued within coping research (and maybe this is much more than one of the myths in coping research) that one successful, and by no means infrequently used, mode of dealing with loss and trauma is to construe *positive changes*, to draw benefits from one's fate, or to replace losses by gains. This point can be illustrated by findings reported by Affleck, Tennen, Croog, and Levine (1987) which, at first glance, seem to be rather contraintuitive: According to their results, middle-aged men who had survived a second heart-attack were more likely than men who had not had second heart-attacks to report benefits from their disease. To put it differently: Perceived instability can be – and obviously is – compensated for by inferring positive changes and by denying negative changes. Thus, what is often referred to elsewhere in terms of "making sense out of one's fate" or "search for meaning" (Silver, Boon, & Stones, 1983), is conceptualized here from a divergent theoretical point of view.

Quite in contrast to research on social comparisons and despite the strong theoretical arguments as presented here, however, an empirical proof of temporal comparisons in the face significant life changes is almost nonexistent. One exception is a study by Lieberman (1992), who used data from the Chicago Transition Study in which more than 2000 adults between 16 and 65 years of age had been enrolled. Subjects were a subsample of individuals who had undergone normative transitions and/or eruptive events between two waves of measurement (separated by 4 years). They were asked to rate how much each event had changed their lives and how much it had changed the way they felt about themselves. Liebermann found that the various events differed markedly in their impact on how people perceived changes in the self. Events that brought about high perceptions of change in the self included divorce, changes in one's job situation, or marriage. Completely in contrast, becoming a grandparent, experiencing a major decrement in one's self, or child-bearing obviously had little subjective impact on the self-image. In particular, deterioration in personal health had a substantial impact on perceptions of changes in one's life situation, yet, only rarely were they perceived as evoking changes in the self. From a superficial point of view, this finding seems to indicate nothing more than that different events have different consequences for the self-system. From a psychological point of view, this implies that the self-system differs with regard to its implicative capacity across various life-change transitions and that the various processes that take place to protect the self from inconsistent self-related information are not equally effective across all domains.

Defending Self-Consistency as a Means of Coping with Cancer

There are good reasons for assuming that the onset of severe and chronic disease is one of the most traumatic events in life, particularly when it occurs nonnormatively in early or middle adulthood, that is, during the so-called "best years" of life. First of all, this might have to do with the fact that people in our culture normally are not "educated" to deal with disease and death. They are not taught such things at school, nor do they usually learn from "models" how to handle threats to life. Even if models are available in their social worlds, people prefer to look at the sunnier sides of life. According to the widely held belief in one's invulnerability and "unrealistic optimism," as already mentioned above, people usually do not consider the onset of chronic disease as one of the possible experiences and realities that will occur in their lives. Thus, neither does anticipatory socialization in whatever setting with regard to such traumatic experiences take place, nor do people, in general, voluntarily engage in ways of anticipatory coping with potential threats to their health or even lives. In that respect, one could borrow a term from cognitive psychology and characterize the diagnosis of cancer as a "weakly scripted situation" (Abelson, 1981), for which instrumental responses (let aside "behavioral routines") are not readily at hand.

In addition, whereas other negative life experiences (e. g., loss of a loved one) are embedded, at least partially, into culturally shaped ways of responding (e. g., by public rituals or mourning customs; see Averill, 1968; Stroebe, Stroebe, & Hanson, 1993), thus, sometimes facilitating the coping process, the initial diagnosis of a severe and possibly life-threatening disease is accompanied by high degrees of behavioral disorganization and, in many cases, by the disruption and breakdown of social ties (for evidence of "defensive distancing from victims of serious illness," see Pyszczynski, Greenberg, Solomon, Cather et al., 1995). Threats to health and life induced by the diagnosis of cancer, by definition, represent existential plights (Weisman, 1979). This might be particularly true for people confronting cancer, because it is cancer – in contrast to other diseases like cardiac heart diseases – that seems to be surrounded by a variety of negatively connoted "myths and metaphors" (Sontag, 1979). Finally, cancer is mostly far beyond the (primary) control of those suffering from it and, at least in many cases, even beyond physicians' control; patients often are exposed to their diagnosis in a completely unpredictable way, taking into consideration that the detection of cancer often simply occurs "by chance." Furthermore, severe and life-threatening diseases generally interfere with a large spectrum of goals people have set for themselves, necessitating disengagement from commitments and their replacement with new options and goals, "coping tasks" that are particularly painful to accomplish and often exceed people's capabilities (see below). And even more painful, to be diagnosed as a cancer patient nearly always means a threat to fundamental beliefs about the self (e. g., being a strong, powerful, effective, or "fully functioning" person) that might have guided individual courses of action in the past. According to our view, the frequent need to make dramatic alterations to the self-system does contribute to the diagnosis of cancer(as to other severe diseases) as being one of the most negative life experiences, in general.

Taken together, there are quite a few arguments for conceiving the diagnosis of cancer as a particularly traumatic event, and one is tempted to give a quick answer to the question as to whether anything "could be worse" in people's lives by simply saying "no" (Filipp, 1992). Yet, simple questions, by no means, allow simple and premature answers. One needs to carefully investigate how successfully patients, in fact, cope with their life-threatening disease and as to what, in particular, defending self-consistency or having construed positive changes in the coping process might contribute to emotional well-being and adjustment. This issue was addressed within the "Trier Longitudinal Study of Coping with Chronic Disease" for a subsample of $N = 100$ cancer patients (for details, see Klauer & Filipp, in press; Klauer, Ferring, & Filipp, in press).

In this study temporal comparisons of the actual self and the current life situation as opposed to the past have been investigated by asking these patients to rate the amount of change resulting from the fact of having been diagnosed a cancer patient on a total of 17 domains (e. g., intellectual functioning, self-confidence, marital satisfaction). For comparison purposes a sample of patients who had recently suffered a myocardial infarction were also recruited as subjects. These explicitly induced temporal comparisons had to be reported using an instrument that we introduced to our subjects as a *"changeometer"*, a scale ranging from 0 (no change at all) to 100 (maximum of change). In addition, after having indicated the amount of perceived change (if change indeed was perceived in a particular domain), its desirability and its controllability were assessed in order to explore the nature of perceived changes. These ratings were used to derive various indicators of perceived change, for example, the number of domains, that were perceived to be affected by one's disease (change prevalence), the ratio of positively versus negatively valenced changes, or the mean intensity of perceived change across all domains.

In general, the perception of changes in the self and in one's life proved to be fairly prominent within both samples of patients with a mean value for change prevalence of $M = 12.12$; $SD = 4.55$ (given a range of scores from min $= 0$ to max $= 17$). Thus, on the level of means, being diagnosed as a cancer patient or having experienced myocardial infarction resulted in perceptions of an "an altered self" and of an "altered life" on a variety of domains. These various domains, however, differed clearly in terms of their "change sensitivity", that is, whether or not changes in the respective domain were indeed perceived. Physical fitness and physical well-being, not too surprisingly, were the domains that yielded the most frequent and most intense self-perceived changes. However, physical attractiveness, self-confidence, and even intellectual functioning were domains that – according to many patients' views – underwent considerable change as well. In contrast, perceived social integration as well as religious beliefs appeared to be fairly unaltered in subjective terms.

With regard to the quality of these changes – aggregated across all domains – the number of negatively valued changes clearly outweighed the number of

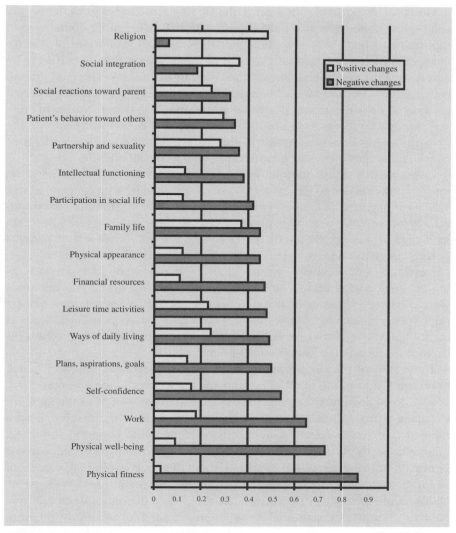

Figure 2. Perceived positive and negative life changes in a sample of cancer patients (relative frequencies).

positively valued changes, in particular, within the sample of cancer patients. Nonetheless, it is remarkable to note that more than one-third of the patients experienced positive changes in at least one of the domains. For example, it was not unlikely for patients to perceive positive changes in the quality of family life, in social integration, and particularly in religion and attitudes toward life (see Figure 2).

However, of particular interest is the finding that change prevalence and desirability of changes interrelated positively, that is, the more domains were reported as having changed, the higher the (relative) proportion of *positive* changes. This result is, at first glance, a nice confirmation of Albert's (1977) assumption, as mentioned above, when victims of life crises are not able to construe self-consistency, they will develop a tendency to evaluate perceived changes in a positive manner. In other words: Inferring many changes in one's self through temporal comparisons in the face of a dramatically altered life situation seems clearly to result in the insight that the self has undergone considerable improvement in important domains of self and life.

Consequently, these various temporal comparison activities should be meaningfully related to indicators of "successful" coping with cancer and to a variety of adaptive outcomes. First, since perceptions of stability are considered to be preferred over perceptions of change, those patients with low scores in change prevalence should be better adjusted to their disease than patients perceiving many changes in their selves and their lives. In addition, however, perceiving a large number of *positive* changes should be considered as indicating effective coping and to be related to adaptive outcomes. Two measures were considered here as indicating effective coping and adaptation, namely hope versus hopelessness (assessed by a German version of the Beck-Scale, as mentioned above; Krampen, 1979) and self-perceived coping effectiveness (as derived from patients' ratings on a 9-point scale).

The results of the various analyses can be summarized as follows: Change prevalence, that is, the number of domains for which change was perceived, proved to be completely unrelated to hopelessness as well as to the measure of coping efficacy. Thus, at first glance, perceiving changes in the self in a large number of domains does not seem to be detrimental to restoring and maintaining hope; to put it differently: the maintenance of self-consistency in the aftermath of being diagnosed a cancer patient did not contribute to successful adaptation. However, a different picture emerges when one looks at the desirability vs. undesirability of perceived changes: When the (absolute or relative) number of *negative* changes in the self were considered, significant relationships to hopelessness emerged that took the expected direction: Many negative changes were significantly related to high levels of hopelessness. Admittedly, this finding is not particularly surprising. However, what appears to be much more inconsistent with theoretical expectations is the finding that the number of perceived *positive* changes was completely unrelated to hopelessness. Thus our data did not support the widely held notion that perceiving positive changes and construing gains in the face of loss and trauma have adaptive consequences. With regard to the preservation of hope (but also with regard to coping efficacy), these patients obviously did not draw any benefits from their attempts to construe "meaning" and to see their selves as having undergone a variety of positive changes. Rather, one gets the impression from these data that successful adaptation to the threat imposed by severe and chronic disease seems to be facilitated much more by minimizing or "overlooking" the negative changes that might have, in fact, occurred rather than through constructing positive changes and gains. Certainly, these results – as many others – are highly limited in their generalizability, in particular, with regard to the issue as to whether they might be applied to other types of stressful life events, as well, (e. g., conjugal bereavement; see Maercker, Bonanno, Horowitz, & Znoj, in press).

Construing "Interpretative Reality" Through Ruminative Thinking

It is highly likely to assume, as mentioned above, that attempts at construing and shaping one's perceptive reality by defending positive illusions and/or engaging in palliative comparisons might have to give way to construals of what is a stake that come increasingly close to objective reality. This might be true, in particular, when being exposed to traumatization occurs across larger periods of time, as in severe and chronic disease, and when "bad news," over and over again, runs counter to an individual's "reality negotiations." Accordingly, palliative construals of a perceptive reality have, in many cases, give way to focusing one's attention on a reality "as it is." This, in turn, is seen to result in and followed by ruminative thought – an assumption that has been addressed from various theoretical perspectives.

Ruminative Thoughts Related to Processing "Bad News"

Ruminations, often considered to be automatic and intrusive in nature, have been linked to the Freudian theory of "working through" and the compulsive repetition subsequent to traumatic events. Within this approach, researchers' attention has focused mainly on the inordinate length of time for which ruminations persist, and persistence of ruminative thought has been viewed as symptomatic of an event that has not been discharged or coped with sufficiently (Tait & Silver, 1989). Recurrence of ruminations, in itself, presumably depends on the ongoing implications of the event, the amount of changes in life circumstances brought about by its occurrence, and how the event interferes with or precludes the realization of plans, aspirations, and goals in which an individual may have heavily invested.

Within Horowitz's (1975, 1982) model of coping with traumatic events, the value of ruminative (here: intrusive) thought is highlighted as an important

stage in the coping process, during which the threatening information sur-
rounding loss and trauma has to be assimilated with old information. In contrast to other conceptions of rumination in which both, automatic and controlled, thought processes are included (as summarized in Uleman & Bargh,
1989), a focus is here on the latter, that is, individuals are seen to be able to
distract themselves from rumination for a while; thus, in alternation with periods of denial, event-related ruminations should allow the individual to gradually tolerate increasing doses of distressing aspects of the event (for the sample
case of conjugal bereavement; see Bonanno, Keltner, Holen & Horowitz,
1995). From that perspective, ruminations are believed to play an integral role
and necessary step in the working-through of negative events, by which an
individual gradually comes to terms with them.

Persistent ruminations in victims of life crises are also believed to represent
attempts to integrate inconsistent information related to the self. Accordingly,
the amount and affective quality of perceived changes in the aftermath of
trauma, rather than being solely linked to time per se (as was observed by
Klauer et al., in press) should also prove to be related to patients' modes of
coping with their disease, in particular to ruminative thinking. This was one
issue within our study of coping with cancer, to which we referred to several
times throughout this chapter. In fact, rumination, defined in terms of frequently reasoning on the presumed causes of one's disease or on whether others are
"telling the truth" (just to quote two marker items of this scale), proved to be
positively and significantly related to the number of domains in which change
in the self was perceived (see Klauer & Filipp, in press). Ruminative thought
obviously led to the perception that one's self has changed in many domains
and that these changes were primarily undesirable. In addition, high scores on
rumination proved to be completely unrelated to the number of positive
changes. Thus one can conclude, though with caution, that to ruminate frequently does not necessarily facilitate the construction of positive changes and
gains from one's disease.

Ruminative Thoughts Related to Unattainable Goals

Beyond this focus on how victims of life crises cope with loss and trauma, the
concept of rumination has recently been elaborated by Martin and Tesser
(1989; 1996) from a broader perspective. In short, these authors argue that
rumination can be considered to cover a heterogeneous class of mental activities (including problem-solving, anticipations, and intrusive thinking), which
arise from "some sort of discrepancy" (Martin & Tesser, 1996, p. 6), in particular, from the unexpectedly low rate of progress toward a desired goal. Accordingly, the core of their theory suggests that when an "undesirable experi-

ence" blocks a goal, this goal will then dominate the person's thought content until disengagement has taken places; thus, rumination is considered to be motivationally driven until individuals either satisfy a blocked or frustrated goal or disengage themselves from this goal – a notion that comes quite close to Klinger's (1975) work on the "commitment-disengagement cycle." In that sense, rumination is a conscious thought process that results from the disruption of important goals, i. e., those that are perceived as central to one's well-being, and it involves attempts to find alternative means to reach these unattained goals or, of this is not possible, to reconcile oneself to not attaining these goals.

Furthermore, they argue that rumination is comprised of a sequence of responses following the frustration of an important goal, namely the repetition of (simple) instrumental behaviors, perhaps with greater intensity and frequency followed by heightened problem-solving centered around finding alternative instrumental responses to attain the frustrated goal. If this has not been accomplished, then the stage of endstate thinking is entered, conceived of as the *prototype of rumination* by most authors in that it is not instrumental, tends to have a strong emotional overlay, and appears, at first glance, to be nonadaptive; endstate thinking means that after individuals have not found instrumental behaviors that will return them to their goal, they start thinking about the goal objects themselves and the feelings associated with them. this might enter into the stage of negotiation, where individuals may have learned that the goal remains unattainable. Thus, disengaging and giving up the goal or investing in a substitute goal would end the rumination process. It becomes obvious, then, that the timing of goal abandonment has implications for subsequent rumination, that is the longer the ruminative process about some particular goal object, the more likely that the object will remain in conscious awareness, even when the goal has been satisfied or substituted. And although ruminative thoughts often do recur unintentionally, these authors claim that ruminations are not necessarily unwanted or disruptive.

However, giving up goals may often be difficult and extremely painful – a notion that is, often only implicitly, inherent in almost all coping theories. This is due to the fact, as Martin and Tesser (1996) claimed, that goals are embedded in a hierarchical structure and that, consequently, higher-order goals may become unattainable, as well. Moreover, it was shown that even everyday stressors or daily hassles (e. g., just having missed the bus) which presumably pose threats only to lower order goals (e. g., being in one's office in time), might have a tremendous impact on higher order goals as well (e. g., being valued by others as a reliable person). This tendency to interpret everyday stressors as threats to higher-order goals has been reported from individuals called "linkers" who, in turn, were likely to experience more ruminative thoughts and

higher levels of depression following minor stressors as compared to "nonlinkers" (McIntosh, Harlow, & Martin, 1995).

Finally, giving up goals might be difficult also because people often are not
very much aware of their own plans and goal hierarchies, thus, misperceiving
what they are really ruminating about and what they really might be wanting
– an observation that is not unfrequently reported by those who are working
with victims of trauma through crisis intervention (see Slaikeu, 1984). When
an individual has not yet found a satisfactory way of meeting the goal nor has
abandoned the frustrated goal, a last stage, according to Martin and Tesser
(1989), is entered in this sequence; in fact, this is seen as the stage of learned
helplessness in that it is dominated by the individual's experience of his or her
powerlessness and loss of control, and, thus, by the breakdown of almost all
positive illusions.

Exposure to stressful or traumatic experiences does not only bring about
the blocking of important goals, as can be addressed from the model just described, but it often results also in a person's questioning the kind of individual
he or she is, thus, challenges central postulates of the individual's self-theory
(sensu Epstein, 1977). This assumption nicely parallels the idea that the disruption of organized behavior sequences through stressful events focuses a
person's attention on the "bad parts" of his or her self that has been made
"incomplete" by the interruption (Horowitz, 1982). If the disrupted part of the
self cannot be repaired easily (which is true in most cases of traumatization),
the person will become more and more likely to engage in (ruminative)
thoughts about the disrupted part of the self. These thoughts are nothing other
than attempts to repair what is deficient, to make up for what is lost, or to
symbolically complete the self until substitutes can be found for what has been
lost. However, in taking the sample case of coping with the diagnosis of severe
and chronic disease, by which most patients are extremely overwhelmed, it is
often less likely that these individuals can easily find "substitutes" to complete
their selves. In these cases ruminative thoughts may, in fact, be more adaptively
centered around the rearrangement of goals and options or adaptation is facilitated "simply" by palliative temporal comparisons of the present self and
past selves, as outlined above.

Ruminative Thoughts Related to Explaining What Happened

So far ruminative thought in the aftermath of victimization by loss and trauma
has been considered to be mainly centered around blocked goals, incomplete
selves, or lost selves; yet, it certainly may also be considered a main constituent
of what is elsewhere called "attributional processes" (e. g., Hewstone, 1989)
and to serve important functions in finding answers to the "Why me" questions

that obviously confront so many victims of life crises (see Bulman & Wortman, 1977). "Metaphorically speaking, rumination is a form of looking. It persists until people find what they are looking for.[. . .] It differs from nonruminative thought primarily in that it takes longer for people to find what they are looking for" (Martin & Tesser, 1996, p. 11). Indeed, evidence suggests that victims of life crises engage in a concerted effort to identify potential causes for their fate, with the number of causal attributions sometimes seen to be roughly proportional to the severity of the perceived threat. Ruminative thoughts, then, are considered to play a crucial role in finding explanations for what has happened to oneself.

Yet, when studying attributional processes in the context of victimization, the differentiation between causes and reasons – which traces back to the philosophy of the ordinary language in Great Britain – needs to be particularly highlighted (see Buss, 1978; Kruglanski, 1979). In general, (perceived) causes are things which (are seen to) have brought about a change in one's life, whereas reasons are that *for which* a change was brought about (e. g., goals, purposes). Thus, reasons can be interpreted as a specific type of explanation (notably teleological explanation), whereas cause is interpreted as explanation in the generic sense. In addition, reasons often appear in a justificatory context, and Buss (1978) has argued that, for "propaganda" purposes, justificatory reasons are often passed off as causes, as also illustrated in common speech through the substitution of "need" for "want." In this respect, the clinical approach of Frankl (1973) and the sociological perspective of Antonovsky (1979) have been combined with the attributional focus within social psychology (see for an overview Graham & Folkes, 1990).

Despite these considerations it is highly likely to assume in the context of coping with loss and trauma that attributions for what has happened are, in fact, to be equated mainly with *teleological* explanations. This should hold particularly true when retrospective accounts of what brought about a stressful event are of minor value in anticipating of and coping with what might happen in the future, as is the case for objectively uncontrollable causal factors. This can be nicely illustrated by, again, taking the diagnosis of cancer as a sample case (see Filipp, in press): Patients suffering from cancer of various sites (except lung cancer) were asked, first in a highly unstructured manner, to describe retrospectively the thoughts that came into their mind, when they had focused their attention upon their disease at various points in time. When these patients referred to the day or week, during which they had been told their diagnosis, denial-like responses as well as all forms of "outcry" proved to be overwhelmingly salient in their reports. Yet, when adopting a temporal frame of reference later in the course of their disease, the search for teleological explanations clearly outweighed any other thought content, in particular causal reasoning (for details, see Filipp, in press). Later in the interview causal explanations were addressed rather directly by asking as to whether the patient had thought about the factors that presumably contributed to his or her disease and, if so, what kind of answers he or she had found. Yet although almost all patients confirmed that they had, somehow, been engaged in some kind of causal reasoning, their explanations proved to be "weak," i. e., were later scored by independent raters to be less well-articulated, less elaborated, and less subjectively valid, as compared to teleological explanations that had been evoked during the interview in a similar manner.

In contrast, a nonpatient sample that was recruited and interviewed for "comparison" purposes (that is, with regard to their illness conceptions related to cancer) particularly focused on etiological factors considered to contribute to or even cause the onset of cancer. The various causal explanations were well-articulated, presented rather confidently, and were – though our evidence is weak on this point – obviously also in the service of bolstering our subjects' beliefs in their own invulnerability. Teleological explanations, on the contrary, proved to be scarce in this sample and efforts to "vicariously" find meaning in the misfortune of severe and chronic disease were seldom found. Thus, despite some confusion in the literature on these two distinct kinds of attributional processes, we consider only teleological explanations to allow for construing personal significance of traumatic events and their implications; it is teleological (rather than causal) reasoning that reflects and, potentially fulfills the individual's need to interpret or appraise the meaning in his or her fate – based on the consideration of meaning as the crucial organizing principle in human behavior (Frankl, 1973). To put it yet differently: Constructions of an "interpretative reality," in which victims of life crises can safely move and continue to live in the aftermath of loss and trauma, can only be built upon teleological explanations.

Nevertheless, traumatic events in themselves often are extremely difficult to be interpreted in meaningful terms and teleological explanations cannot be found, at all, as was shown for the sample cases of incest or loss of child (see Wortman, Silver, & Kessler, 1993). Thus, a meaningful and acceptable interpretation is often not forthcoming, and the search for meaning will persist for extended periods of time, contributing to ongoing rumination about the event. This has been recently confirmed by Maercker and Schützwohl (1997) based on a sample of political prisoners from the former German Democratic Republic. According to their results, intrusions – including dreams and nightmares – were highly common symptoms in these victims even six years later together with remarkably fewer indicators of "avoidance" than have been reported in other studies. In addition, social responses to the individual's victimization and to his or her need to discuss the event's implications might play a fundamental role here, as well. Rumination about an event and discussing its occurrence with others may represent the two sides of a coin, namely personal and social aspects of the same process of "working through" and making sense out of one's fate (see also King & Pennebaker, 1996). However, the literature suggests that the need for discussion may frequently go unmet by an unsupportive environment (see Aymanns, Filipp, & Klauer, 1995), This is in line with results reported from a study on victims of a criminal assault (Schützwohl & Maercker, 1997) pointing to a zero relationship between perceived social support and recovery from victimization. In these cases, ruminations about the event in terms of involuntary, intrusive, and distressing thoughts may continue and may be experienced by a person for days, weeks, and sometimes even years (see also Lepore, Silver, & Wortman, 1996).

The Adaptive Value of Ruminative Thinking

It is not surprising, then, that ruminative thought in terms of a consistent search for meaning has been sometimes found to be inversely related to psychological recovery and positively related to negative affect, long-term unhappiness, and depression (see Nolen-Hoeksema, Parker, & Larson, 1994). On the other hand, it has been claimed a common theme underlying diverse theories of adjustment to loss and trauma "... that healthy adjustment is the result of *repeated confrontation with the memories* of the trauma and its subjective meaning ..." (Greenberg, 1995, p. 1263; italics added). Based on his review of various theoretical accounts, this author has concluded as follows: "Mentally reviewing past traumas may be beneficial only to the extent that such a review (a) reduces physiological strain associated with deliberate effort to inhibit such material and produces cognitive insight [...], (b) produces more constructive appraisals of the traumatic memory or more effective coping strategies [...], or (c) results in less physiological reactivity to and less threatening appraisals of reminiscent stimuli associated with the trauma ..." (Greenberg, 1995, p. 1264). Obviously, in considering the adaptive value of rumination in coping with loss and trauma, it is necessary to adopt a highly differential perspective with regard to *who* derives profit from ruminating and *under which conditions* this is likely to occur; in addition, as has been proposed in many earlier notions, one has to take into account how often ruminative thought recurs unintentionally and how long this persists. Unfortunately, however, longitudinal (e. g., follow-through) studies or, at least, cross-sectional studies in which the time elapsed since the traumatic event is systematically taken into account, are still too scarce in order to find satisfying answers to this issue (for exceptions, see Filipp, 1992; Silver et al., 1983).

Nevertheless, there is no doubt that rumination has a powerful impact on affective states and proved to be consistently related to negative affect. Since the objects of ruminative thought in victims of life crises have negative valence (e. g., "lost selves" or "blocked goals"), simply thinking about these objects should intensify their negative valence; this assumption is derived from propositions made by Tesser (1988) for the polarization of feelings that become observable when people think about objects with either a positive or a negative valence. In addition, it is well documented that self-focused attention in the face of loss or threat intensifies negative feelings (for an overview, see Filipp, Klauer, & Ferring, 1993; Ingram, 1990). Yet, the causal ordering of ruminative thoughts and affective states is still open to dispute, i. e., whether ruminative thoughts contribute to or arise from high levels of negative affect, or whether the inverse relation between them is attributable to the influence of other factors. Martin and Tesser (1996) argue in favor of the latter by claiming that rumination and negative affect covary primarily, because the two are influenced by many of the same factors (e. g., importance of an unattainable goal). On the other hand, experimental evidence has repeatedly shown (see Blaney, 1986) that mood states increase the accessibility of *mood-congruent* information in memory. That is, individuals in a bad mood are more likely to recall negative events in their lives, as opposed to individuals in a good mood being more likely ro recall positive events (for details, see also Strack & Schwarz, 1991). Thus, it is not unlikely to assume that this might also apply to ruminative thinking, i. e., ruminative thoughts to be triggered by, rather than resulting in, negative affective states. Results reported by Filipp et al. (1990) can be interpreted in support of this notion.

These authors investigated the effectiveness of various coping modes in a sample of cancer patients. In particular, self-reported frequency of ruminative thoughts was related to measures of emotional well-being, hopefulness, and other indicators of adjustment. Patients had to report for each item how often they had shown each response within the last four weeks. Frequency ratings were preferred over typicality ratings in order to allow for a more process-oriented, episodic measure of coping, using a longitudinal, multiwave design, in which the process of coping with the diagnosis of cancer was observed over a time span of one year (with an additional follow-up two years later), the application of causal modeling techniques was allowed for, as well (see Rogosa, 1980). Some modes of coping under study (e. g., threat minimization or distracting oneself by affiliating with others), in fact, proved to be highly "effective," that is were causally prior to (or more precisely: predictive of) low levels of hopelessness and high levels of emotional well-being over the time span under study. On the other hand, rumination proved to be significantly and negatively related to all indicators of emotional well-being, thus, at first glance, indicating that rumination is to be considered a "maladaptive" response to severe disease. Yet, this would have been a premature conclusion had one adopted only a synchronous perspective, since a different picture emerged from a diachronic perspective: rumination proved to be the only mode of dealing with cancer that was predicted by, rather than resulting in, low levels of emotional well-being and hopefulness. Based on these results one can conclude that negative affect triggers ruminative thoughts rather than being caused by it.

In addition, interindividual differences in these patients' tendencies to engage in ruminative thought proved to be highly stable over the time span under study. Accordingly, one might consider rumination also a "trait-like" response style that either might have been learned in earlier years of the life span (maybe due to the absence of models in children's social environments exhibiting more "adaptive" strategies to handle stress; see Nolen-Hoedsema, 1991) or that is reflective of a habitual tendency in these patients to experience negative affect, which in turn, results in a higher frequency of ruminative thoughts.

Unfortunately the empirical evidence that is available up to now, is fairly insufficient in order to allow for more general conclusions about the nature and adaptive value of ruminative thinking. Nevertheless, it is still highly likely to assume that, in victims of life crises and trauma, the transformation of objective reality into their "interpretative realities" can only be accomplished by ruminative thinking. Ruminative thoughts that center around the search for teleological explanations, around how, what has been lost, can be "replaced," or how the traumatic event can be meaningfully related to and integrated into a coherent and stable conceptual system of the one's self, are a necessary, though by no means a sufficient step on the long way to recovering from loss and trauma.

Summary and Conclusions

The present chapter tries to outline three types of process that are considered to play a crucial role in how victims of life crises gradually come to terms with their lot. In contrast to other propositions and because of the paucity of empirical evidence from longitudinal studies, no assumptions have been made with regard to either the sequential order or the overall adaptive value of these various processes. Our considerations are based primarily on what has been reported repeatedly in the literature as well as on conclusions drawn from some of our own studies with patients suffering from life-threatening disease.

A core argument in the present chapter is that the best and perhaps only way to understand coping with loss and trauma is when it is taken as a process by which, step by step, people gain an understanding of what has happened in their lives. We have considered this process in terms of attentive and comparative processes that result in the construction of victims' "perceptive realities." In other words: Given the fact that, in many cases, overwhelmingly "bad news" accompanies these various events, it is highly plausible to consider coping as process in which individuals, over longer periods of time, attempt to maintain a delicate balance between their "objective reality" and a "perceptive reality" that allows them to carry on living at relative peace with themselves. At some point in time they may be able to work on constructing their "interpretative realities," that is, they may start to engage in various types of ruminative thinking, namely related to finding teleological explanations (in terms of "For what reason did all this happen?") or related to how to "replace" the loss of illusions, hopes, plans, options, or past selves. In addition, they may be forced to revise their internal models of who they are in order to integrate their experiences into conceptions of their selves and the world more meaningfully. It may well be true that, in their daily lives people are quite reluctant about accepting changes in their selves; and even victims of life crises who have undergone considerable change often appear to be – in terms of Greenwald and Banaji (1989) – "cognitively conservative." Yet, in the face of traumatic life change, as associated with the onset of severe and chronic disease, adaptive functioning and psychological survival make it necessary to maintain a delicate balance between changing the self (possibly by reconstructing self-views in less central domains) and preserving self-consistency and continuity over time.

We have tried to integrate some propositions derived from different approaches, for example, from temporal comparison theory, from research on ruminative thinking, or research on defending positive illusions, based on our conviction that these are heuristically valuable and extremely helpful in studying responses to traumatic life changes. These propositions were used as conceptual tools in order to gain a better understanding of what, in fact, constitutes "coping" and how it might be related to adaptive outcomes. At various points in our line of reasoning, we have presented preliminary evidence that, in some cases, is quite in line with theoretical expectations, for example, longitudinal observations of terminally ill patients who successfully defended positive illusions and strove for hope over a considerable amount of time. In other cases evidence completely contradicted theoretical expectations; this was particularly true for propositions borrowed from temporal comparison theory. In fact, individuals' attempts to maintain self-consistency and to "overlook" changes in their lives prove to be completely unrelated to adaptive outcomes; even more surprisingly, to perceive positively valenced changes and to infer "gains" from one's fate also does not to be an effective mode of coping in victims of severe disease. Thus the current state of research indicates that attempts aimed at construing benefits from loss and trauma or at finding meaning by reframing losses as gains seem to be highly limited with regard to their adaptive value. It is, by all means, certainly necessary to replicate such a finding in other samples and perform a cross-validation to other types of crises; yet, we are tempted to provisionally conclude that modern coping research is still too often filled with myths, including the widespread assumption that successfully coping with loss and crisis might be either equated with perceiving "gains" or even be an opportunity for personal growth. And even when victims of life crises do experience positive changes in the aftermath of victimization, this obviously does not help them to regain or strengthen hope.

To sum up, it seems that there may be many avenues – at least, certainly more than two main roads – that many, if not most, victims of life crises travel in order to overcome loss, trauma, and other negative aspects of their lives. Simply minimizing the implications of these negative aspects for their selves rather than reframing these aspects and converting them into positive ones, might be an avenue that deserves closer attention in future research. These maneuvers may help people to live the lives they have productively. In this latter sense, to borrow a metaphor used by Higgins and Snyder (1991): "Our outcome in the game of life depends not only on the cards that we have been dealt, but also on how we play out our hands" (p. 91).

References

Abelson, R.P. (1981). Psychological status of the script concept. *American Psychologist, 36*, 715–729.

Affleck, G., Tennen, H., Croog, S., & Levine, S. (1987). Causal attribution, perceived benefits, and morbidity after a heart attack: An eight year study. *Journal of Consulting and Clinical Psychology, 55*, 29–35.

Albert, S. (1977). Temporal comparison theory. *Psychological Review, 84*, 485–503.

Aldwin, C.M., Sutton, K.J., & Lachman, M. (1996). The development of coping resources in adulthood. *Journal of Personality, 64*, 837–871.

Alloy, L.B., & Abramson, L.Y. (1988). Depressive realism: Four theoretical perspectives. In L.B. Alloy (Ed.), *Cognitive processes in depression* (pp. 223–265). New York: Guilford.

Antonovsky, A. (1979). *Health, stress, and coping.* San Francisco: Jossey-Bass.

Averill, J.R. (1968). Grief: Its nature and significance. *Psychological Bulletin, 70*, 721–748.

Aymanns, P., Filipp, S.-H., & Klauer, T. (1995). Family support and coping with cancer: Some determinants and adaptive correlates. *British Journal of Social Psychology, 34*, 107–124.

Baltes, P.B. (1979). Life-span developmental psychology: Some converging observations on history and theory. In P.B. Baltes & O.G. Brim Jr. (Eds.), *Life span development and behavior* (pp. 255–279). New York: Academic Press.

Blaney, P.H. (1986). Affect and memory: A review. *Psychological Bulletin, 99*, 229–246.

Bonanno, G.A., Keltner, D., Holen, A., & Horowitz, M.J. (1995). When avoiding unpleasant emotions might not be such a bad thing: Verbal-autonomic response dissociation and midlife conjugal bereavement. *Journal of Personality and Social Psychology, 69,* 975–989.

Brown, G.W., & Harris, T.O. (1989). *Establishing causal links: The Bedford College studies of depression.* London: Hyman.

Brown, J.D. (1991). Accuracy and bias in self-knowledge. In C.R. Snyder & D.R. Forsyth (Eds.), *Handbook of social and clinical psychology. The health perspective* (pp. 158–179). New York: Pergamon.

Bulman, R.J., & Wortman, C.B. (1977). Attributions of blame and coping in the "real world": Severe accident victims report to their lot. *Journal of Personality and Social Psychology, 35,* 351–363.

Buss, A.R. (1978). Causes and reasons in attribution theory: A conceptual critique. *Journal of Personality and Social Psychology, 36,* 1311–1321.

Buunk, B.P. (1994). Social comparison processes under stress: Towards an integration of classic and recent perspectives. *European Review of Social Psychology, 5,* 211–241.

Clark, L.F., & Collins, J.E. (1993). Remembering old flames: How the past affects assessments of the present. *Personality and Social Psychology Bulletin, 19,* 399–408.

Davidson, J.R.T., & Foa, E.B. (Eds.). (1993). *Posttraumatic stress disorder: DSM-IV and beyond.* Washington, DC: American Psychiatric Press.

Davis, C.G., & Lehman, D.R. (1995). Counterfactual thinking and coping with traumatic life events. In N.J. Roese & J.M. Olson (Eds.), *What might have been: The social psychology of counterfactual thinking* (pp. 353–374). Hillsdale, NJ: Erlbaum.

Elder, G.H., & Caspi, A. (1988). Economic stress in lives: Developmental perspectives. *Journal of Social Issues, 44,* 25–45.

Epstein, S. (1973). The self-concept revisited, or a theory of a theory. *American Psychologist, 28,* 404–416.

Erikson, E.H. (1959). Identity and the life cycle. *Psychological Issues, 1,* 1–165.

Filipp, S.-H. (1992). Could it be worse? The diagnosis of cancer as a prototype of traumatic life events. In L. Montada, S.-H. Filipp, & M. Lerner (Eds.), *Life crises and experiences of loss in adulthood* (pp. 23–52). Hillsdale, NJ: Erlbaum.

Filipp, S.-H. (in press). *Subjektive Krankheitstheorien* [Subjective theories of illness]. Göttingen: Hogrefe.

Filipp, S.-H., & Klauer, T. (1986). Conceptions of self over the life span: Reflections on the dialectics of change. In M.M. Baltes & P.B. Baltes (Eds.), *The psychology of control and aging* (pp. 167–207). Hillsdale, NJ: Erlbaum.

Filipp, S.-H., & Ferring, D. (in press). Befindlichkeitsregulation durch temporale und soziale Vergleichsprozesse im Alter? [Regulation of well-being by temporal and social comparison processes in old age]. *Zeitschrift für Klinische Psychologie – Sonderheft "Altern."*

Filipp, S.-H., & Klauer, T. (1991). Subjective well-being in the face of critical life events: The case of successful copers. In F. Strack, M. Argyle, & N. Schwarz (Eds.), *Subjective well-being* (pp. 213–234). New York: Pergamon.

Filipp, S.-H., Klauer, T., & Ferring, D. (1993). Self-focused attention in the face of adversity and threat. In H.W. Krohne (Ed.), *Attention and avoidance* (pp. 267–294). Seattle: Hogrefe & Huber.

Filipp, S.-H., Klauer, T., Freudenberg, E., & Ferring, D. (1990). The regulation of subjective well-being in cancer patients: An analysis of coping effectiveness. *Psychology and Health, 1990,* 305–317.

Foa, E.B., & Kozak, M.J. (1986). Emotional processing of fear: Exposure to corrective information. *Psychological Bulletin, 99,* 20–35.

Frankl, V.E. (1973). *Der Mensch auf der Suche nach Sinn. Zur Rehumanisierung der Psychotherapie* [Man in search of meaning. On the re-humanization of psychotherapy]. Freiburg: Herder.

Frese, M. (1992). A plea for realistic pessimism: On objective reality, coping with stress, and psychological dysfunction. In L. Montada, S.-H. Filipp, & M.J. Lerner (Eds.), *Life crises and experiences of loss in adulthood* (pp. 81–93). Hillsdale, NJ: Erlbaum.

Goethals, G.R., Messick, D.M., & Allison, S.T. (1991). The uniqueness bias: Studies of constructive social comparison. In J. Suls & T.A. Wills (Eds.), *Social comparison. Contemporary theory and research* (pp. 149–176). Hillsdale, NJ: Erlbaum.

Graham, S., & Folkes, V.S. (Eds.). (1990). *Attribution theory: Applications to achievement, mental health, and interpersonal conflict.* Hillsdale, NJ: Erlbaum.

Greenberg, M. (1995). Cognitive processing of traumas: The role of intrusive thoughts and reappraisals. *Journal of Applied Social Psychology, 25,* 1262–1296.

Greenwald, A.G., & Banaji, M.R. (1989). The self as a memory system: Powerful, but ordinary. *Journal of Personality and Social Psychology, 57,* 41–54.

Haan, N. (1977). *Coping and defending: Processes of self-enviroment organization.* New York: Academic Press.

Heckhausen, J., Dixon, R.A., & Baltes, P.B. (1989). Gains and losses in development throughout adulthood as perceived by different adult age groups. *Developmental Psychology, 25,* 109–121.

Heckhausen, J., & Schulz, R. (1995). A life-span theory of control. *Psychological Review, 102,* 284–304.

Hewstone, M. (1989). *Causal attribution: From cognitive processes to collective beliefs.* Worcester: Billings.

Higgins, R.L., & Snyder, C.R. (1991). Reality negotiation and excuse making. In C.R. Snyder & D.R. Forsyth (Eds.), *Handbook of social and clinical psychology. The health perspective* (pp. 79–96). New York: Pergamon.

Holmes, T.H., & Rahe, R.H. (1967). The Social Readjustment Rating Scale. *Journal of Psychosomatic Research, 11,* 213–218.

Horowitz, M.J. (1975). Intrusive and repetitive thoughts after experimental stress. *Archives of General Psychiatry, 32,* 1457–1463.

Horowitz, M.J. (1982). Stress response syndromes and their treatment. In L. Goldberger & S. Breznitz (Eds.), *Handbook of stress* (pp. 711–733). New York: Free Press.

Janoff-Bulman, R.J. (1979). Charactereological versus behavioral self-blame: Inquiries into depression and rape. *Journal of Personality and Social Psychology, 37,* 1798–1809.

Ingram, R.E. (1990). Self-focused attention in clinical disorders: Review and a conceptual model. *Psychological Bulletin, 107,* 156–176.

Janoff-Bulman, R., & Brickman, P. (1982). Expectations and what people learn from failure. In N.T. Feather (Ed.), *Expectations and actions* (pp. 207–237). Hillsdale, NJ: Erlbaum.

Janoff-Bulman, R., & Schwartzberg, S.S. (1991). Towards a general model of personal change. In C.R. Snyder & D.R. Forsyth (Eds.), *Handbook of social and clinical psychology. The health perspective* (pp. 488–509). New York: Pergamon.

King, L.A., & Pennebaker, J.W. (1996). Thinking about goals, glue, and the meaning of life. In R.S. Wyer Jr. (Ed.), *Ruminative thoughts* (pp.9 7–106). Mahwah, NJ: Erlbaum.

Klauer, T., & Filipp, S.-H. (in press). Life change perception in cognitive adaptation to life-threatening illness. *European Review of Applied Psychology.*

Klauer, T., Ferring, D., & Filipp, S.-H. (in press). "Still stable after all this ...?" Temporal comparisons in coping with life-threatening disease. *International Journal of Behavioral Development (Special issue on "Coping and Development across the Life-span.")*

Klinger, E. (1975). Consequences of commitment to and disengagement from incentives. *Psychological Review, 82,* 1–25.

Krampen, G. (1979). Hoffnungslosigkeit bei stationären Patienten: Ihre Messung durch einen Kurzfragebogen (H-Skala) [Hopelessness in inpatients: Its assessment by a brief questionnaire (H-scale)]. *Medizinische Psychologie, 5,* 39–49.

Kruglanski, A.W. (1979). Causal explanation, teleological explanation: On radical particularism in attribution theory. *Journal of Personality and Social Psychology, 37,* 1447–1457.

Lazarus, R.S. (1983). The costs and benefits of denial. In S. Breznitz (Ed.), *The denial of stress* (pp. 1–34). New York: International Universities Press.

Lazarus, R.S., & Folkman, S. (1984). *Stress, appraisal, and coping.* New York: Springer-Verlag.

Lepore, S.J., Silver, R.C., & Wortman, C.B. (1996). Social constraints, intrusive thoughts, and depressive symptoms among bereaved mothers. *Journal of Personality and Social Psychology, 70,* 271–282.

Lerner, M.J., & Gignac, M.A. (1992). Is it coping or is it growth? A cognitive-affective model of contentment in the elderly. In L. Montada, S.-H. Filipp, & M.J. Lerner (Eds.), *Life crises and experiences of loss in adulthood* (pp. 321–340). Hillsdale, NJ: Erlbaum.

Lieberman, M.A. (1992). Perceptions of changes in the self, the impact of life events, and large group awareness training. In Y. Klar, J.D. Fisher, J.M. Chinsky, & A. Nadler (Eds.), *Self change* (pp. 43–61). New York: Springer-Verlag.

Maercker, A., & Schützwohl M. (1997). Long-term effects of political imprisonment: A group comparison study. *Social Psychiatry and Psychiatric Epidemiology, 32,* 435–442.

Maercker, A., Bonanno, G.A., Horowitz, M.J., & Znoj, H. (in press). Positive and negative themes in complicated grief. *Journal of Clinical Psychology.*

Martin, L.L., & Tesser, A. (1989). Toward a motivational and structural theory of ruminative thought. In J.S. Uleman & J.A. Bargh (Eds.), *Unintended thought* (pp. 306–326). New York: Guilford.

Martin, L.L., & Tesser, A. (1996). Some ruminative thoughts. In R.S. Wyer Jr. (Ed.), *Ruminative thoughts* (pp. 1–47). Mahwah, NJ: Erlbaum.

McIntosh, W.D., Harlow, T.F., & Martin, L.L. (1995). Linkers and nonlinkers: Goal beliefs as a moderator of the effects of everyday hassles on rumination, depression, and physical complaints. *Journal of Applied Social Psychology, 25,* 1231–1244.

Miller, S.M. (1992). Monitoring and blunting in the face of threat: Implications for adaptation and health. In L. Montada, S.-H. Filipp, & M.J. Lerner (Eds.), *Life crises and experiences of loss in adulthood* (pp. 255–270). Hillsdale, NJ: Erlbaum.

Montada, L., Filipp, S.H., & Lerner, M.J. (Eds.). (1992). *Life crises and experiences of loss in adulthood.* Hillsdale, NJ: Lawrence Erlbaum.

Muthny, F.A. (1989). *Freiburger Fragebogen zur Krankheitsverarbeitung (FKV) – Manual* [Freiburg Questionnaire on Coping with Illness – Manual]. Weinheim: Beltz.

Nolen-Hoeksema, S. (1991). Responses to depression and their effects on the duration of depressive episodes. *Journal of Abnormal Psychology, 100,* 259–282.

Nolen-Hoeksema, S., Parker, L.E., & Larson, J. (1994). Ruminative coping with depressed mood following loss. *Journal of Personality and Social Psychology, 67,* 92–104.

Pyszczynski, T., Greenberg, J., Solomon, S., Cather, C., Gat, I., & Sideris, J. (1995). Defensive distancing from victims of serious illness: The role of delay. *Personality and Social Psychology Bulletin, 21,* 13–20.

Rahe, R. (1988). Recent life changes and coronary heart disease: 10 years' research. In S. Fisher & J. Reason (Eds.), *Handbook of life stress, cognition and health* (pp. 317–335). Chichester: Wiley.

Rogosa, D. (1980). A critique of cross-lagged correlation. *Psychological Bulletin, 88*, 245–258.

Ross, M. (1989). Relation of implicit theories to the construction of personal histories. *Psychological Review, 96*, 341–357.

Rothbaum, F., Weisz, J.R., & Snyder, S.S. (1982). Changing the world and changing the self: A two-process model of perceived control. *Journal of Personality and Social Psychology, 42*, 5–37.

Ryff, C.D. (1982). Self-perceived personality change in adulthood and aging. *Journal of Personality and Social Psychology, 42*, 108–115.

Schützwohl, M., & Maercker, A. (1997). Posttraumatische Belastungsreaktionen nach kriminellen Gewaltdelikten [Posttraumatic stress reactions due to criminal victimization]. *Zeitschrift für Klinische Psychologie, 26*, 258– 268.

Silver, R.L., Wortman, C.B., & Klos, D.S. (1982). Cognitions, affect, and behavior following uncontrollable outcomes: A response to current human helplessness research. *Journal of Personality, 50*, 480–514.

Silver, R.L., Boon, C., & Stones, M.H. (1983). Searching for meaning in misfortune: Making sense of incest. *Journal of Social Issues, 39*(2), 81–102.

Slaikeu, K.A. (1984). *Crisis intervention: A handbook for practice and research.* Boston: Allyn and Bacon.

Snyder, C.R. (1989). Reality negotiation: From excuses to hope and beyond. *Journal of Social and Clinical Psychology, 8*, 130–157.

Snyder, C.R., Irving, L.M., & Anderson, J.R. (1991). Hope and health. In C.R. Snyder & D.R. Forsyth (Eds.), *Handbook of social and clinical psychology. The health perspective* (pp. 285–309). New York: Pergamon.

Sontag, S. (1979). *Illness as metaphor.* New York: Farrar Strauss & Giroux.

Staudinger, U.M., Freund, A.M., Linden, M., & Maas, I. (1996). Selbst, Persönlichkeit und Lebensgestaltung im Alter: Psychologische Widerstandsfähigkeit und Vulnerabilität [Self, personality, and creation of life in old age: Psychological resistance and vulnerability]. In K.U. Mayer & P.B. Baltes (Eds.), *Die Berliner Altersstudie* [The Berlin study of old age] (pp. 321–350). Berlin: Akademie Verlag.

Strack, F., & Schwarz, N. (1991). Evaluating one's life: A judgement model of subjective well-being. In F. Strack, M. Argyle, & N. Schwarz (Eds.), *Subjective well-being* (pp. 27–47). New York: Pergamon.

Stroebe, M.S., Stroebe, W., & Hanson, R.O. (1993). *Handbook of bereavement, theory, research, and intervention.* Cambridge: Cambridge University Press.

Suls, J.M., & Mullen, B. (1982). From the cradle to the grave: Comparison and self-evaluation across the life-span. In J. Suls (Ed.), *Psychological perspectives on the self* (pp.9 7–128). Hillsdale, NJ: Erlbaum.

Swann, W.B., Jr., & Hill, C.A. (1982). When our identities are mistaken: Reaffirming self-conceptions through social interactions. *Journal of Personality and Social Psychology, 43*, 59–66.

Swann, W.B. (1983). Self verification: Bringing social reality into harmony with the self. In J. Suls & A.G. Greenwald (Eds.), *Psychological perspectives on the self (Vol. 2)* (pp. 33–66). Hillsdale: Erlbaum.

Tait, R., & Silver, R.C. (1989). Coming to terms with major negative life events. In J.S. Uleman & J.A. Bargh (Eds.), *Unintended thought* (pp. 351–382). New York: Guilford.

Taylor, S.E. (1984). Issues in the study of coping: A commentary. *Cancer, 53*, 2313–2315.

Taylor, S.E., & Brown, J.D. (1988). Illusion and well-being: A social psychological perspective on mental health. *Psychological Bulletin, 103*, 193–210.

Taylor, S.E., & Lobel, M. (1989). Social comparison activity under threat: Downward evaluation and upward contact. *Psychological Review, 96*, 569–575.

Uleman, J.S., & Bargh, J.A. (Eds.). (1989). *Unintended thought*. New York: Guilford.

Viorst, J. (1986). *Necessary losses: The loves, illusions, dependencies and impossible expectations that all of us have to give up in order to grow*. New York: Fawcett Gold Medal.

Watzlawick, P. (1976). *How real is real?* New York: Random House.

Webster, J.D., & Cappeliez, P. (1993). Reminiscence and autobiographical memory: Complementary contexts for cognitive aging research. *Developmental Review, 13*, 54–91.

Wegner, D.M. (1988). Stress and mental control. In S. Fisher & J. Reason (Eds.), *Handbook of life stress, cognition, and health* (pp. 683–697). Chichester: Wiley.

Weisman, A. D. (1979). *Coping with cancer*. New York: McGraw-Hill.

Wills, T.A. (1981). Downward comparison principles in social psychology. *Psychological Bulletin, 90*, 245–271.

Wills, T.A., & Suls, J. (1991). Commentary: Neo-social comparison theory and beyond. In J. Suls & T.A. Wills (Eds.), *Social comparison. Contemporary theory and research* (pp. 395–411). Hillsdale, NJ: Erlbaum.

Wong, P.T., & Watt, L.M. (1991). What types of reminiscence are associated with successful aging? *Psychology and Aging, 6*, 272–279.

Wortman, C.B., & Silver, R.C. (1992). Reconsidering assumptions about coping with loss: An overview of current research. In L. Montada, S.H. Filipp, & M.J. Lerner (Eds.), *Life crises and experiences of loss in adulthood*. Hillsdale, NJ: Erlbaum.

Wortman, C.B., Silver, R.C., & Kessler, R.C. (1993). The meaning of loss and adjustment to bereavement. In M.S. Stroebe, W. Stroebe, & R.O. Hansson (Eds.), *Handbook of bereavement: Theory, research, and intervention* (pp. 349–366). New York: Cambridge University Press.

PART II:
FROM CHILDHOOD
TO ADULTHOOD

Children in War: Soldiers Against Their Will

Zahava Solomon and Tamar Lavi

Introduction

Traumatic events have consistently been shown to have profound and long lasting pathogenic effects. Whether the event is flood or auto accident, rape or assault, war or terror, there is ample evidence of the psychological damage of such events in whatever country and culture they occur, to young and old alike (APA, 1994). Yet while a good deal has been learned about the symptoms, duration, and course of traumatization, little is known about the interaction of traumatic stressors with the various stages of the life cycle. That is we do not know whether a trauma will have different effects on children and adolescents, adults and the aged, and if it does, how it will manifest itself in each age group.

This chapter addresses the relationship between age and traumatization issue through the perspective of the impact of war on children. Most of our knowledge of the traumatic effects of war relates to adults, that is the soldiers who fight it. But the increasing involvement of children in wars makes it imperative to explore the impact of war on young people.

Children are exposed to wars both passively and actively (e. g., Frazer, 1974; Garbarino, 1992; Punamaki, 1990). They may be separated from their fathers and older brothers who go out to fight; they may lose them, or have them return physically or emotionally disabled. In the increasingly frontless wars of the latter part of this century – the Gulf War, the fighting in Lebanon, Yugoslavia and Ruwanda, and others – they may be shot at, injured or killed themselves, may see their homes destroyed or be forced to flee them. They may see their parents killed, taken away, humiliated, or tortured. Their education is disrupted, as is the entire order of their lives. Even worse, younger and younger children have become active participants in wars that were once reserved for adults. Ten-year-old children wielded RPGs in Lebanon; Palestinian children hurled stones and molotov cocktails in the Intifada; Children were drafted into the armies of Iran and Iraq and into the rebel forces of Zaire and other countries in Africa. There are parts of the world that are, or have been, in an unremitting state of frontless war for decades, so that the children who are caught up in them know no other reality (e. g., Frazer, 1974; Garbarino, 1992).

Studies of adults, both soldiers and civilians, have shown that the impact of war is wide ranging and multi-faceted. It may effect all areas of the personality: emotional, cognitive, and behavioral. In the emotional sphere its most common and conspicuous expression is PTSD (APA, 1994), which itself has both cognitive and behavioral consequences and is often accompanied by depression and anxiety. In the cognitive sphere, concentration, memory, and learning ability may all be impaired, and internalized cognitive schemes and world views may be shattered (Janoff-Bulman, 1989). In the behavioral sphere, social, family, and occupational functioning may be compromised (e. g., Solomon, 1993).

The question we address here is whether and how children's emotional and cognitive immaturity effects their reaction to trauma. Does it shield and protect them from the psychological wounds of war because they cannot grasp or anticipate the dangers? Or does it make them more vulnerable because they lack the defenses and resources to cope with the threat?

Researchers disagree about children's vulnerability to traumatic stress. Lifton and Olson (1976) argue that a severe flood produced strikingly similar psychological disturbances in virtually everyone exposed to it. Terr (1985) observes that children of five to fourteen responded with "amazing similarity" across age groups to being abducted in their school bus. Pynoos and Eth (1985), on the other hand, based on their study of children caught up in a shooting accident, contends that age is implicated in shaping children's reactions to trauma. At each age – preschool, school, and adolescence – their cognitive immaturity functions as both a protective and risk factor and their cognitive level leads to different pathological manifestations.

Below we will examine the question of how the trauma of war has affected Israeli, Palestinian, and Lebanese children.

Growing up in the War-Stricken Middle East

The ongoing dispute in the Middle East has meant that both Jewish and Arab children have been exposed to a long period of violent conflict, whether in the form of official wars, undeclared wars, terrorism, or civil uprising.

Israeli Children

In its fifty years of statehood, Israel has known seven organized wars and countless terrorist attacks. With the exception of the War of Independence in 1948 and the Gulf War of 1991, most of the official wars were fought largely beyond the country's borders. Nonetheless, virtually every child living in Israel has been exposed to the threat of war. Most have had or will have one or more family members serving in the army either in regular or reserve forces, and almost every boy knows that when he turns 18 he will be conscripted (Breznitz, 1983).

Moreover, children living near the borders experienced shelling in several wars. In the War of Attrition, for example, the towns, kibbutzim, and moshavim along Israel's northern and eastern borders were repeatedly shelled. The shelling posed an immediate life threat and forced them to spend most of their time in underground shelters. Homes and other buildings were destroyed, and people were wounded and killed.

In the Gulf War, both children and adults in the densely populated Central regions were sitting ducks to 18 Iraqi scud attacks, while the Israeli Army was prevented from counter-attacking by the government's policy of restraint. Though there was hardly any loss of life and relatively little substantial damage in comparison to other wars, the life of the country was disrupted for several weeks. Schools, nurseries, community centers, and places of recreation were closed. Israelis of all ages walked about with gas masks and hurried to shelter when the air raid sirens sounded. At nightfall – scud time – most people rushed indoors and stayed there. Many families left Tel Aviv to go abroad or to parts of the country that were not being shelled. Perhaps worst of all, the fear of chemical attack was constantly in the air.

Numerous studies were conducted on the responses of Israeli children to war, most of them during or immediately after the Gulf War. The following table presents the findings of studies carried out among Israeli children in the War of Attrition (1968–70), the Yom Kippur War (1973), and the Gulf War (1991):

Table 1. Israeli children's reactions to war and shelling.

Authors/year	Method	Findings
The War of Attrition		
A. Ziv R. Israeli 1973	*N* = 193 *age:* 10 *place:* shelled & nonshelled kibbutzim *measures:* 1. The children's manifest anxiety scale (Castaneda, McCandless, & Palermo, 1956).	No significant difference in anxiety levels of shelled and nonshelled Kibbutzim or of gender were found.

The Yom Kippur War		
Milgram & Milgram, 1976	*N* = 85 *age:* 10–12 *place:* Tel Aviv *measures:* 1. The Wallach & Kogan (1965) version of the Sarason scale of General anxiety. 2. The Tennessee self concept scale. 3. Questionnaire assessing personal stress.	Children's general anxiety level nearly doubled, with those who reported the lowest peacetime anxiety level reporting the highest war-time level. Rise in anxiety level was related to sex and social class but not to personal war stress or self-concept.
The Gulf War		
Levi-Shiff, Hoffman & Rosenthal, 1993	*N* = 99 mothers *age:* 4–36 months. *place:* Tel Aviv & comparison nontargeted area. *measures:* semistructured interviews of mothers measuring children's distress reactions during initial alarm states; coping reactions during initial alarm states; reactions over time; family's initial reactions; & family's reactions over time.	Almost two thirds exhibited a negative alarm state characteristic by crying, aggression or fright. Many showed signs of distress or were upset at the sound of the sirens, the sight of their parents with masks and at the stay in the sealed rooms. More than half showed changes in eating and sleeping habits and responded with adjustment difficulties. A small percentage demonstrated a regression in patterns of behavior. A small percentage showed cooperative behavior. Habituation was detected among some of the infants. Older toddlers reacted more strongly but adjusted more quickly.
Rosenbaum & Ronen, 1992	*N* = 277 *age:* 5th, 6th grade *place:* Tel Aviv *measures:* 1. Coping behaviors during the war: anxiety, routine activities, coping perceptions 2. Children's Self-Control Scale (Rosenbaum & Ronen, 1991) 3. Parental training methods from self control.	All subjects reported higher anxiety in week 1 than week 5 and greater anxiety at night than during the day. Children's anxiety was lower than the relatively high level of their mothers'. Pre-adolescents' anxiety was similar to the relatively low level of their fathers' during the day, but higher at night.
Klingman, 1992	*N* = 657 *age:* 7th, 10th, 12th grade *place:* Tel Aviv & Haifa *measures:* 1. Stress reaction scale referring to adverse emotional reactions, cognitive impairment & physiological disturbance.	Fear of being hit, refraining from enjoyable activities and difficulty in falling asleep were common. A pattern of habituation was observed from week 1 to week 4. Symptoms differed with age, gender, and level of exposure.

Mintz, 1992	$N = 313$ *age:* 7th & 10th grads *place:* High & Low risk areas *measures:* 1. The Spielberger State Trait Anxiety Inventory.	Anxiety levels were positively related to age. Girls and children who lived closer to the attacked areas reported higher anxiety levels.
Ronen & Rahav, 1992	$N = 316$ *age:* 2nd, 6th grade *place:* Tel Aviv *measures:* 1. Prewar: Kendall & Wilcox Self-Control Rating Scale (1979). 2. Wartime: Self report symptom frequency.	An increase in stress-related symptoms during the war was observed, especially, a high increase in sleep disorders. A moderate change in frequency of behavioral problems was noted. These findings were positively related to age and prewar problems.
Zeidner, Klingman, & Itskovitz, 1993	$N = 170$ *age:* 4th, 5th grade *place:* Ramat Gan, Haifa, Tybirias *measures:* A situation specific adaptation of the Bar Ilan picture test for children (Itskowitz & Strauss, 1982, 1986).	Most preadolescents expressed fear and anxiety, along with a sense of control. About a third expressed loneliness and sadness. Very few expressed extreme feelings such as panic, confusion and helplessness. No significant association was found between the respondents' psychological distress and their proximity to missile target area.
Weisenberg et al., 1993	$N = 492$ *age:* 5th, 7th, 10th graders *place:* Tel-Aviv (high exposure) Nathanyia (low exposure) *measures:* 1. Emotional reactions and coping behaviors 2. Stress reaction questionnaire 3. Global symptom score.	Children focusing on the threat reported more psychological stresses than did children who focused on avoidance and distraction. Children reported mainly optimistic feelings. Activity in the sealed room was oriented towards information seeking. Children from the shelled area reported more coping activities than did children in the nonshelled area. Younger children were engaged more in activity oriented towards the threat.
Schwarzwald et al., 1994	$N = 329$ *age:* 6th, 8th, 11th graders *place:* shelled and nonshelled cities *measures:* 1. Stress reaction questionnaire. 2. Global symptoms score.	A large drop in stress reactions was obtained with the lapse of time. Residual long-term stress reactions were found to be associated with higher immediate (4-weeks) stress reactions, a greater degree of exposure and younger age.

Palestinian and Lebanese Children

Palestinian and Lebanese children were exposed to yet different war induced stressors.

Palestinian children were dragged into the Intifada, the Palestinian uprising in the Israeli occupied territories between 1987 and 1994, when the Oslo Accords were signed. The Intifada was a popular rebellion in which Palestinians struck out with stones, burning tires, molotov cocktails, light arms, and other means against Israeli soldiers and settlers in the Gaza Strip and Judea and Samaria. The lives of the children, as of the entire Palestinian population, were disrupted by the conflict. As Palestinian shopkeepers closed their stores in days of protest and the Israeli government imposed curfews and closures which limited Palestinians' movement and prevented those who worked in Israel from going to their jobs. Hunger became a daily reality. Schools were shut for long periods both by the Israelis and the Palestinians themselves, and other daily routines were disrupted.

Violence was rampant. Palestinian children, organized and egged on by their elders, actively participated in harassing Israeli soldiers, often in the front lines of violent demonstrations. In consequence, some were killed and many were wounded. Others saw their parents, relatives, and friends killed or injured. At all hours of the day and night, their homes were invaded by Israeli soldiers searching for terrorists. Not a few children were separated from their fathers and elder brothers who were imprisoned or detained. Nor were they safe from their own people, as Palestinian extremists tortured and murdered those in their midst suspected of collaborating with the Israelis, while others took the opportunity to settle accounts with their enemies. Neither home nor street was secure.

Lebanese children were caught up in a ten year civil war, in which the country's various ethnic groups (Shi'ites, Sunni, Druse, and Christians), who had formerly lived in a delicate balance with one another were suddenly at each others' throats. From a commercial, banking, and tourist center, the "Switzerland of the Middle East," Lebanon fell into complete disarray. Its civil administration, economy, and social and cultural services, from schools and hospitals through garbage collection, all collapsed. Neighbors who had lived side by side peacefully became violent enemies. As armed militias sprung up, the simplest activities – going shopping, going to church or mosque, going to school – became fraught with danger. People were shot crossing the street, sometimes as direct targets, sometimes merely caught in the crossfire between armed groups. Kidnapping was commonplace. Many who had the means immigrated.

While, in comparison to Palestinian children, relatively few Lebanese children were actively involved in fighting, they were exposed to all the disruptions

of the war and civil breakdown. They were personally threatened by the violence, witnessed or experienced the death of family members and friends, experienced separation and displacement, and saw their parents' afraid and unable to cope.

Table 2 presents some of the studies carried out among the Palestinian and
Lebanese children.

Table 2. Palestinian children's reaction to the Intifada.

Authors	Method	Findings
Baker, 1990	$N = 796$ *age:* 6–15 *place:* West Bank & Gaza *measures:* 1. Observed symptoms rating scale-filled by mothers. 2. The Nowicki-Stickland Locus of Control Scale for Children. 3. The Cooper-Smith Self-Esteem Inventory.	High levels of fears and depression were detected though no serious pathologies were reported. Increased Behavioral problems such as: disobedience, disturbing others, fighting, sleep disturbances (these varied according to age) as well as strengthened self-esteem were found.
Punamaki & Suleiman, 1990	$N = 66$ *age:* 8–14 *place:* West Bank & Gaza *measures:* 1. Children's Coping Modes Picture Test 2. Children's Psychological Symptoms Checklist (modified from Tutter, Shaffer, & Shefherd, 1975) 3. A short version of Castaneda's Form of Manifest Anxiety Scale. 4. Political hardships 5. Locus of control (by Rotter, 1966) 6. Mothers coping modes 7. Psychological symptoms (Gurin, Veroff, & Feld's screening test, 1960)	High levels of anxiety were found among children whose mothers reported external locus of control. Aggressiveness, withdrawal and nervousness increased with the exposure to political hardships. Predictors of children's psychological symptoms were political hardships and mother's psychological symptoms.
Garbario & Kostelby, 1996	$N = 150$ children & their mothers *age:* 6–9, 12–15 *place:* West Bank *measures:* 1. Demographic and life history information. 2. Achenbach Child Behavior Checklist 3. Violence Questionnaire. 4. Conflict Tactics Scale (Straus & Gelles, 1987) 5. Parenting Stress Index (Abidin, 1983)	Palestinian children displayed more behavioral problems than did similar children in the US. Behavioral problems increased with the increase of political violence but family negativity exert a greater influence. Being female and older moderated the effect.

S. Qouta; R.L. Punamaki; E. El-Sarraj, 1995a	$N = 64$ *age:* 11–12 *place:* Gaza *measures:* 1. The Traumatic Events Checklist. 2. Eysenck Neuroticism Scale 3. Self-esteem development of Rosenberg's scale 4. Participation in flag-raising festivities questionnaire. 5. The Saleh Picture IQ Test 6. The Abraham Creativity Test. 7. Political Activity During the Intifada (a picture questionnaire)	Levels of neurotics found among children decreased after the peace treaty. Exposure to traumatic experiences decreased self-esteem and increased neuroticism. Yet participation in the flag raising festivities and personal creativity correlated with low neuroticism and high self-esteem.
S. Qouta; R.L. Punamaki; E. El-Sarraj, 1995b	$N = 108$ *age:* 11–12 *place:* Gaza	Exposure to traumatic experiences positively related to concentration, attention and memory problems. An interaction effect was found between level of exposure and active participation. In high exposure conditions, active children suffered less. An opposite trend was found in low exposure conditions. High neuroticism was related to a high level of traumatic experiences, active Intifada participation and being a boy. Active participation was related to lowest levels of self-esteem and could not moderate between traumatic experiences and emotional well-being.
Macksoud & Aber, 1996	$N = 224$ *age:* 10–16 *place:* Lebanon *measures:* 1. The Childhood War Trauma Questionnaire (Macksoud, 1992) 2. The Child Behavior Inventory (Macksoud, Aber, Dyregrov, & Raundalen, 1990) 3. The Post-Traumatic Stress Reaction Checklist (Macksoud, Aber, Dyregrov, & Raundalen, 1990).	Being a victim of violent acts, having lost someone close and being exposed to heavy shelling as well as number of traumatic events related to PTSD. Children separated from family were more likely to report depression. Separation from parents and witnessing a violent act increased prosocial and planful behavior. Age predicted only planful and prosocial behavior outcomes. Level and type of exposure experiences, separation, exposure to shelling, victims of or witnessing violent acts and emigration vary with age and gender.

The two tables reveal an extraordinary variety of responses. Children in all three population groups – Israelis, Palestinians, and Lebanese – showed both pathogenic and salotogenic responses to the war stresses they experienced. At the same time, for all the many differences in the intensity, type, duration, and context of the war stresses to which they were exposed, there was a good deal of similarity in the responses of the three groups. This picture of intra-group variation and inter-group similarity is consistent with observations of children in wars in many other places in the world: Croatia (Saric, Zuzul, & Kerestes, 1994), Cambodia (Garbarino, 1992; Sack et al., 1994), Kuwait (Nader & Fairbanks, 1994; Llabre & Hadi, 1994), Central America (Masser, 1992) and more.

The studies presented above are quite different from one another. They used different measures, examined children of different ages, and examined different outcomes. Moreover, the stressors that the children endured in the various wars differed in their intensity, duration, and social, political, and cultural meanings. Nonetheless, taken together their findings all point in similar directions.

Virtually all the studies show that the children, of all three nationalities, of all ages (from infancy through teens), and in all the wars, experienced elevated levels of distress. Most of the studies also revealed the onset or exacerbation of various stress related behavioral and emotional problems (Ronen & Rahav, 1992; Qouta et al., 1995a). These included fear, anxiety, and depression (Baker, 1990; Punamaki & Suleiman 1990), increased aggression, disobedience (Baker, 1990; Punamaki & Suleiman 1990; Garbarino & Kostenly, 1996) and increased cognitive and learning problems (Qouta et al., 1995b). In addition, a minority of children showed signs of one or another diagnosable disorder. PTSD was recorded among some Israeli children during and after the Gulf War (Schwarzwald et al., 1994) and some Lebanese children during the Lebanon War (Macksoud & Aber, 1996). Severe anxiety was observed among Israeli children in the Yom Kippur War (Milgram & Milgram, 1976). These findings are consistent with findings throughout the world on the impact of war on children (Garbarino & Konstenly, 1996; Milgram, 1993).

On the other hand, the findings clearly show that most children, both Israeli, Palestinian, and Lebanese were able to respond adaptively, despite the threat and uncertainty, the external disorganization of their lives, the disruption of normal routines, and the loss of important sources of social support. There were hardly any reports of panic (e. g., Zeidner, Klingman, & Itzkovitz, 1993); nor were there any published reports of reactive psychosis or epidemics of anxiety reactions (e. g., Baker 1990). In fact, in the Gulf War the proportion of children brought to emergency rooms in the high exposure area of Tel Aviv dropped, though it is difficult to know whether this was due to a special war time effort on the part of the children and their parents to handle their problems or their own or to the temporary departure from Tel Aviv of a large number of families with children.

The children's responses over time were more complex. All the studies that assessed responses over time of Israeli children in the Gulf War showed that most of the children, like most of the adults, showed a pattern of amelioration (e. g., Solomon, 1995). In fact, these studies reveal a gradual process of habituation (Klingman, 1992; Rosenbaum & Ronen, 1992). For example, levels of anxiety, depression, and general distress declined as the war wore on. Fewer children reported somatic symptoms of fear and more and more children indicated that they felt a sense of mastery and ability to cope (e. g., Rosenbaum & Ronen, 1992). These adjustments occurred despite the fact that the danger remained imminent. Similar processes were observed in the Yom Kippur War (Milgram & Milgram, 1976) and the War of Attrition (Ziv & Israeli, 1973). Milgram explains the adaptation by the children's learning to deal constructively with the danger. Another explanation, offered by Helson (1964), is that the danger became part of the children's lives.

Findings also indicate that a gradual process of stress evaporation took place with the end of the Gulf War. Thus, while studies carried out a month or so after the the Gulf War found discernible stress residues (Zeidner, Klingman, & Itskovitz, 1993; Weisenberg et al., 1993, Schwarzwald et al., 1994), a few months later, the war was no longer uppermost in children's concerns (Greenbaum, Erlich, & Toubiana, 1992) and a year later most ill effects had evaporated (Schwarzwald et al., 1994). Both general stress symptomatology and PTSD rates had significantly declined (Solomon, 1995).

Palestinian children of the Intifada responded somewhat differently. During the Intifada, most of them showed increasing distress and emotional problems. Baker (1990) found that levels of depression among Palestinian children living in the occupied territories increased significantly between 1988 and 1989, and that these levels were much higher than the levels of depression found among Palestinian children residing in Israel. He also reported that their fear of leaving the house and fear of Israeli soldiers increased in the course of the Intifada.

With the signing of the Oslo peace accords their responses were more similar to those of the Israeli children, but not identical. Qouta et al. (1995) found a decline in neuroticism and rise in self-esteem when the accords were signed. However, he also found that the psychological damage of their long exposure to violence still remained high. In addition, he found that the greatest amelioration occurred among those children who participated in the peace festivities, that is among those who accepted and looked forward to peace with Israel. Here we see both the persistence of strong distress, even as the level declines, and the mitigating effect not only of time, but also of circumstances.

These differences in the two groups show a clear relationship between the intensity and duration of the stressors and the children's outcomes. The Palestinian children of the Intifada were subjected to considerably greater external stress than the Israeli children who were studied. For unlike the Israeli wars, which were all limited in time and intensity, the Intifada combined pervasive, chronic violence with severe economic and social deprivation for an extended period of time.

Salutary Findings

The trauma literature, on children and adults both, assumes a pathogenic perspective, in which negative events, especially man made ones, carry the risk for a host of pathological outcomes. But there is also another approach, thus far little reflected in the literature, which focuses on effective coping and healthy responses to stress (Antonovsky, Bernstein, 1986). Research that takes this salutogenic perspective into account suggests that under certain circumstances children may emerge from war not only psychologically healthy, but more empathic, more moral, and with an enhanced sense of self. Some of the studies discussed in this chapter also present salutary findings.

Macksoud and Aber (1996) found increased prosocial behavior among Lebanese children who were separated from their parents and had witnessed violent acts, such as people in their communities being killed or injured or the intimidation of family members by soldiers. The researchers suggested that such behavior may be the outcome of the empathy that these children learn to feel from their experience and/or that it helps them to master their feelings of pain. Increased prosocial behavior was similarly found by Saric et al. (1994) among five- and six-year-olds in Zagreb, whom they assessed both before and after the Yugoslavian civil war. Nor did these children register any increase in aggression. Earlier moral development (Cole, 1987) and accelerated abstract thinking (Magwaza, Killian, Peterson, & Pillay, 1993) were observed among South African children exposed to the violence of apartheid.

Macksoud and Aber (1996) also found increased planful behavior among Lebanese children who lost someone close to them. They explained this finding by the idea that their loss created a need for them to take more control over their lives.

Baker (1990) found that, along with depression, the youth of the Intifada exhibited heightened self-esteem and a more internal locus of control. He attributes these findings to the active role that the young people took in confronting the Israeli Army and to the social commendation they won from adults and peers for their "bravery." His explanation is supported by empirical findings that children who participated actively in the Intifada emerged with elevated pride, importance, self-esteem (Punamaki, 1990), and readiness to take risks (Hein, Qouta, Thabet, & El Sarraj, 1993). Similar increases in self-esteem and risk-taking were found among Irish children exposed to the Protestant – Catholic violence (McWhirter & Trew, 1981; Lyons, 1989).

Sources of Variability in Children's Vulnerability and Resilience

Put together, the above findings reveal a substantial amount of variability in children's responses to war. Not only do different children respond differently, with some suffering more of war's negative psychological consequences than others, but the same child may respond in different ways. For example, the child who suffers from depression may also exhibit heightened prosocial behavior, accelerated moral development; and, contrary to expectations, even depression (Baker, 1990). The child who suffers from anxiety may also develop greater self-esteem. Researchers who adopt either the pathogenic or salutogenic perspective, to the exclusion of the other, tend to miss the complexity of children's responses to war.

Some of the variance both across and within children may be explained by a range of factors that may foster either vulnerability or resilience. In addition to the all important intensity of the stressor (Macksoud & Aber, 1996; Solomon, 1995), these include personality, age & gender (Baker, 1990, Garbarino & Kostenly, 1996; Macksoud & Aber, 1996), socio-economic status (Milgram & Milgram, 1976; Macksoud & Aber, 1996), social support (e. g., Ziv & Israeli, 1973), the child's (Garbarino & Kostenly, 1996; Punamaki, 1990) and his/her parents' coping, ideological conviction (Punamaki, 1990), and others.

Here we will focus on age. Unfortunately, few of the studies of the Middle East wars made a comparative assessment of children of different age groups, and those that did employ a somewhat limited age range. Nonetheless, the findings consistently show that younger children were more adversely affected than older ones. In the Gulf War, babies demonstrated more maladjustment than older toddlers (Levi-Shiff, Hoffman & Rosenthal, 1993); elementary school children showed more stress symptomatology (Klingman, 1992; Mintz, 1992; Raviv & Raviv, 1991) and PTSD (Schwarzwald et al., 1993) than junior high schoolers; and junior high schoolers demonstrated more stress (Klingman, 1992) and more PTSD (Schwarzwald et al., 1994) than high schoolers. Similar findings were reported among Lebanese (Macksoud & Aber, 1996) and Palestinian children (Garbarino & Kostenly, 1996; Baker, 1990; Punamaki, 1990).

As pointed out earlier, professionals disagree as to whether older or younger children are more vulnerable to war. The findings reported here are most consistent with those of Pynoos and Eth (1985), and similarly suggest that it is the immaturity of their cognitive and coping skills that puts younger children at risk. According to Pynoos and Eth, the more developed cognitive skills of adolescents enable them to conceive of a greater range of possible reappraisals and plans of action, which may allow for more flexible and effective coping.

The utility of adolescents' greater coping skills was demonstrated among both Israeli and Palestinian children. In both groups, the older children, who were better able to employ situation-appropriate coping strategies, and consequently fared better psychologically.

In the Gulf War, families locked themselves into sealed rooms when the air raid sirens sounded and could do nothing effective to avert the threat of the scuds. The children who suffered the least severe psychological residuals were those who adopted coping strategies of distraction, such as talking, reading, and thinking about things unrelated to the war, while those who sought parental reassurance and tried to monitor the situation showed greater distress both during and after the war. Significantly, the choice of coping strategies corresponded with age, with adolescents using distraction, the most appropriate and effective modes of coping, while younger children sought reassurance and attempted to monitor a situation that could not be controlled.

The Intifada, with its on the ground fighting, called for more active coping strategies. Not only were children mobilized to street fights; they were also required to take responsibility at home when their fathers were detained or their mothers could not cope. According to Baker (1990), the children who fared best psychologically were those who adapted active coping strategies. For example, the children whose self-esteem was most enhanced were those who actively engaged in the events of the Intifada. Clearly, this engagement was more pronounced among adolescents than younger children. Punamaki (1995) similarly found that older Palestinian children employed more purposive coping strategies than younger children, who were more helpless in responding to stressful situations. On the other hand, in an earlier publication, she also reported that active coping was not associated with more salutary psychological outcomes, possibly because the youths who actively engaged the Israeli soldiers suffered from more reprisals (Punamaki & Sulieman, 1990).

Macksoud and Aber's work on Lebanese children confirm Baker's findings. The authors explained the more adaptive behaviors of the older children as due to their greater capacity to engage in more planful and prosocial behavior as they make the transition from concrete to formal operational intelligence (Macksoud & Aber, 1996).

References

American Psychiatric Association. (1994). *Diagnostic and statistical manual of mental disorders (DSM-IV)*. Washington, DC: Author.

Baker, A.M. (1990). The psychological impact of the Intifada on Palestinian children in the occupied Westbank and Gaza: An exploratory study. *American Journal of Orthopsychiatry, 60*, 496–505.

Breznitz, S. (1983). The many faces of stress. In S. Breznitz, (Ed.), *Stress in Israel*. New York: Van Nostrand Reinhold.

Clarke, G., Sack, W., & Goff, B. (1993). Three forms of stress in Cambodian adolescent refugees. *Journal of Abnormal Child Psychology, 21*, 65–77.

Cole, R. (1987). *The political life of children*. Boston: Houghton Mifflin.

Frazer, M. (1974). *Children in conflict*. England: Penguin.

Garbarino, J., Kostenly, K., & Dubrow, N. (1991). What children can tell us about living in danger. *American Psychologist, 46*, 376–383.

Garbarino, J., Kostenly, K., & Dubrow, K. (1992). *No place to be a child*. Toronto: Lexington Books.

Garbarino, J., & Kostenly, K. (1996). The effects of political violence on Palestinian children's behavior problems: A risk accumulation model. *Child Development, 67*, 33–45.

Greenbaum, C., Erlich, C., & Toubiana, Y. (1992). *Sex differences in delayed effects of exposure to Gulf War stress by Israeli city settler children*. Paper presented at the Ministry of Education Conference on Stress Reaction in Children in the Gulf War, Ramat Gan. In *Journal of Personality Assessment, 60*, 435–457.

Hein, F., Qouta, S., Thabet, H., & El Sarraj, E. (1993). Trauma and mental health of children in Gaza. *British Medical Journal, 306*, 1130–1131.

Helson, H. (1964). *Adaptation level theory: The experimental and systematic approach to behavior*. New York: Harper & Row.

Hoffman, M.A., & Bizman A. (1996). Attributions and responses to the Arab-Israeli conflict: A developmental analysis. *Child Development, 67*, 117–128.

Israelshvili, M. (1992). *The effect of the Gulf War on the feeling of youth and their willingness to serve in the Israel Defense Forces*. Unpublished paper, School of Education, Tel Aviv University.

Janoff-Bulman, R. (1989). Assumptive worlds and the stress of traumatic events: Applications of the schema construct. *Social Cognition, 7*, 113–136.

Klingman, A. (1992). Stress reaction of Israeli youth during the Gulf War: A quantitative study. *Professional Psychology, Research Practice, 23*, 521–527.

Levi-Shiff, R., Hoffman, M. A., & Rosenthal, M. (1993). Innocent bystanders: Young children in war. *Infant Mental Health Journal, 14*, 116–130.

Lifton, R.J., & Olson, E. (1976). The human meaning of total disaster: The Buffalo Creek Experience. *Psychiatry, 39*, 1–18.

Llabre, M., & Hadi, F. (1994). Health-related aspects of the Gulf crisis experience of Kuwaiti boys and girls. Special issue: War and stress in the Middle East. *Anxiety, Stress and Coping, 7*, 217–228.

Lyons, J.A. (1989) Posttraumatic stress disorder in children and adolescents: A review of the literature. In S. Chess & M.E. Hertzig (Eds.), *Annual progress in child psychiatry and development* (pp. 451–467). New York: Brunner/Mazel.

Macksoud, M.S., & Aber, J.L. (1996). The war experience and psychosocial development of children in Lebanon. *Child Development, 67*, 70–88.

Magwaza, A.S., Killian, B.J., Peterson, I., & Pillay, Y. (1993). The effects of chronic violence on preschool children living in South African townships. *Child Abuse and Neglect, 17*, 22–35.

Masser, D. S. (1992). Psychosocial functioning of Central American refugee children. *Child Welfare, 71*, 439–456.

McCloskey, L., Southwick, K., Fernandez-Esquer, M., & Locke, C. (1995). The psychological effects of political and domestic violence on Central American and Mexican immigrant mothers and children. *Journal of Community Psychology, 23*, 95–115.

McWhirter, L., & Trew, K. (1981). Children in Northern Ireland: From "aggression" to "troubles." In A.P. Goldstein & M.H. Segall (Eds.), *Aggression in global perspective* (pp. 367–400). New York: Pergamon.

Milgram, R., & Milgram, N. (1976). The effect of the Yom Kippur War on anxiety level in Israeli children. *The Journal of Psychology, 94*, 107–113.

Milgram, N. (1993). War related trauma and victimization: Principles of traumatic stress prevention in Israel. In J.P. Wilson & B. Raphael (Eds.), *International handbook of traumatic stress syndromes*. New York: Plenum.

Mintz, M. (1992, January). *A comparison between children in two areas following the Gulf War.* Paper presented at the Ministry of Education Conference on Stress Reactions of Children in the Gulf War, Ramat Gan.

Nader, K., & Fairbanks, L. (1994). The suppression of reexperiencing: Impulse control and somatic symptoms in children following traumatic exposure. *Anxiety, Stress and Coping, 7*, 229–239.

Punamaki, R.J. (1990). Can ideological commitment protect children's well-being in situations of political violence? *Child Development, 67*, 55–69.

Punamaki, R.L., & Sulieman, R. (1990). Predictors and effectiveness of coping with political violence among Palestinian children. *British Journal of Social Psychology, 29*, 67–77.

Pynoos, R.S., & Spencer, E. (1985). Developmental perspective on psychic trauma in childhood. In C.R. Figley (Ed.), *Trauma and its wake* (pp. 36–52). New York: Brunner/Mazel.

Qouta, S., Punamaki, R. L., & El-Sarraj, E. (1995a). The impact of the peace treaty on psychological well-being: A follow-up study of Palestinian children. *Child Abuse and Neglect, 19*, 1197–1208.

Qouta, S., Punamaki, R. L., & El-Sarraj, E. (1995b). The relations between traumatic experiences, activity, and cognitive and emotional responses among Palestinian children. *International Journal of Psychology, 30*, 289–304.

Raviv, A., & Raviv, A. (1991). *Telephone survey during and after the Gulf War.* Unpublished report, Tel Aviv University, Department of Psychology, Department of Statistics.

Ronen, T., & Rahav, G. (1992). *Children's behavior problems during the Gulf War.* Paper presented at the Ministry of Education Conference on stress reaction of children in the Gulf War, Ramat Gan, Israel.

Rosenbaum, M., & Ronen, T. (1992, January). *How did Israeli children and their parents cope with the threat of daily attack by Scud missiles during the Gulf War?* Paper presented at the Ministry of Education Conference on stress reaction of children in the Gulf War, Ramat Gan, Israel.

Sack, W., McSharry, S., Clark, G., & Kinney, R. (1994). The Khmer adolescent project: Epidemiologic findings in two generations of Cambodian refugees. *Journal of Nervous and Mental Disease, 182*, 387–395.

Saric, Z., Zuzul, M., & Kerestes, G. (1994). War and children's aggressive and prosocial behavior. *European Journal of Personality, 8*, 201–212.

Schwarzwald, J., Weisenberg, M., Solomon, Z., & Waysman, M. (1994). Stress reactions of School-age children to the bombardment by scud missiles: A 1-year follow-up. *Journal of Traumatic Stress, 7*, 657–667.

Solomon, Z. (1993). *Combat stress reaction: The enduring toll of war*. New York: Plenum.

Solomon, Z. (1995). *Coping with war induced stress*. New York: Plenum.

Terr, L.C. (1985). Psychic trauma in children and adolescents. *Psychiatric Clinics of North America, 8*, 815–835.

Weisenberg, M., Schwarzwald, J., Waysman, M., Solomon, Z., & Klingman, A. (1993). Coping of school age children in the sealed room during Scud missile bombardment and post war stress reaction. *Journal of Consulting and Clinical Psychology, 61*, 462–467.

Zeidner, M., Klingman, A., & Itskovitz, R. (1993). Children's affective reactions and coping under threat of missile attack: A semiprojective assessment procedure. *Journal of Personality Assessment, 60*, 435–457.

Ziv, A., & Israeli, R. (1973). Effects of bombardment on the manifest anxiety levels of children living in the kibbutz. *Journal of Consulting and Clinical Psychology, 40*, 287–291.

Childhood Sexual Abuse and Long-Term Sequelae

Frauke Teegen

The aim of our study was to investigate sequelae of childhood sexual abuse and to analyze development and maintenance of clinical symptoms. Research data reports of 541 women who experienced sexual abuse in their childhood and were willing to answer a questionnaire about their family background, characteristics of the sexual abuse, distress and symptoms as well as coping strategies in childhood, adolescence and adulthood. I will briefly address prevalence and summarize the studies that confirmed the impact of child sexual abuse and were the basis for the development of our research instrument. After reporting on the main results of our study I will indicate some treatment implications.

Prevalence of Childhood Sexual Trauma

Child sexual abuse (CSA) can be defined as involving children and not yet mature youths in sexual activities (such as exposing and touching genitals; digital, oral, anal and vaginal penetration) to which they could not responsibly give their consent due to their phase of development. The perpetrators are usually males who take advantage of their position of power (Engfer, 1992).

Finkelhor (1994) reported on an international study of child sexual abuse. After recollecting the data on CSA from 21 countries (from Europe, the United States, Canada, South America, South Africa, New Zealand) he found CSA rates of 7–36% for women and 3–29% for men. Higher rates were usually due to more detailed and sensible screening questions. Most studies found females to be abused 1½–3 times the rate of males. The results confirm that sexual abuse of children is an international problem. Epidemiological studies of CSA in Europe and the United States identified with marked degree of comparability that 10–15% of the women and 5–19% of the men experienced sexual abuse at least once before age 16 (Ernst, 1997).

The literature suggests that childhood sexual abuse is not randomly distributed through the population in Western societies. Victimization is more likely to occur to children from a problematic and dysfunctional family background (Finkelhor & Baron, 1986; Gelles & Cornell, 1990). Family characteristics as inadequate care, alcohol abuse, marital discord and violence as well as parentification of the children appear to be more important than demographic variables as risk factors for abuse.

The Impact of Sexual Childhood Trauma: A Review of the Literature

Cole and Putnam (1992) assume that the lack of development, or loss of self-regulatory process in abused children leads to severe problems with self-definition: disturbances of the sense of self (such as a sense of separateness or stigma, loss of autobiographical memories and disturbances of the body image), poorly modulated affect and impulse control (including aggression against self and others), and insecurity in relationships (such as distrust, suspiciousness, lack of intimacy, and isolation).

The loss of self-regulation is possibly the most far reaching effect of sexual abuse and may be expressed in many different ways. The most common immediate reaction of most victimized children is anxiety. Many children experience shame, guilt, feelings of inferiority, lack of worth, and develop fears of abuse reminders. Some develop sexualized behavior, aggression, depression, physical complaints or evidence symptoms of reexperiencing, arousal, and avoidance which comprise posttraumatic stress disorder (PTSD) (Beichmann et al., 1991; Browne & Finkelhor, 1986; Bagley & Ramsey, 1986; Carraiola & Schiff, 1988; Conte & Schuerman, 1987; Goodwin, 1985; Green, 1983).

Children who developed severe and complex symptom patterns were more likely to have been abused for a longer period of time by close family members with force or penetration. 21–30% of the victims did not develop symptoms. These children were more likely to have been abused only once or twice without force by someone who was not a father figure and who had the support of a well functioning family (Finkelhor, 1990). A delayed onset of symptom development may peak during adolescence or adulthood with various "developmental triggers" (Downs, 1993). According to Courtois (1988) half of the incest victims made attempts to disclose at the time of the abuse. Most of the disclosures were unfavorably received: other family members often suppressed or denied the reality and effects of the abuse.

Sexually victimized children appear to be at a four fold increased lifetime risk for any psychiatric disorder (Finkelhor & Dzubia Leatherman, 1994). When studied as adults, CSA victims demonstrate impairment in comparison with non victimized counterparts; about one fifth evidence serious psychopathology (Browne & Finkelhor, 1986). Although only a minority of CSA victims become psychiatric patients, a large proportion (40–70%) of adult psychiatric patients are survivors of chronic abuse (Herman, 1992).

Reviews of disorders in women with a CSA history evidence a variety of symptomatic profiles (Bagley, 1991; Briere & Runtz, 1983; Ensink, 1992; Gelinas, 1983; Herman, 1992; Russel, 1986). The following symptom patterns are often described: *altered emotionality* (fearfulness and elevated anxiety, pre occupation with control, depression); *alexithymia, dissociation and avoidance* (due to feelings of vulnerability and the urge to disengage from distressing memories and affect); *impaired self-reference* (low self-esteem, shame, guilt, self-blame); *disturbed relatedness* (role confusion, poor social adjustment, distrust in others, difficulty sustaining relationships, difficulty with sexual intimacy, increased risk of revictimization); *self-destructive behavior* (substance abuse, binging, self-mutilation, suicidality). Several studies describe histories of child sexual abuse (in conjunction with alexithymia and dissociative processes) in women with *somatoform disorders* (Loewenstein, 1990; Morrison, 1989; Walker et al., 1992). Widom (1989) observed that mothers with a CSA history often maintain an emotional distance from their children which in some cases set the stage for *repeating their own victimization.*

Abuse survivors manifest a constellation of disorders which is not fully captured by the criteria of PTSD. The theory behind PTSD does not fully adapt to the experience of sexual abuse. CSA may occur under conditions of threat and violence, but it is much more characteristic for the perpetrators to misuse their authority and act with the child's trust. Sexual child abuse is less of an "event" than a situation, relationship, and process which often continues for a period of time. And the traumatization may derive from the distorted socialization in the abuse relationship.

Conceptual Basis of the Assessment and Sample Characteristics

Dissociative amnesia for emotional and cognitive material seems to be age and dose related and childhood sexual abuse seems to result in the highest proportions of victims with amnesia prior to memory retrieval. The younger the children were at the time of victimization and the more prolonged and severe the trauma was, the greater the likelihood of significant amnesia (Briere & Conte, 1993; Herman & Schatzow, 1987). The issue of memory impairment considering childhood trauma may lead to report biases. To obtain adequate information on sexual abuse experiences and sequelae we decided to recruit only individuals who were already aware of their traumatization. We advertized our research project in various media (primarily women's magazines) in German-speaking European countries and asked people who were aware of having been sexually abused during their childhood to support the project by means of requesting and filling out a self-report questionnaire.

The extensive questionnaire was developed by Teegen, Beer, Parbst, and Timm (1992) for a non clinical sample. As most available instruments which measure psychological dysfunction were developed without reference to sexual abuse they are less sensitive to abuse related specific symptoms. Therefore, the various aspects were ascertained by means of easily answerable – mostly nominally scaled – items. For the purpose of extensive data analyses subject-specific items were summarized by means of factor analyses.

The main subjects of the questionnaire are: (1) demographic variables; (2) distress and conflict regulation in the original family; (3) characteristics of childhood sexual abuse (age at onset, duration, severity of abuse, physical injuries, perpetrators, threat, disclosure, and social support); (4) revictimization; (5) distress and symptoms in childhood (5–11), adolescence (12–17) and adulthood (i. e., trauma related fears, avoidance, sexualized behavior, obsessive compulsive behavior, dissociative symptoms, eating, and sleeping disorders, substance abuse, self-mutilation, suicidality); (6) current view towards life, self, and others (FAPK scales 1 + 3, Koch, 1981: reality contact and alexithymia; self-concept, social attitudes, intimacy, sexuality, body awareness, body image drawing); (7) coping strategies (i. e., counseling, psychotherapy, self-help groups, literature, diary, creativity, affiliation, and social support).

Approximately 1000 women requested the questionnaire; 541 women (54%) sent in a questionnaire that we could evaluate. The average study participant was 34 years old (SD: 9.1). Approximately half of the women were married or in a steady relationship and had children. The educational level of the sample was relatively high: more than half of the women had high school diplomas. 57% worked outside the home and approximately 50% worked in a social profession. 68% of the women reported to have undergone psychotherapy (primarily outpatient client centered therapy). 40–60% of the women evidenced on aspects which Gelles and Cornell (1990) found in profiles of sexually abusive families – a high level of spouses quarrels, alcoholism, violence, and parentification of the children. A third reported patterns pointing to generation overlapping violence.

Sexual Abuse Characteristics and Early Coping Strategies

The women were 7 years old on the average (SD: 3.82) when the abuse began and the abuse lasted an average of 7 years (SD: 2.17). Most women were abused by close family members; in 60% of the cases the abuse was incest. The women reported primarily male perpetrators (92%), frequently their own (step) fathers (60%). 4% reported female perpetrators, most frequently their own mothers. Almost 50% were abused at the hands of more than one (2–9) perpetrators. 88% of the women suffered from very serious sexual abuse, i. e., anal, oral or vaginal penetration and 23% reported serious physical injuries which result from violent penetration of the body boundaries (i. e., bleeding of anus and vagina). The children were forced into silence primarily by means of guilt accusation towards the child and threat of love withdrawal. 23% reported threat of violence and 13% murder threats.

During childhood and adolescence only one-third of the women dared to disclose about the abuse and to ask for help from family members or institutions. Most of them were confronted with disbelief and were not taken into protection. A fourth tried to avoid the abuse by running away from home. 40% developed sexualized behavior (i. e., masturbation in public, sexual play with younger children). Frequently the women provided information which pointed to self-regulation by means of numbing perceptions and sensations: 79% evidenced depersonalization, 22–42% reported on substance abuse, eating disorders, and self-mutilation. More than 60% reported on suicidal ideation and 20% have attempted to commit suicide one or more times.

Long-Term Sequelae

In comparison to healthy control persons approximately 1/3 of the women show significant mean deviances in test scales which measure realistic problem solving and alexithymia. Approximately half of the women describe their current views towards life, themselves, and others as very negative; they are mistrusting, isolate themselves socially, avoid emotional and sexual intimacy, or continue to live in dependent relationships. They suffer from negative self-concept: low self-esteem, feelings of shame, and guilt and reject their own bodies.

Forty percent of the women reexperienced sexual violence in their adulthood one or more times (in a relationship, at work, in therapy). Almost all report voluntary sexual contacts, but only half of them experience sexual contact as enjoyable and satisfactory. 13% of the women evidence having an urge to abuse children, 8% had committed abuse already.

When we take into account that 68% of the women had been in psychotherapy, the great extent of current clinical symptoms is surprising: Even today 93% of the women still suffer from trauma related fears which are triggered by abuse reminders. 68% have sleeping disorders (45% report repetitive nightmares). 79% suffer from dissociative symptoms (along with depersonalization flashbacks in particular). 51% engage in repetitive washing. 29% report eating disorders, substance abuse, and self-mutilation. 43% evidence suicidal ideation and 14% have made suicidal attempts. Nearly all suffer from somatic disorders; they suffer particularly from chronic muscle tension/pain and illness in stomach/intestinal areas.

Predictors of Current Clinical Symptoms

With a partial least square path analysis model, Teegen and Böttcher (1996) tried to explain the current clinical symptomatology. Eighteen latent concepts were included. As nearly all women reported patterns of fear and anxiety as well as somatic disorders. These variables could not be included due to nearly zero variance.

In the path analyses model more than 60% with a stability of 97% ($0^2/R^2$-ratio) of the current clinical symptomatology could be explained by the following constructs: characteristics of sexual traumatization; problems in the original family; coping strategies in childhood/adolescence and adulthood; avoidance of social interaction and contact; avoidance of intimacy and sexuality; distorted self-concept, body awareness. The main predictors for the current symptomatology are:

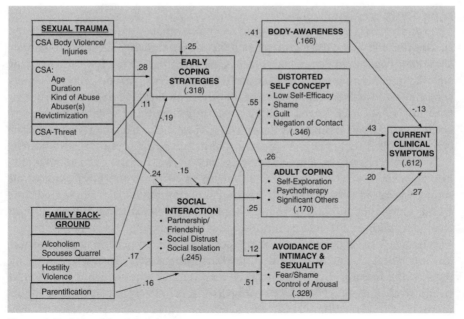

Figure 1. Path Analyses Model.

1) *Distorted self-concept:* low self-efficacy, unassertiveness, feelings of helplessness, shame, guilt, self-blame, distrust in others and social isolation, dysfunctional performance attributions. It should be noted that this most important predictor variable seems to be uninfluenced by any form of professional help.

2) *Avoidance of emotional and sexual intimacy* in order to control fear, shame, guilt, disgust.

3) *Adult coping strategies:* counseling and psychotherapy; self-exploration by reading significant literature, diary, creativity; low amount of disclosure, affiliation, and social support by friends, husband/partner.

4) *Body awareness:* inability to sense the body or certain parts of it, negative body oriented feelings, and attributions.

The important latent variable *social contact and interaction during and after sexual traumatization* consists of four constructs which describe a dysfunctional family background (alcoholism, marital discord, parentification of the child and her worrying for mothers well being), characteristics of the sexual traumatization and additional experience of violence.

The results point to the fact that the sexual traumatization is aggravated by early beginning and long duration of incestuous abuse which includes penetration and additional physical violence and takes place in a dysfunctional family atmosphere. Under these conditions the child tries to cope by numbing and dissociation of affect and sensation. She develops a deep rooted feeling of insecurity in social relationships and distrust in others and isolates herself from social contact. The disturbed relatedness is associated with disturbances of the self-image and clinical symptoms.

Social isolation as well as the avoidance of emotional and sexual intimacy serve the function of reducing the possibility of being confronted with cues that may trigger the trauma matrix. By avoiding the trauma related cues, the women try to control the possibility of reexperiencing speechless terror and loss of self-regulation. But due to this avoidance, the evaluation, differentiation and modification of dysfunctional cognitive schemas and the integration of the impact of the trauma becomes impossible and severe symptoms persist.

Comparison of Women with High and Low Amounts of Current Symptomatology

Figures 2 and 3 show body image drawings which are characteristic for two extreme groups of the sample. The groups, each 50 in number, were selected

Figure 2. Body image drawings of women with high amount of current clinical symptoms.

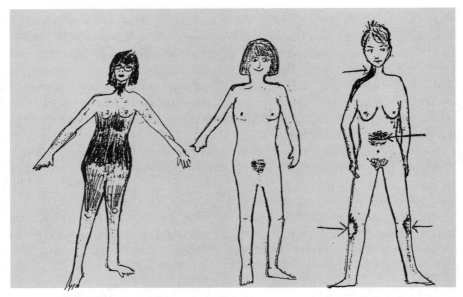

Figure 3. Body image drawings of women with low amount of current clinical symptoms.

according to high and low amounts of current clinical symptoms. The groups were comparable according to age, level of education and abuse characteristics and represented the entire sample regarding these aspects. Besides the significantly different amounts of current symptomatology the groups showed highly significant differences in the four main predictor variables we found in the path analysis model as well (Teegen, 1997b).

Figure 2 shows body image drawings of women who still suffer from a high amount of clinical symptoms and evidence a severely disturbed self-concept as well as high amount of avoidance of intimacy. Nearly all of them have undergone psychotherapy, but only 30% disclosed about the trauma in adulthood towards significant others. Most of them report that they try to deal with emotional conflicts by suppression. Only 8% feel supported in a good relationship. Characteristic of their drawings is the child like proportioning of the body and other artistic expressions which are more typical for children under 8 years and evidence a lack of development of the body schema. With red, blue, and black colors feelings of pain, tension, disgust, and hate are emphasized.

The drawings in Figure 3 are characteristic for women who reported less clinical symptoms as well as less distortions of their self-concept and avoidance of intimacy. Only 40% of this group had undergone psychotherapy, but 71% disclosed about the trauma in adulthood and experienced social support from significant others. Most of them deal with emotional conflict by affiliation and 57% evidence a good marriage or love relationship. In their drawings one can also see slight distortions of the body image (disproportioning of a shoulder, shortened arms, missing body boundary in the genital area) and an emotional emphasis (red, blue, black color) which reflects somatic memories of abuse and chronic tension. Yet on the whole these drawings evidence a clearly developed body concept. They show adult female figures and radiate a positive sense of self.

The differences between the two extreme groups which are reflected in these drawings cannot be attributed to different abuse experience, as the groups were comparable in this regard. All women survived long-term and severe intrafamilial abuse at the hands of 1.8 perpetrators on the average. But women with a high amount of current symptomatology reported more violence in their family which may have contributed to the development of highly dysfunctional attitudes toward themselves and others.

Most of the women who still suffer from severe clinical symptoms and show severe distortions of their self-concept have undergone psychotherapy. It can be assumed that the therapy possibly helped the women to become aware of the abuse trauma and to cope in some aspects. But according to our results these treatments – mostly individual outpatient client centered or psychoanalytical therapy, often long-lasting – were not effective and may not be specific enough to restructure dysfunctional cognitive schemata, emotional and social competence and to reduce trauma related symptomatology.

Treatment Implications

Because abuse survivors were mostly maltreated by authority figures they often approach psychological assessment procedures with fear and distrust. Therefore the clinician must provide a safe and non judgmental environment and approach the issue of childhood abuse in a gradual and careful manner (Curtois, 1995). A learned tendency to avoid distress and arousal may decrease the victims response and lead to an underrepresentation of abuse history and abuse related symptomatology. Avoidance may also be represented in the form of dissociative amnesia. With regard to impaired memory recall a clear diagnosis will often take 5–12 sessions (Herman, 1992). For the recent concerns of "false memories" of abuse it is also possible for individuals to confabulate abuse memories as a result of the demand characteristics associated with the inappropriate use of hypnosis, overly directive and suggestive interventions (Briere, 1993; Lindsey, 1994).

Herman (1993) has offered a clinical profile for individuals who experienced prolonged and repeated exposure to interpersonal violence. Her concept of "Complex PTSD" was supported for survivors of sexual abuse by the research of Zlotnick et al. (1996). Van der Kolk et al. (1996) and Pelcovitz et al. (1997) reframed Herman's concept into the diagnostic category "Disorders of extreme stress (DES)" and developed a structural interview (SIDES). The expanded diagnostic concept and the interview include somatization; alterations in the regulation of affect and impulse; alterations of attention, consciousness, and self-perception; alteration in relations with others and in systems of meaning. Results of the research suggest that the diagnosis of DES can be a useful tool for the investigation of the complex symptomatology in adult survivors of childhood sexual abuse.

Systematic research of effective treatment for adults with severe alteration in response to CSA is virtually non existent. Research on psychosocial treatments for other trauma populations has focused almost exclusively on combat veterans and rape victims. Of the systematic studies of behavioral treatments, prolonged exposure, and cognitive restructuring appear to be the most effective forms of treatment for patients with PTSD (Solomon, Gerity, & Muff, 1992; Olasov-Rothbaum & Foa, 1996). Results on prolonged exposure may not generalize to survivors of childhood sexual abuse because they primarily address positive PTSD symptoms and do not relate to emotional numbing and avoidance. Because our results point to the fact that disturbed relatedness and dysfunctional schemas are important mediators for the development and maintenance of a complex symptomatology I will focus on some fundamental treatment goals and address cognitive restructuring techniques and group programs in more detail.

The treatment of CSA-survivors makes high demands on the competence and stress endurance of the therapist, who should protect him/herself from secondary traumatization by taking part in a good supervision group. In order to build up a stable therapeutic relationship, the therapist must be able to enter the traumatic reality of the client and view it through the eyes of the victim. Yet in order to make the treatment effective, she must be able to keep a clinical perspective. The congruence between her verbal and nonverbal behavior is particularly important for incest survivors who have developed an extreme sensitivity to dishonest interpersonal messages. Herman (1992) has recommended a "first stage" of treatment that emphasizes safety, stabilization, education, and stress management skills. The treatment should be flexible, should clarify traumatic material from the past while creating a new framework for interpreting the experiences for the present and future. Traumatic experiences are often not connected with verbal expression. Thus, nonverbal media (drawings, designs in sand tray or with clay) and imagery instructions make the expression and the step by step verbalization easier. Pictures are encoded in more detail, more deeply and with more meaning than verbal material (Craik & Llockhardt, 1972) and create more associations to the cognitive structures. Creative drawings and guided imagery can thus be helpful in memory retrieval as well as in reframing dysfunctional cognitions.

Jehu et al. (1986) and Jehu (1989) describe the distorted beliefs of women with a history of CSA as well as cognitive interventions. They used "corrective" information, logical analyses, socratic dialog, decatastrophying, and reattribution to restructure especially self-blame and self-denial. They emphasize that a positive prognostic expectance, acceptance, support, and empathic understanding are vital to enable women to continue the restructuring process.

The restructuring of deeply rooted beliefs and assumptions is easier for a client if she first experiences by means of guided imagery how she created these assumptions as a child to explain a very threatening reality. The experience that these child cognitions are not "wrong," "irrational," or "crazy" per se, but still need to be closely addressed increases the acceptance for the interventions mentioned above. At the same time the client usually develops a fundamental understanding for developmental deficits and a willingness to accept and integrate her own role and actions as a child (Teegen, 1994, 1997a).

The restructuring of dysfunctional cognitions is often more difficult with incest victims because they are missing very basic positive parental messages and concepts for normal developmental processes. In contrast to child therapy, a direct "post parenting" for "adult children" is only possible in the therapeutic relationship to a limited extent and can quickly lead to projection problems and trespassing the lines of the client/therapist relationship. This can cause clients to repeat traumatic relationship patterns. Basic positive messages which support the client's self-esteem can be experienced with the help of kinesthetic emotional imagery. A collection of "healing stories" by Wallas (1991), which allow various developmental phases to be experienced anew, can be of inspiration. The goal of this kind of imagery is to convey positive, parental messages to the client in a way that makes it possible for her to accept herself as lovable and adequate and encourage her to trust herself.

A variety of diverse group treatment approaches (both short and long-term) have been used to confront the isolation which is characteristic for the survivors of CSA trauma (Brandt, 1989; Brende, 1994; Cole Kreidler & Burns England, 1990; Gold-Steinberg & Buttenheim, 1992; Herman & Schatzow, 1984; McBride & Emerson, 1989; Mennen & Meadow, 1992; Resick & Schnicke, 1992; Robert & Lie, 1989; Zlotnick et al., 1997). The amount of structure varies greatly and may include a clear agenda of topics for each meeting or specific topics set for the first meetings and the discussion for topics in later sessions to be determined by the group members (usually 4–8). Most clinicians propose that women, who are suicidal or who suffer from substance abuse or self-mutilation should be screened out. Zlotnick et al. (1997) report drop outs with higher dissociative symptomatology as well as higher levels of pretreatment. But at this point there are no clear comparative outcome studies to examine the different treatment formats, nor the selection criteria.

A good example of a clearly structured psycho-educational group program was developed by Brende (1994). It introduces the participants with 12 basic topics for an understanding of their problems in 12 weeks. They are introduced step by step:

1) clarifying trauma related memories, attitudes, and behaviors;

2) setting goals for coping with the symptoms and their further development;

3) planning changes, and

4) practicing new behaviors.

The psycho-educational measures should create a framework for understanding traumatic experiences and their related symptoms and train self-help possibilities for stabilization. The clear structure and the training paradigm in which the participants are not forced to open themselves protects them against destructive group interaction which may occur very quickly in unstructured sessions. Brende reports that the program in general has also been successful for clients with dissociative disorders and substance abuse.

The elaboration of treatment milieu concepts which are applied to short term hospital care (21 days) in a 23-bed psychiatric unit for adult CSA survivors is demonstrated by Bloom (1994). The patients receive daily individual psychotherapy sessions and attend four groups: *Psycho-educational groups* are designed to provide didactic information about trauma and its effects. *Stress management groups* help the patient to learn new coping skills to replace self-destructive habits. *Re-enactment groups* focus on the ways patients reenact their traumatic scenarios in the context of the community. *Discharge planning groups* prepare individuals to utilize the insight they have gained during their admission to anticipate and prepare for problems after discharge. *Psychodrama*, *art therapy*, *occupational therapy*, and *movement therapy* help the patient express emotions nonverbally, translate nonverbal into verbal expression that can be shared, and rehearse new behaviors. Patients with destructive symptoms are placed on *special agendas* to help manage problems on eating disorder, self-mutilation, dissociation, and traumatic reenactment. In order to be admitted to the unit, patients must be willing to make a commitment to transforming self-destructive habits. In discussing on issues of safety for incest survivors with severe and complex symptomatology Bloom (1994) writes:

A morally safe environment must be a place to freely and openly discuss issues of life's purpose and meaning, existential dilemmas and spiritual impasses without fear of condemnation and censure. Thus, there must be room for hope, love, and atonement. Thus, the most fundamental obligation in the therapeutic milieu is to provide an environment in which honesty combined with compassion represents the overall therapeutic stance (p. 481).

References

Bagley, C. (1991). The long-term psychological effects of child sexual abuse: A review of some British and Canadian studies of victims and their families. *Annuals of Sex Research*, *4*, 25–48.

Bagley, C., & Ramsey, R. (1986). Sexual abuse in childhood. Psychosocial outcomes and implications for social work practice. *Journal of Social Work and Human Sexuality*, *4*, 33–47.

Beichman, J.H., Zucker, K.J., Hood, J.E., daCosta, G.A., & Akmann, D. (1991). A review of the short-term effects of child sexual abuse. *Child Abuse and Neglect*, *15*, 537–565.

Brandt, L.M. (1989). A short term group therapy model for treatment of adult female survivors of childhood incest. *Group*, *2*, 74–82.

Brende, J.O. (1994). A twelve theme psycho educational program for victims and survivors. In M.B. Williams & J.F. Sommer (Eds.), *Handbook of posttraumatic therapy* (pp. 231–149). Westport, CT: Greenwood.

Bloom, S. (1994). The sanctuary model. Developing generic impatient programs for the treatment of psychological trauma. In M.B. Williams & J.F. Sommer (Eds.), *Handbook of posttraumatic therapy* (pp. 474–491). Westport, CT: Greenwood.

Briere, J. (1995). Science versus politics in the delayed memory debate. A commentary. *Counseling Psychologist, 23*, 290–293.

Briere, J., & Conte, J. (1993). Self-reported amnesia for abuse in adults molested as children. *Journal of Traumatic Stress, 1*, 21–31.

Briere, J., & Runtz, M. (1983). Childhood sexual abuse. Long term sequelae and implications for psychological assessment. *Journal of Interpersonal Violence, 8*, 392–330.

Browne, A., & Finkelhor, D. (1986). Impact of child sexual abuse: A review of the research. *Psychological Bulletin, 1*, 66–77.

Caraiola, A.A., & & Schiff, M. (1988). Behavioral sequelae of physical and/or sexual abuse in adolescence. *Child Abuse and Neglect, 12*, 181–188.

Cole, P., & Putnam, E.W. (1992). Effect of incest on self and social functioning: A developmental psychopathology perspective. *Journal of Counseling and Clinical Psychology, 60*, 174–184.

Cole Kreidler, M., & Burns England, D. (1990). Empowerment through group support: Adult women who are survivors of incest. *Journal of Family Violence, 1*, 35–41.

Conte, J., & Schuerman, J. (1987). The effects of sexual abuse on children. A multidimensional view. *Journal of Interpersonal Violence, 4*, 380–390.

Courtois, C.A. (1988). *Healing the incest wound. Adult survivors in therapy.* New York: Norton.

Courtois, C. (1995). Assessment and diagnosis. In C. Classen (Ed.), *Treating women molested in childhood* (pp. 140–157). San Francisco: Jossey Bass.

Craik, E.L., & Lockhurt, R.C. (1992). Levels of processing: A framework for memory research. *Journal of Verbal Learning and Verbal Memory, 11*, 671–684.

Downs, W. (1993). Developmental considerations for the effects of childhood sexual abuse. *Journal of Interpersonal Violence, 8*, 331–345.

Engfer, D. (1992). Kindesmißhandlung und sexueller Mißbrauch [Child maltreatment and sexual abuse]. *Zeitschrift für Pädagogische Psychologie, 6*, 165–174.

Ensink, B.J. (1992). *Confusing realities. A study on child sexual abuse and psychiatric symptoms.* Amsterdam: VU University.

Ernst, C. (1997). Zu dem Problem der epidemiologischen Erforschung des sexuellen Mißbrauchs [On the problem of the epidemiologic investigation of sexual abuse]. In G. Amann & R. Wipplinger (Eds.), *Sexueller Mißbrauch. Überblick zu Forschung, Beratung und Therapie.* [Sexual abuse: An overview on research, counseling, and therapy] (pp. 56–77). Tübingen: DGVT Verlag.

Finkelhor, D. (1990). Early and long-term effects of child sexual abuse. An update. *Professional Psychology, Research and Practice, 5*, 325–330.

Finkelhor, D. (1994). The international epidemiologic of child sexual abuse. *Child Abuse and Neglect, 19*, 409–417.

Finkelhor, D., & Baron, L. (1986). Risk factors for child sexual abuse. *Journal of Interpersonal Violence, 1*, 43–71.

Finkelhor, D., & Dzuiba Leatherman, J. (1994). Victimization of children. *American Psychologist, 3*, 173–183.

Gelinas, D. (1983). The persisting negative effects of incest. *Psychiatry, 46*, 312–332.

Gelles, R., & Cornell, C. (1990). *Intimate violence in the family.* Beverly Hills: Sage.

Gold Steinberg, S., & Buttenheim, M.C. (1993). Telling one's story in the incest survivors's group. *International Journal of Group Psychotherapy*, *43*, 173–189.

Goodwin, J. (1985). Posttraumatic symptoms in incest victims. In S. Eth & R.S. Pynoos (Eds.), *Posttraumatic stres disorder in children* (pp. 157–168). Washington, DC: American Psychiatric Press.

Green, A.H. (1983). Dimensions of psychological trauma in abused children. *American Journal of Psychiatry*, *22*, 231–237.

Herman, J.L. (1992). *Trauma and recovery*. New York: Basic Books.

Herman, J.L. (1993). Sequelae of prolonged and repeated trauma. Evidence to a complex posttraumatic syndrome (DESNOS). In J.R. Davidson & E.D. Foa (Eds.), *Posttraumatic stress disorder: DSM IV and beyond* (pp. 213–228). Washington, DC: American Psychiatric Press.

Herman, J.L., & Schatzow, E. (1984). Time limited group therapy for women with a history of incest. *International Journal of Grouptherapy*, *34*, 603–618.

Herman, J.L., & Schatzow, E. (1987). Recovery and verification of memories of childhood sexual trauma. *Psychoanalytic Psychology*, *4*, 1–14.

Jehu, D. (1989). Mood disturbances among women clients sexually abused in childhood. *Journal of Interpersonal Violence*, *2*, 164–184.

Jehu, D., Klassen, C., & Gazan, M. (1986). Cognitive restructuring of distorted beliefs associated with childhood abuse. *Journal of Social Work and Human Sexuality*, *4*, 49–69.

Koch, C. (1981). *Fragebogen zur Abschätzung Psychosomatischen Krankheitserlebens (FAPK)* [Questionnaire on the Appraisal of Processes of Psychosomatic Disturbances]. Weinheim: Beltz.

Lindsay, D.S. (1994). Contextualizing and clarifying criticism of memory work. The recovered memory/false memory debate. *Consciousness and Cognition*, *3*, 436–437.

Loewenstein, R.J. (1990). Somatoform disorders in victims of incest and child abuse. In R.P. Kluft (Ed.), *Incest-related syndromes of adult psychopathology* (pp. 75–112). Washington, DC: American Psychiatric Press.

McBride, M.C., & Emerson, S. (1989). Group work with women who were molested as children. *The Journal of Specialists of Group Work*, *1*, 25–33.

Mennen, F.E., & Meadow, D. (1992). Process of recovery: in support of long-term groups for sexual abuse survivors. *International Journal of Group Psychotherapy*, *42*, 29–44.

Morrison, J. (1989). Childhood sexual histories of women with somatoform disorder. *American Journal of Psychiatry*, *146*, 239–241.

Olasov Rothbaum, B., & Foa, E.B. (1996). Cognitive behavioral therapy for posttraumatic stress disorder. In A.C. van der Kolk, A.C. McFarlane & L. Weisaeth (Eds.), *Traumatic stress. The effects of overwhelming experiences on mind, body, and society* (pp. 491–501). New York: Guilford.

Pelcovitz, D., van der Kolk, B., Roth, S., Mandel, F., Kaplan, S., & Resick, P. (1997). Thematic resolution, PTSD, and complex PTSD. The relationship between meaning and trauma-related symptoms. *Journal of Traumatic Stress*, *1*, 3–16.

Resick, P.A., & Schnicke, M.K. (1992). Treating symptoms of adult victims of sexual assault. *Journal of Interpersonal Violence*, *5*, 466–506.

Roberts, L., & Lie, G.Y. (1989). A group therapy approach to the treatment of incest. *Social Work with Groups*, *3*, 77–90.

Russel, D. (1986). *The secret trauma. Incest in the lives of girls and women*. New York: Basic Books.

Solomon, S.D., Gerrity, E.T., & Muft, A.M. (1992). Efficacy of treatments for posttraumatic stress disorder. An empirical review. *Journal of the American Medical Association*, *5*, 633–638.

Teegen, F. (1994). *Körperbotschaften. Selbstwahrnehmung in Bildern* [Messages of the body: Self-perception by drawings]. Hamburg, Germany: Rowohlt.

Teegen, F. (1997a). Behandlung dissoziativer Symptome. Ein kognitiv behavioraler Ansatz [Treatment of dissociative symptoms. A cognitive-behavioral approach]. In A. Amann & R. Wipplinger (Eds.), *Sexueller Mißbrauch. Überblick zu Forschung, Behandlung und Therapie* [Sexual abuse: An overwiew of research, counseling, and treatment] (pp. 535–557). Tübingen, Germany: DGVT Verlag.

Teegen, F. (1997b, June). *Coping with sexual childhood trauma*. Paper presented at the 5th European Conference on Traumatic Stress, Maastricht, The Netherlands.

Teegen, F., Böttcher, S. (1996, June). *Child sexual abuse and long-term sequelae*. Paper presented at the 2nd World Conference of the International Society on Traumatic Stress Studies, Jerusalem, Israel.

Teegen, F., Beer, M., Parbst, B., & Timm, S. (1992). Sexueller Mißbrauch von Jungen und Mädchen. Psychodynamik und Bewältigungsstrategien [Sexual abuse of boys and girls. Psychodynamic and coping strategies]. In M. Gegenfurtner, W. Keukens (Eds.), *Sexueller Mißbrauch von Kindern und Jugendlichen* [Sexual abuse of children and juveniles] (pp. 19–31). Essen: Westarp.

Van der Kolk, B.A., Pelcovitz, P., Roth, S., Mandel, F.S., McFarlane, A., Herman, J.L. (1996). Dissociation, somatization and affect dysregulation. The complexity of adaptation to trauma. *American Journal of Psychiatry*, *153*, 83–93.

Walker, E.E., Laton, W.J., Hevaas, R., Jemelka, R.P., & Massoth, D. (1992). Dissociation in women with chronic pelvic pain. *American Journal of Psychiatry*, *141*, 532–537.

Wallas, I. (1991). *Stories that heal. Reframing adult children of dysfunctional families with hypnotic stories*. New York: Norton.

Widom, C.S. (1989). The cycle of violence. *Science*, *144*, 160–165.

Zlotnick, C., Shea, T.M., Rosen, K., Simpson, E., Mulrenin, K., Begin, A., Pearlstein, T. (1997). An affect management group for women with posttraumatic stress disorder and histories of childhood sexual abuse. *Journal of Traumatic Stress*, *3*, 414–436.

Zlotnick, C., Zakriski, A.L., Shea, M.T., Costello, E., Begin, A., Pearlstein, T., Simpson, E. (1996). The long-term sequelae of sexual abuse. Support for a complex posttraumatic stress disorder. *Journal of Traumatic Stress*, *2*, 105–205.

Prevalence and Comorbidity of Traumatic Events and Posttraumatic Stress Disorder in Adolescents and Young Adults*

Axel Perkonigg and Hans-Ulrich Wittchen

Introduction

Clinical wisdom and many psychopathological theories of mental disorders suggest that traumatic events and the subsequent way how people deal with them, play a crucial role in the development of not only posttraumatic stress disorder (PTSD) but also many other mental disorders. More recent epidemiological surveys, almost exclusively conducted in the United States, have provided at least some support for the potentially critical role of traumatic events, by demonstrating the considerable frequency of traumatic events throughout the life span and substantial prevalence estimates of full-blown posttraumatic stress disorders as well as high rates of comorbidity in PTSD sufferers (Breslau, Davis, Andreski, & Peterson, 1991; Kessler, Sonnega, Brommet, & Nelson, 1995; Resnick, Kilpatrick, Dansky, Saunders, & Best, 1993).

The general picture resulting from epidemiological studies, however, is quite confusing, primarily due to considerable variations in findings. Prevalence rates for a lifetime history of PTSD varied from 1.0% DSM-III PTSD in the Epidemiologic Catchment Area survey (St. Louis; Helzer, Robins & McEvoy, 1987) to 12.3% DSM-III-R PTSD from a telephone survey in a national prob-

* This paper is part of the Early Developmental Stages of Psychopathology Study (EDSP), a 5-year prospective collaborative epidemiologic investigation of the prevalence, causes, and consequences of mental and substance use disorders in Munich, Germany. The EDSP is supported by the Bundesministerium für Bildung, Forschung und Wissenschaft as part of the collaborating epidemiological ANEPSA program (Analytical Epidemiology of Psychopathology and Substance Abuse). Collaborators are Dr. Ron Kessler, Harvard Medical School, Boston, USA; Dr. Cathy Merikangas, Genetic Epidemiology, Yale, New Haven, USA; Dr. Jules Angst, Psychiatrische Universitätklinik, Zürich, Switzerland; Dr. Jürgen Margraf, Universität Dresden, Klinische Psychologie und Psychotherapie; Dr. Neumärker, Kinderpsychiatrische Universitätsklinik der Charité, Berlin; Dr. Gerhard Bühringer, Institute of Therapy Research (IFT), München.

ability household sample of adult women (Resnick et al., 1993). In the most recent study by Kessler et al. (1995) as part of the National Comorbidity Survey (NCS) a lifetime prevalence of DSM-III-R PTSD of 7.8% was reported.

Differences in sampling frame especially gender and age of respondents, the assessment of traumatic events and PTSD symptoms may be responsible for this wide range of prevalence estimates (Kessler et al., in press; Norris, 1992). It is also quite likely that the many changes in the definition of PTSD as well as PTSD qualifying events (DSM-III, DSM-III-R), might be held responsible for some of this variation. To illustrate, since the codification of diagnostic criteria in the third edition of the Diagnostic and Statistical Manual of Mental Disorders (DSM-III) for psychopathological stress responses after traumatic experiences as posttraumatic stress disorder with rather vague general criteria, considerable conceptual refinements and revisions were subsequently made, especially with regard to the essential features of traumatic events (Davidson & Foa, 1993). In DSM-IV (APA, 1994) for example, the DSM-III-R phrase describing qualifying traumatic event as "outside the range of normal human experience" has been deleted, because data had shown that it was unreliable and not specific enough, leading to inflated prevalence estimates. A diagnosis of PTSD according to DSM-IV now requires unlike to DSM-III-R an exposure to a traumatic event that involved "actual or threatened death or serious injury, or a threat to the physical integrity of self or others" (criterion A1 of DSM-IV) and a victim's response that involves "intense fear, helplessness, or horror" (criterion A2). Further a new criterion for clinically significant distress or impairment was added (criterion F in DSM-IV), besides a minor change in the reorganization of diagnostic elements (physiological reactivity on exposure to cues).

Given the considerable variation in definitions of qualifying events and PTSD, emphasis more recently has shifted from merely reporting PTSD prevalence rates to studying the conditional probabilities of traumatic events leading to PTSD (Kessler, Sonnega, Brommet, & Nelson, 1995). These types of analyses offer the important advantage of identifying the frequency and type of those traumatic events, that are most likely to be associated with the further development of PTSD. The most common type of trauma in the NCS was witnessing someone being injured or killed, being involved in a fire, flood, or natural disaster; and being involved in a life-threatening accident. The risk (conditional probability) for PTSD developing as a consequence of these events however differed markedly with rape being the most powerful.

Types of trauma as well as the risk for PTSD, however, also varied by gender with men reporting more of the three as well as physical attacks and combat experiences and women reporting more rape and sexual molestation. Despite a higher number of traumatic events in men, women were more than twice as likely as men to develop PTSD. Besides gender differences which were also reported from other studies (Breslau et al., 1991) social class and history of past trauma exposure were found to be important moderators of these effects. Previous studies have suggested that only 25% of the people exposed to a traumatic event will develop PTSD (Bromet et al., 1998). But some risk factors seem to predict only trauma exposure and others seem to be significantly related to conditional risks of PTSD after exposure (Kessler, Sonnega, Bromet, Hughes, Nelson, & Breslau, in press).

With regard to comorbidity the results of epidemiological studies have shown that PTSD is a highly comorbid disorder. Rates of lifetime comorbidity between 62% and 92% have been reported in epidemiological surveys suggesting strong relationships with affective and anxiety disorders and also with substance use disorders (Yehuda & McFarlane, 1995; Cottler, Compton, Mager, Spitznagel, & Janca, 1992). It is not clear whether overlapping criteria are responsible for these high comorbidity rates or whether the relationships between PTSD and other disorders may allow for causal explanations of underlying vulnerabilities. Some studies have shown that specific other psychiatric disorders are primary and increase the risk of subsequent traumatic events or PTSD (Breslau, Davis, Peterson, & Schultz, 1997; Kessler et al., 1995). Other studies have shown that PTSD influenced the risk of subsequent other disorders (Breslau et al., 1997).

Most past and current literature of PTSD concerns adults. In children, adolescents and young adults systematic studies of trauma victims started only in the last 15 years (Parry-Jones & Barton, 1995; Shannon, Lonigan, Finch, & Taylor, 1994; Pelcovitz, Kaplan, Goldenberg, Mandel, Lehare, & Guarrera, 1994). Most of these studies refer to populations exposed to a particular traumatic event as a natural disaster, war, displacement, abuse or violence. They have shown that traumatic events can have a profound influence on current and future behavior of children that is not only restricted to the same symptoms of PTSD as in adults but also to other comorbid psychiatric conditions and even more developmental consequences, which may have long-term implications of childhood and adolescents trauma for later adult personality (Goenjian et al., 1995; Pynoos, Steinberg, & Goenjan, 1996). Additionally early traumatization as childhood sexual and physical abuse seems to be a stronger predictor of PTSD and other mental disorders than later traumatic experiences (Shalev, 1996).

But epidemiological evidence about the frequency of traumatic events and PTSD in young age groups of the general population is available from two studies only: The NCS estimated a lifetime prevalence of DSM-III-R PTSD in 15–24 olds of 2.8% in men and 10.3% in women. Similarly high prevalence estimates were also reported from Breslau et al. who found in a study of an urban population with young adults that 11.3% of young women and 6% of young men had a lifetime history of DSM-III-R PTSD. Risk factor analysis revealed that among the young adults, those with poor education, blacks, and those with high neuroticism and extraversion were more likely than others to be exposed to traumatic events and were at greater risk for PTSD. Neither of these studies however reported in detail about the conditional probabilities from traumatic events to PTSD in these age groups, nor were age-group specific comorbidities reported.

Aims

This paper primarily reports – similar to Kessler's above mentioned paper – the prevalence of traumatic events and PTSD with specific focus on determining which types of events carry the strongest risk of PTSD development in these young age group. Also we will examine the risk for particular PTSD symptoms after specific types of events to see which symptoms are more strongly associated with specific types of events as a more practical issue of this analysis. Additionally we are interested in correlates of traumatic events and PTSD and age specific comorbidity to allow a comparison of the results with older age groups. Unlike to previous studies we use DSM-IV diagnostic criteria, however retaining largely comparability with DSM-III-R criteria, in order to allow for cross-study comparisons. Our study is also limited to adolescents and young adults (aged 14–24), in an attempt to examine more closely the role of traumatic events early in the life cycle.

Methods

Sample

The data presented here come from the first wave of the Early Developmental Stages of Psychopathology Study (EDSP), a study funded by the German Ministry of Research and Technology. The sample was drawn from 1994 government registries of all residents in metropolitan Munich (1990 population 3.2 million, Statistisches Jahrbuch, 1994) expected to be 14–24 years of age at the time of interview during the first half of 1995. Because the special interest was in early developmental stages of psychopathology, 14–15-year-old adolescents were sampled at twice the rate of persons 16–20 years of age and 21–24-year-old young adults were sampled at nearly half this rate. From 4809 sampled individuals, 4263 were located. The response rate was 71%. A total of 3021 interviews were completed. This response rate is among the highest ever achieved in Germany. Slightly higher proportions of refusals were found among women. Details about sampling procedure and non respondents are presented elsewhere (Wittchen et al., in press). The data has been adjusted by age, sex, and geographic location to match the distribution of the sampling frame. Approximately two-thirds of the sample is currently attending or has attended gymnasium (secondary education preparing students for possible entrance to university) and are currently living with their parents. Twenty-three percent of the sample live alone. Seventy-five percent of the sample live in suburban Munich.

Interviewing Procedures

The survey staff was highly experienced and consisted of 10 clinical interviewers and 25 full-time professional health research interviewers from Infratest-Gesundheitsforschung, a survey company specializing in health interview research. They received two full weeks of training in use of the study instrument. This training period was followed by at least 10 practice interviews that were closely monitored by our staff. Immediately prior to the beginning of the study, one day of prefield training was done to stress important points and techniques and increase the motivation of the interviewers. After contacting the probands, a time and setting for the interview was established although most interviews took place at the time of first contact in the home of the probands. At the beginning of the interview the written data protection explanation was given to the probands and a gift was given as an incentive for participation. The standard gift was two telephone cards each worth DM 12 (US$ 8). For quality assurance and editing the interviewers had to contact the editors after having completed three to five interviews in the beginning of the study and, throughout the field period, when handling over completed interviews. This gave interviewers an opportunity to receive help with regards to technical and content aspects of the interview. Interviewers were closely monitored throughout the field period by both the Infratest field staff as well as specially trained clinical editors with clinical experience. This procedure ensured that within a week of submission to the clinical editor interviews were checked according to a standard procedure for both formal consistency as well as appropriate recording techniques. During these weekly editing sessions, detailed feedback was given to every interviewer to avoid errors in later interviews. The correct administration was also checked by random follow-up phone calls to probands.

Instrument and Diagnostic Assessment

Psychopathological as well as diagnostic assessment was based on the Munich version of the Composite International Diagnostic Interview (M-CIDI-DIA-X, Wittchen et al., 1995a). The M-CIDI is an updated version of the World Health Organization (WHO) CIDI version 1.2 supplemented by questions of WHO-CIDI version 2.0 developed to cover DSM-IV and ICD-10 criteria (Wittchen & Pfister, 1997; Lachner et al., submitted; Reed & Schuster, 1995). The M-CIDI allows for the assessment of symptoms, syndromes, and diagnoses of 48 mental disorders (not counting various subtypes of main disorders) along with information about onset, duration, clinical, and psychosocial severity*.

The section N of the M-CIDI refers to DSM-IV Posttraumatic stress disorder and is based on a modified version of the revised DIS (Robins et al., 1989). It starts with a screening question about traumatic stressors. We decided not to ask directly about these experiences. Instead we presented a list of 8 groups of specifically described traumatic events and an open ended question about any other terrible event (Figure 1) in a booklet with the question: "Now I'd like to ask you about extremely stressful or upsetting events that most people never experience – experiences that are distressing or upsetting to almost anyone. Please look at list N1. Have you ever experienced one of these situations? If yes: Please give me their letters." These procedure was also chosen by Kessler et al. (1995) because respondents are sometimes reluctant to admit the occurrence of embarrassing and stigmatizing traumas, such as rape and sexual abuse. All responses that did refer to specific traumatic events and involved intense fear were coded if qualifying under criterion A. If a respondent reported more than three events, the age at which the experience first occurred was asked for the three worst events. An additional question asked for associations between the reported events to avoid double coding.

As Kessler et al. (1995) and differing from the DIS criteria B through D were evaluated for the most "upsetting event" (nominated by the respondent). This restriction means that estimates of lifetime prevalence are lower-bound estimates but as Kessler et al. (1995) pointed out, only a small number of

---

* Developmental work on the M-CIDI started in 1993. The full package containing the M-CIDI lifetime and 12-month versions (paper-and-pencil, computer-administrated personal interview (CAPI) versions) along with respondents booklets, data entry, and diagnostic programs as well as training package, became available in end of 1994 in time for use in this study. The complete computerized M-CIDI package with screening questionnaires, interviewer, and respondents booklet, the computer-administered personal interview (CAPI) and the computer programs were published under the name Diagnostic Expert System (DIA-X) by Swets and Zeitlinger in 1997. The English as well as other language versions of this package is available on request by writing to the authors.

Terrible experiences and catastrophes:
1 You've had a terrible experience during a war.
2 You were seriously physically threatened (for example, with a weapon), attacked, injured or tortured.
3 You were the victim of a rape attack.
4 You were sexually abused as a child (that is, before the age of 14), that is, someone forced you to commit sexual acts against your will or such acts were done to you.
5 You were the victim of a natural catasthrophe.
6 You had a serious accident.
7 You were imprisoned, were taken hostage or were the victim of a kidnapping.
8 You witnessed one of the events above happen to another person.
Whom: ....
Which of the events listed above?
Number: [ ][ ][ ][ ][ ][ ][ ][ ]
9 Was there another terrible event or catastrophe that hasn't been mentioned?
Which: ....

Figure 1. Questions about events and experiences that qualified as traumas according to DSM-IV.

respondents who fail to meet PTSD diagnostic criteria are likely to meet these criteria for any other event. If respondents reported at least one PTSD symptom the age of onset, the duration resp. how long the symptoms continued and the last occurrence of PTSD symptoms were recorded.

Diagnostic analysis is based on the M-CIDI diagnostic package DSM-IV diagnostic algorithms (Pfister & Wittchen 1995). Diagnostic findings reported in this paper are based on the M-CIDI DSM-IV algorithms without using the DSM-IV hierarchy rules, unless otherwise stated in the text.

Analysis Procedures

The results are based on weighted data. Prevalence analysis were stratified by sex. Zero-order odds ratios (ORs) for comorbidity analyses were derived by exponentiating the coefficients of univariate logistic regression models. Estimates of the confidence intervals were generated by using the SE's and the logistic regression coefficients from the same regression analyses. Coefficients of correlates of PTSD are based on multivariate logistic regression models. The LOGISTIC program in the SPSS software package (Version 6.1.3) was used for these analyses. The age of onset curve for events was generated by means of the survival analysis methods operationalized in the SURVIVAL program in the SPSS software package.

Results

Prevalence of Traumatic Events and PTSD

Table 1 shows that women (2.2%) were more than five times as likely than young men (0.4%) to fulfill DSM-IV criteria for PTSD in their life. Gender differences were apparent in all age groups. The highest lifetime prevalence for PTSD was found in 18- to 24-year-old women (2.8%). 12-month prevalence estimates were considerable lower (0.1% for males and 1.3% for females) with a high proportion of persistent PTSD, which means an onset before the last 12 months.

18.6% of young men and 15.5% of young women reported at least one qualifying traumatic event (according to the A1 and A2 DSM-IV criterion), with considerably higher estimates in the older age groups. Unlike as to the gender difference for PTSD diagnosis, here males are reporting slightly higher rates of traumatic events than females. But women are considerably more likely to develop PTSD after qualifying traumatic events than males. The last column of Table 1 indicates that 14.5% of women, but only 2.2% of men developed PTSD as a consequence of traumatic events.

Because findings of studies about PTSD had shown that it may be difficult for children and adolescents to validly report about the PTSD criterion of "diminished interest in significant activities and constriction of affect" (PTSD, C-criterion, APA, 1994) we additionally created an additional subthreshold diagnosis which required only one symptom of the DSM-IV C-criterion. All other DSM-IV-PTSD criteria including duration and impairment were fulfilled. The inclusion of those "subthreshold PTSD" cases increases the overall prevalence in women from 2.2% to 3.5% and in men from 0.4% to 0.7%.

Table 1. Lifetime and 12-month prevalence of traumatic events and PTSD[1].

	DSM-IV PTSD diagnosis		DSM-IV traumatic events		
	% lifetime	% 12 months	% persistence lt: 12 months	% any event	% PTSD among those with events
Men, total	0.4	0.1	0.1	18.7	2.2
14–17 years	0.2	0.0	0.0	15.9	1.4
18–24 years	0.5	0.2	0.2	20.2	2.4
Women, total	2.2	1.3	1.0	15.4	14.5
14–17 years	1.1	0.7	0.4	10.9	10.0
18–24 years	2.8	1.6	1.2	17.4	15.5

[1]weighted number of respondents and percentages

Table 2. Lifetime prevalence of traumatic events by gender[1].

		Lifetime Prevalence			
		A1 events		A2 events	
		N	%	N	%
Any traumatic event:	– men	377	25.2	279	18.7
	– women	271	17.7	235	15.4
	– total	648	21.4	514	17.0
Physically attacked:	– men	211	14.1	151	10.1
	– women	82	5.4	75	4.9
	– total	293	9.7	226	7.5
Serious accident:	– men	146	9.8	99	6.6
	– women	89	5.8	65	4.3
	– total	235	7.8	164	5.4
Wittness:	– men	90	6.0	68	4.6
	– women	44	2.9	40	2.6
	– total	134	4.4	108	3.6
Sexual abuse as a child:	– men	5	0.3	5	0.3
	– women	58	3.8	56	3.7
	– total	63	2.1	61	2.0
Rape:	– men	0	...	0	...
	– women	41	2.7	35	2.3
	– total	41	1.4	35	1.2
Sudden (threat of) death of associate:	– men	11	0.7	11	0.7
	– women	13	0.9	11	0.7
	– total	24	0.8	22	0.7
Natural catastrophe:	– men	9	0.6	6	0.4
	– women	6	0.4	6	0.4
	– total	15	0.5	12	0.4
Other qualifying event:	– men	6	0.4	4	0.3
	– women	5	0.3	5	0.3
	– total	11	0.4	9	0.3
Terrible experience in war:	– men	3	0.2	2	0.1
	– women	7	0.5	6	0.4
	– total	10	0.3	8	0.3
Imprisoned, taken hostage, kidnapped:	– men	3	0.2	3	0.2
	– women	1	0.1	1	0.1
	– total	4	0.1	4	0.1
No. of traumatic events:	1 event				
	– men	294	19.6	223	14.9
	– women	216	14.1	188	12.4
	– total	510	16.9	411	13.6
	2 events				
	– men	61	4.1	44	2.9
	– women	41	2.7	36	2.4
	– total	102	3.4	80	2.6
	>3 events				
	– men	22	1.5	12	0.8
	– women	14	0.9	11	0.7
	– total	36	1.2	23	0.8

[1]based on weighted data

Prevalence of Specific Traumatic Events

Table 2 shows the lifetime prevalence of specific traumatic events separately for young men and women according to A1 and A2 criteria. 25.2% of young men and 17.7% of young women reported at least one A1 event (serious threat). The types of A1-events, experienced by the largest proportions of re-spondents were physical attacks (9.7%) and serious accidents (7.8%). Men reported more physical attacks (14.1% vs. 5.4%), serious accidents (9.8% vs. 5.8%) and witnessing a traumatic event happening to another person (6.0% vs. 2.9%) while women reported more sexual abuse as a child (3.8% vs. 0.3%) and rape (2.7% vs. 0%).

The groups of A2-traumatic events, that means those involving intense fear, helplessness or horror, experienced by the largest proportions of respondents were also physical attacks (7.5%) and serious accidents (5.4%) with as for A1 events women reporting more often than men rape and sexual abuse as a child. Men also reported more often than women more than one A1 event and more than one A2 event. But these differences were smaller for A2 events.

Onset of Traumatic Events

For each A2-trauma age of onset was assessed. Hazard rates for onset were estimated with life tables for the onset of four groups of traumatic events*. Figure 2 displays the cumulative incidence curves of the four groups of all A2-traumas. In nearly half of the sexual traumas, onset occurred before the age of 12. The cumulative incidence of these traumas then showed a steeper increase once more between 17 and 19 years, as a closer inspection reveals due to rape. On the other hand the cumulative incidence curve of physical attacks especially showed a very steep increase after the age of 13. Approximately about half of these traumatic events occurred at 17 or younger. All other events also had a median age at 17 years but with lower frequencies. Steep increases for other traumatic events are for serious accidents between 16 and 19 and witnessing traumatic events between 15 and 17 and again 21 and 22 years.

---

* Events which included rape and sexual abuse as a child, events related to severe physical attacks or threats, including attacks or threats with weapons, terrible experiences during war and imprisoned, taken hostage or kidnapped, events related to serious accidents and natural catastrophes and events from witnessing traumatic events happen to another person with those from sudden death of associates. Because of their complex nature including witnessing traumatic events, the category "other" was also included in the group of witnessing traumatic events happen to others.

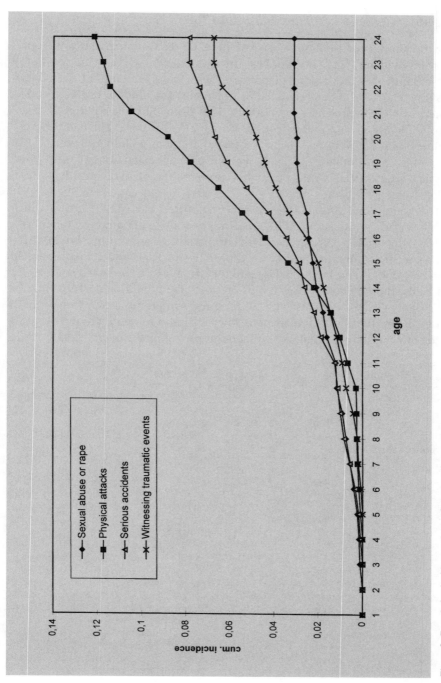

Figure 2. Cumulative incidence of specific traumatic events.

Specific Traumatic Events and Risk for PTSD

For the analysis of conditional probabilities we also summarized some types of events with no PTSD cases or very low frequencies (see previous footnote). Table 3 indicates that among respondents with any qualifying A1 event (serious threat), 74.0% of males and 86.7% of females qualified for the A2 criterion (intense fear, helplessness, or horror). This probability in column 2 varied across the four groups and by gender from 67.7% to 100%. The highest probabilities with 100% in men were for sexual abuse as a child and with 77.6% for witnessing traumatic events. In women rape or sexual abuse (91.9%) and physical attacks (91.1%) had the highest probabilities of involving intense fear, helplessness, or horror.

The conditional probabilities for the "subthreshold PTSD" group which includes also the threshold PTSD cases are overall higher among women with 22.6% compared to 3.9% in men. High probabilities for "subthreshold PTSD" after specific traumatic events are especially for rape and sexual abuse in women (45.3%) and men (25.0%) and for witnessing traumatic events.

Finally, the last column of Table 3 reports the conditional probability of developing DSM-IV PTSD with all required symptoms, at least one month duration and significant impairment when exposed to an qualifying event or to the most upsetting event. For women this probability is overall 14.5% while

Table 3. Conditional probabilities from traumatic events to PTSD.

Types of traumatic events		Conditional probabilities (%) A1 → A2 events	qualifying A2 events → sub-threshold and threshold PTSD	qualifying A2 events → threshold PTSD
Any trauma:	– men	74.0	3.9	2.2
	– women	86.7	22.6	14.5
	– total	79.3	12.5	7.8
Physical attacks:	– men	71.9	2.4	1.6
	– women	91.1	12.7	3.2
	– total	77.5	5.8	2.1
Serious accidents:	– men	67.7	1.3	. . .
	– women	74.7	9.8	. . .
	– total	70.4	4.6	. . .
Witnessing traumatic events:	– men	77.6	8.7	5.8
	– women	90.3	15.2	10.9
	– total	82.2	11.3	7.8
Rape or sexual abuse:	– men	100.0	25.0	. . .
	– women	91.9	45.3	36.0
	– total	92.3	44.3	34.1

only 2.2% of men met all criteria for PTSD. Although witnessing traumatic events which are in most cases a sudden death of associates, witnessing at home or terrible accidents of close associates indicate elevated conditional probabilities especially in men. This finding is clearly dominated by "sexual traumas" in women. Most of these cases suffer from sexual abuse as a child (44.1%) but also rape (35.5%) has an elevated probability of PTSD. Respondents who reported of serious accidents didn't meet criteria for PTSD. Also the association between physical attacks and PTSD was low in the total A2-sample of physical attacks (1.6% for men, 3.2% for women).

Specific Traumatic Events and DSM-IV Diagnostic Criteria for PTSD

Table 4 reports the conditional probabilities for the four groups of traumatic events for each of the DSM-IV diagnostic criteria (reexperiencing, B-criterion, Avoidance, C-criterion, etc.). The highest probabilities were found for symptoms of re-experience, the lowest probabilities were found for avoidance symp-

Table 4. Conditional probabilities of DSM-IV criteria B to F by specific types of traumatic events[1].

Traumatic events	S_x (B) reexperience $pr_{B|A}$%	S_x (C) avoidance $pr_{C|A}$%	S_x(D) arousal $pr_{D|A}$%	S_x(E) duration $pr_{E|A}$%	S_x(F) impairment $pr_{F|A}$%
Any trauma:					
– men	63.4	6.5	32.3	37.3	12.2
– women	83.4	30.6	54.5	57.9	28.9
– total	72.8	17.5	42.4	46.3	19.8
Physically attacked:					
– men	65.1	7.9	31.0	36.5	6.3
– women	75.0	15.6	47.6	50.8	17.2
– total	68.4	10.5	36.3	41.1	10.0
Serious accident:					
– men	57.7	2.6	33.3	41.8	18.9
– women	80.4	2.0	39.2	47.1	21.6
– total	66.2	2.3	35.4	43.8	20.0
Witness:					
– men	68.6	8.6	34.3	32.9	14.5
– women	87.3	19.1	50.0	47.8	15.2
– total	77.4	13.0	40.9	37.4	14.8
Sexual abuse/rape:					
– men	50.0	...	25.0	50.0	25.0
– women	89.3	69.3	72.0	76.0	51.3
– total	87.3	65.8	69.6	74.7	50.6

[1]percentages based on weighted numbers of respondents; [2]conditional on S_x (A2) for qualifying events

toms and impairment. Men have overall lower probabilities for all symptom groups. Sexual abuse as a child or rape in women causes most of the symptoms. Re-experiences have high probabilities in nearly all traumatic events.

The low rate of persistent avoidance in serious accidents (2.6% in men, 2.0% in women) which include also natural catastrophes may reflect the nature of this traumas, which can't be controlled with persistent avoidance despite significant distress or impairment. Few distress and impairment is especially related to physical attacked persons (6.3% in men, 17.2% in women).

Correlates of Traumatic Events, Subthreshold PTSD and PTSD Cases

The results of a multivariate logistic regression analysis (Table 5) describe correlates of subthreshold PTSD and PTSD. Because previous analyses with additional variables as marital status or education showed no significant association with PTSD in this age cohort, we decided to analyze only sex and social class as sociodemographic predictors of the outcome variables. Age at trauma, the presence of more than one trauma and trauma type were analyzed as trauma specific predictors for subthreshold PTSD and PTSD.

Comparable to other studies with adults 14–24 years old men also have a higher significant risk for traumatic events but even more low social class is significantly associated with traumatic events (OR = 2.21). For the group of

Table 5. Correlates of traumatic events, subthreshold PTSD and PTSD.

Variables	Traumatic events OR (95% CI)	Substhreshold or threshold PTSD OR (95% CI)	PTSD OR (95% CI)
Sex:			
– men	1.23* (1.01–1.49)	0.62 (0.22–1.80)	0.43* (0.20–0.90)
– women	1.00 (…)	1.00 (…)	1.00 (…)
Social class:			
– low	2.21* (1.65–2.97)	2.59* (1.07–6.23)	2.20* (1.03–4.71)
– middle/high	1.00 (…)	1.00 (…)	1.00 (…)
Age at traumatic event:			
– < 12 years		3.27* (1.36–7.92)	3.80* (1.90–7.69)
– > 12 years		1.00 (…)	1.00 (…)
No. of traumatic events			
– 1		1.00 (…)	1.00 (…)
– > 1		3.92* (1.63–9.49)	8.54* (4.22–17.12)
Type of event			
– rape or sexual abuse		31.62* (11.59–85.62)	15.30* (7.17–32.79)
– others		1.00 (…)	1.00 (…)

*OR (odds ratio) is significantly different at .05 level (two-tailed) from the reference category value of OR = 1.0

subthreshold and threshold PTSD cases, as for only threshold cases, highest significant odds ratios were found for the variable type of traumatic event. In agreement with the above mentioned findings on the conditional probabilities in Table 3, all outcomes are significantly associated with sexual abuse and rape. Therefore young men have a significant lower risk for PTSD (OR = 0.43) but low social class is also associated with subthreshold and threshold PTSD associations, possibly indicating sexual abuse or rape in lower social class groups or a greater vulnerability for traumatic events and lower resources in combination with higher conditional probabilities for PTSD symptoms after sexual traumas such as rape and sexual abuse. Age at trauma also was also significantly associated with the outcomes and may play a role in combination with sexual abuse. The presence of more than one trauma is significantly associated with all outcomes but especially seems to be a risk for threshold PTSD (OR = 8.54).

Comorbidity

Table 6 shows the lifetime prevalence of DSM-IV disorders and their associations with both qualifying traumatic events and lifetime PTSD. This tabulation indicates that PTSD is strongly associated with a wide range of disorder. 87.5% of PTSD sufferers had at least one additional comorbid condition, 77.5% even two or more. Except for pain disorder all associations were significant. The strongest associations found are those for Panic with or without Agoraphobia (OR = 14.10), GAD (OR = 13.29), Dysthymia (OR = 11.00), and Social Phobia (OR = 10.70).

Less impressive moderate, but nevertheless significant associations, were also found for qualifying traumatic events and most mental disorders examined, except for phobia, NOS, and GAD. The highest odds ratios were found for Dysthymia and OCD.

Because it has often been suggested that the high comorbidity rates in PTSD reflect overlapping diagnostic criteria with other disorders we tried to determine the associations between specific other disorders and PTSD symptoms. For this examination we only looked at respondents, who reported just symptoms after a traumatic event, which also could refer to other types of mental disorders (for example avoidance, depressive syndromes, etc.). No significant associations between specific other anxiety disorders and avoidance in PTSD were found. Also this analysis did not reveal significant associations between depressive disorders and symptoms of numbing of general responsiveness. The only significant association was between symptoms of re-experience and somatoform disorders. 34.9% of respondents with symptoms of reexperience after a traumatic event also fulfilled criteria for any somatoform disorder (OR = 2.14, 95% CI: 1.07–4.21).

Table 6. Associations of traumatic events and lifetime posttraumatic stress disorder (PTSD) with other mental disorders[1].

DSM-IV disorders	Total sample N %		Traumatic events N %		OR (95%CI)[2]	PTSD N %		OR (95%CI)[2]
Affective disorders								
Any depressive disorders	356	11.8	94	18.3	2.00*(1.55–2.56)	15	37.5	3.96*(2.05–7.61)
Dysthymia	91	3.0	37	7.2	3.76*(2.44–5.75)	11	27.5	11.00*(5.28–22.94)
Any bipolar disorder	54	1.8	19	3.7	2.89*(1.63–5.10)	3	7.5	3.53*(1.01–12.43)
Anxiety disorders								
Panic w/, w/o agoraphobia	49	1.6	19	3.7	3.30*(1.82–5.93)	8	20.0	14.10*(6.11–32.79)
Agoraphobia w/o panic	61	2.0	20	3.9	2.70*(1.55–4.66)	7	17.5	8.49*(2.36–20.10)
Social phobia	106	3.5	37	7.2	2.89*(1.92–4.35)	12	30.0	10.70*(5.21–21.98)
Simple phobia	69	2.3	20	3.9	2.12*(1.25–3.60)	6	15.0	5.60*(2.18–14.30)
Phobia NOS	157	5.2	30	5.8	1.24 (.82–1.86)	6	15.0	2.41 (0.96–6.05)
GAD	24	0.8	7	1.4	2.01 (.84–4.85)	3	7.5	13.29*(3.90–45.60)
OCD	22	0.7	10	1.9	4.47*(1.93–10.38)	2	5.0	7.08*(1.60–31.50)
Somatoform disorders								
Undiff. somatoform disorder	298	9.9	77	15.0	1.92*(1.46–2.51)	13	32.5	5.24*(1.81–6.11)
Pain disorder	51	1.7	16	3.1	2.52*(1.38–4.66)	4	10.0	2.66 (0.61–11.59)
Any eating disorder	91	3.0	28	5.4	2.48*(1.58–3.90)	4	10.0	2.63 (0.91–7.61)
Substance use disorders								
Nicotine dependence	568	18.8	155	30.2	2.18*(1.75–2.72)	25	62.5	7.76*(4.06–14.88)
Alcohol abuse/dependence	481	15.9	131	25.5	2.07*(1.63–2.64)	12	30.0	4.63*(2.23–9.58)
Drug abuse/dependence	138	4.6	44	8.6	2.35*(1.62–3.39)	5	12.5	4.13*(1.55–11.02)
Any disorder								
Any other disorder	1464	48.5	337	65.6	2.36*(1.93–2.89)	35	87.5	5.63*(2.97–20.30)
>1 other disorder	662	21.9	190	37.0	2.58*(2.10–3.17)	31	77.5	12.46*(5.92–26.05)

[1]weighted number of respondents; [2]controlled for sex; *OR (odds ratio) is significantly different at the .05 level (two-tailed) from the reference category value of OR = 1.0

Summary and Comment

The findings of this study, conducted in a representative sample of respondents aged 14–24, reveal:

(1) That traumatic events, rigidly defined by the new DSM-IV diagnostic criteria, are frequent phenomena even in this fairly young sample.

Seventeen percent of our sample (18.7 of males and 15.4% of females) had experienced at least one traumatic event in their lifetime. But only 1.4% of respondents – females considerably more frequently (lifetime prevalence of 2.2%) than men (0.4) – developed subsequently a posttraumatic stress disorder (PTSD) according to DSM-IV criteria. These numbers are markedly lower than most of the previous estimates, resulting from US-American population studies with comparable assessment instruments on the basis of DSM-III-R criteria. In the NCS (Kessler et al., 1996) the lifetime PTSD prevalence estimates for the same age group were 2.8% for men and 10.3% for females, Breslau et al. (1997) reported 6% for males and 11.3% for females. Both studies also reported dramatically higher rates for specific events. Since we have used a similar respondents list to assess the types of events as has been used in the NCS, and the fact of our more detailed breakdown of DSM-IV A1- and A2-types of traumatic events it seems to be unlikely that the tremendous difference in number of traumatic events can be explained by methodological differences between studies.

It seems to be more likely that both the considerably lower frequency of qualifying traumatic events as well as the lower prevalence estimates of PTSD more likely reflect a true difference between US-American and German adolescents and young adults. This assumption is supported by a more detailed comparison of events types in both countries. For example in the NCS the frequency of terrible combat experiences which have in men the highest probabilities of being associated with PTSD is much higher. Another important difference is the low rate of natural catastrophes in Germany compared to the United States. Only 1% of our sample had experienced these kind of traumatic event while nearly 17% of the NCS-sample experienced natural disasters especially with fire. Therefore differences in victimization rates between geographic areas and different populations might account for our lower rates of traumatic events.

(2) Disregarding however the differences in victimization rates, the conditional probabilities for traumatic events to subsequent PTSD development were quite similar, if accounting for differences that have occurred as a consequence of the new DSM-IV criteria.

Overall 7.8% of persons, who were exposed to traumatic events developed PTSD. In the NCS 14.0% of persons, who were exposed to traumatic events developed DSM-III-R PTSD. But if we exclude the new DSM-IV criterion of impairment, our conditional probability for PTSD goes up to 12.8%, quite similar to the finding in the NCS. Gender differences in these conditional probabilities are confounded with the type of trauma. Despite an overall lower number of traumatic events, women have higher rates of PTSD which may be due to a higher exposure rates of rape and sexual abuse events as a child. But it may also be that women might have a stronger tendency to report symptoms but less so specific events.

The conditional probabilities of specific traumas are overall higher in our sample than in the NCS sample mostly because of a smaller number of persons with more than one trauma. But the conditional probabilities of specific traumas once selected for assessment are for some traumas similar to the NCS. Rape and sexual abuse as a child have strong association with PTSD in both studies. In our study serious accidents and physical attacks have the lowest probability despite the highest frequencies. It may be that especially these events are considered as traumatic by most people but are not so powerful that they lead to DSM-IV PTSD in adolescents and young adults especially to symptoms of avoidance and impairment or they are powerful but can not be avoided in adolescents and young adults.

Ages of onset were different for types of traumatic events. While traumatic events from sexual abuse as a child and serious accidents were the most frequent in childhood there was a remarkable change in adolescence with physical attacks especially in men becoming more frequent.

(3) The correlates of traumatic events and PTSD are consistent with other studies. Despite a higher risk for traumatic events in men, women have a higher risk of PTSD. But even more the type of trauma was significantly associated with subthreshold PTSD and threshold PTSD. Other factors as multiple and early traumas may also play a role as vulnerability factors for PTSD symptoms in association with trauma type.

(4) Traumatic events are related not only to PTSD development, but also to a wide range of many mental disorders. The associations between traumatic events and other disorders show that traumatic events may play a role as risk factors or consequences of mental disorder together with other factors independently of full threshold PTSD. Further analysis based on time-varying factors might help us to understand the role of traumatic events in these processes. Besides research on other life events research on traumatic events can be

more related to clinical significant outcomes and therefore give us the opportunity to study processes in the development of psychopathology.

Further PTSD is strongly related to any type of mental disorders, most impressively to panic disorders, Dysthymia, and GAD. Even in this fairly young sample 87.5% with lifetime DSM-IV PTSD reported at least one other DSM-IV Disorder, most two or more. It is worth noting that we could demonstrate that these high comorbidity rates are not merely an artefact of partly overlapping symptom criteria. This underlines that traumatic events and PTSD might be important components in the initiation and pathogenic pathways of mental disorders.

Finally, some limitation should be taken into account. The results are based on data that require lifetime recall of traumas and the symptoms associated with them. It is likely that there was some recall failure in respondent reports, leading to underestimation of the lifetime prevalence rates of traumatic events and even more PTSD symptoms. But it is also worth noting that in our sample recall bias might be less critical, compared to the other studies with older respondents. In evaluating the results concerning the types of traumatic experiences associated with PTSD, it is important to remember that criteria B through D were assessed for only one event per person as in the study of Kessler et al. (1995). As a result, the event-specific analyses focused on a subsample of events and not the total sample. This can create an overestimation of the associations of particular events with PTSD especially if there is a high number of respondents with more than one traumatic event. In our young sample with a smaller number of respondents with more than one traumatic event it could be that the association between rape and PTSD resp. sexual abuse and PTSD is overestimated. On the other hand the relationship between PTSD and other traumatic experiences especially in women can be underestimated. Another limitation is especially focused on the correlates for subthreshold PTSD and threshold PTSD and is related to the number of PTSD cases for these analysis.

References

American Psychiatric Association. (1994). *Diagnostic and statistical manual of mental disorders (4th ed.)*. Washington, DC: Author.

Breslau, N., & Davis, G.C. (1987). Posttraumatic stress disorder. The stressor criterion. *Journal of Nervous and Mental Diseases, 175*, 255–264.

Breslau, N., Davis, G.C., Andreski, P., & Peterson, E. (1991). Traumatic events and posttraumatic stress disorder in a urban population of young adults. *Archives of General Psychiatry, 48*, 216–222

Breslau, N., Davis, G.C., Peterson, E.L., & Schultz, L. (1997). Psychiatric sequelae of posttraumatic stress disorder in women. *Archives of General Psychiatry, 54*, 81–87

Bromet, E., Sonnega, A., & Kessler, R. C. (1998). Risk factors for DSM-III-R posttraumatic stress disorders: Findings from the National Comorbidity Survey. *American Journal of Epidemiology, 147*, 353–361.

Cottler, L.B., Compton, III W.M., Mager, D., Spitznagel, E.L., & Janca, A. (1992). Posttraumatic stress disorder among substance users from the general population. *American Journal of Psychiatry, 149*, 664–670

Davidson, J.R.T., Hughes, D., Blazer, D., & George, L.K. (1991). Posttraumatic stress disorder in the community. An epidemiological study. *Psychological Medicine, 21*, 713–721

de Girolamo, G., & McFarlane, A.C. (in press). Epidemiology of posttraumatic stress disorders. A comprehensive review of the literature. In A.J. Marella, M. Friedman, E. Gerrity & R. Scurfield (Eds.), *Ethnocultural aspects of posttraumatic stress disorder. Issues, research, and directions*. Washington: American Psychological Association.

Goenjian, A., Pynoos, R.S., Steinberg, A.M., Najarian, L.M., Asarnow, J.R., Karayan, I., Ghurabi, M., & Fairbanks, L.A. (1995). Psychiatric co-morbidity in children after the 1988 earthquake in Armenia. *Journal of the American Academy of Child and Adolescent Psychiatry, 34*, 1174–1184.

Helzer, J.E., Robins, L.N., & McEvoy, L. (1987). Posttraumatic stress disorder in the general population. *New England Journal of Medicine, 317*, 1630–1634.

Kessler, R.C., Sonnega, A., Brommet, E., & Nelson, C.B. (1995). Posttraumatic stress disorder in the National Comorbidity Survey. *Archives of General Psychiatry, 52*, 1048–1060

Kessler, R.C., Sonnega, A., Bromet, E., Hughes, M., Nelson, C.B., & Breslau, N. (in press). Epidemiologic risk factors for trauma and PTSD. In R. Yehuda (Ed.), *Risk factors for posttraumatic stress disorder*. Washington, DC: American Psychiatric Association Press.

Lachner, G., Wittchen, H.U., Holly, A., & Pfister, H. (submitted). Test-retest reliability and sources of variance of a standardized diagnostic expert system (M-CIDI-DIA-X).

March, J.S. (1993). What constitutes a stressor. The "criterion A" issue. In J.R.T. Davidson & E.B. Foa (Eds.), *Posttraumatic stress disorder. DSM-IV and beyond* (pp. 147–172). Washington, DC: American Psychiatric Press.

Norris, F.H. (1992). Epidemiology of trauma. Frequency and impact of different potentially traumatic events on different demographic groups. *Journal of Consulting and Clinical Psychology, 60*, 409–418

Parry-Jones, W., & Barton, J. (1995). Posttraumatic stress disorder in children and adolescents. *Current Opinion in Psychiatry, 8*, 227–230

Pelcovitz, D., Kaplan, S., Goldenberg, B., Mandel, F., Lehare, J., & Guarrera, J. (1994). Posttraumatic stress disorder in physically abused adolescents. *Journal of the American Academy of Child and Adolescent Psychiatry, 44*, 305–312

Pfister, H., & Wittchen, H.U. (1995). *M-CIDI Computerprogramm* [M-CIDI computer program]. München: Max-Planck-Institut für Psychiatrie.

Pynoos, R.S., Steinberg, A.M., & Goenjian, A. (1996). Traumatic stress in childhood and adolescence. Recent developments and current controversies. In B.A. van der Kolk, A.C. McFarlane, & L. Weisaeth (Eds.), *Traumatic stress* (pp. 331–358). New York: Guilford.

Reed, V., & Schuster, P. (1995). *Instructions for use of the computerized version of the M-CIDI. Version 2.0, 6/95* (English version). München: Max-Planck-Institut für Psychiatrie.

Resnick, H.S., Kilpatrick D.G., Dansky, B.S., Saunders B.E., & Best, C.L. (1993). Prevalence of civilian trauma and posttraumatic stress disorder in a representative national sample of women. *Journal of Consulting and Clinical Psychology, 61*, 984–991.

Robins, L.N., Helzer, J.E., Cottler, L., & Golding, E. (1989). *NIMH Diagnostic Interview Schedule, Version III Revised.* St. Louis, MO: Washington University.

Shalev, A.V. (1996). Stress versus traumatic Stress. In B.A. van der Kolk, A.C. McFarlane, & L. Weisaeth (Eds.), *Traumatic stress* (pp. 77–101). New York: Guilford.

Shannon, M.P., Lonigan, C.J., Finch, A.J., & Taylor, C.M. (1994). Children exposed to disaster. I. Epidemiology of posttraumatic symptoms and symptom profiles. *Journal of the American Academy of Child and Adolescent Psychiatry, 33,* 80–93

Wittchen, H.U., Nelson, C.B., & Lachner, G. (in press). Prevalence of mental disorders and psychosocial impairments in adolescents and young adults. *Psychological Medicine.*

Wittchen H.U., & Pfister, H. (1997). *Munich Composite International Diagnostic Interview (M-CIDI-DIA-X).* Frankfurt: Swets and Zeitlinger.

Yehuda, R., & McFarlane, A.C. (1995). Conflict between current knowledge about posttraumatic stress disorder and its original conceptual basis. *American Journal of Psychiatry, 152,* 1705–1713.

PART III:
FROM ADULTHOOD
TO OLD AGE

Aging in the Shadow of War

Zahava Solomon and Karni Ginzburg

Introduction

Reciprocal Relations between Trauma and Age

With the exception of trauma experienced in childhood, relatively little attention has been paid to the interplay of the traumatic event and the survivor's developmental stage. The tendency may stem from the fact that much of the theory and study of trauma is rooted in psychoanalytic theory, which postulates that personality is by and large determined in childhood and that human development virtually terminates in adolescence. The outcome of this assumption is that the trauma literature does not adequately take into account our present understanding that people continue to develop throughout the life cycle and that every stage has its particular resources and concerns, which may affect how individuals respond to a trauma.

This chapter examines how the elderly respond to trauma. The first part explores the effect of this developmental stage on adjustment to current trauma, asking whether the elderly cope with and adjust to such trauma differently from younger adults. The second part explores whether prior experiences, including earlier exposure to trauma, affect one's adjustment to aging – that is whether the aging process of trauma victims differs from that of persons who had the good fortune to have been spared earlier trauma.

The Impact of Current Trauma in Old Age

Traumatic Experiences in Old Age

The literature offers three distinct views, each supported by empirical evidence, of the impact of traumatic events on the psychosocial adjustment of the elderly.

One view claims that the aged are largely a weak and vulnerable group, have fewer resources than younger persons to cope with traumatic stress, and are at particularly high risk for adjustment difficulties following traumatic events. It further maintains that the aged are rigid in their responses, and use regressive and nonadaptive defense mechanisms. In accordance with this view, Friedsman (1961) and Bolin and Klenow (1982–83) reported that older victims tend to react with a greater sense of deprivation than younger victims to roughly equivalent losses. Others reported that the elderly have specific age-related problems and needs following a disaster. These include difficulty in coping with the heavy physical work of clean-up and repair (Huerta & Horton, 1978); the need for selected support services, such as transportation and shopping, to help them extend their life-space beyond the home (Poulshock & Cohen, 1975); and, frequently, the need for more help than younger persons in dealing with the financial, legal, and tax issues that arise following a disaster (Huerta & Horton, 1978). The "vulnerability perspective" is further supported by studies showing high levels of depression (McNaughton, Smith, Patterson, & Grant, 1990) among elderly victims of stressful experiences, a low level of perceived quality of life (Melick & Logue, 1985–86), increased use of sedatives and tranquilizers (Melick & Logue, 1985–86), and poorer immune function (McNaughton et al., 1990).

A second view regards the aged as a resilient population that can adjust better than younger persons to traumatic experiences. The "resilience perspective" is supported by studies showing that elderly persons adjust better than their juniors in the aftermath of trauma. Elderly victims have reported better recovery than younger victims following a major tornado (Bolin & Klenow, 1988). They have been found to express less fear, worry, and despair than younger survivors in the aftermath of a natural disaster, and more positive emotions, such as security, cheerfulness, and contentment (Bell, 1978; Huerta & Horton, 1978). Studies show less family and emotional disruption among elderly disaster victims (Bolin & Klenow, 1982–83), as well as lower alcohol consumption (Miller, Turner, & Kimball, 1981). Following an earthquake, elderly victims reported less intrusion of the experience into their lives, in the form of unsolicited recollections, thoughts and dreams of the event, than their juniors, though the PTSD rates were much the same (Goenjian, Majarian, Pynoos, Steinberg, Manoukian, Tavosian, & Fairbanks, 1994).

These salutary findings can be attributed to a number of possible factors. One is that the aged usually experience less disruption of their daily routine and work following disaster than do younger victims (Bolin & Klenow, 1982–83). They would thus perceive the disaster as less stressful than younger victims, who are subject to more secondary stressors (such as financial loss derived from the disruption of work). A related factor might be that being more restricted to their homes, more occupied with themselves, and less involved in the external world, including in postdisaster rescue efforts, than younger victims, the aged are less exposed to the full brunt of the trauma. Their exposure is more confined to their own losses and they are relatively shielded from the suffering of others. This too could lead them to experience the situation as less stressful. Lastly, some professionals have argued that their more extensive life experience, including prior exposure to trauma, might make the aged more resilient to traumatic stress. Various scholars hold that stressful life events serve as an "immunizer" by contributing to the development of useful coping mechanisms (Epstein, 1983; Meichenbaum, 1985).

A third view holds that vulnerability and resilience to stress are not age-related. This view is supported by studies showing that there were no age-related differences in the levels of worry, anxiety, depression, avoidance, sleep disturbances, nightmares, intrusiveness, forgetfulness, and lack of confidence experienced after a disaster (Ollendick & Hoffmann, 1982; Miller et al., 1981; Hagstrom, 1995). It is also supported by the finding that the same percentage (33%) of elderly and younger victims of a disaster reported positive changes in their lives or emotional functioning as result of the events related to a disaster (Ollendick & Hoffmann, 1982).

In short, the literature is highly inconsistent on the impact of trauma on the elderly. At least part of the problem may derive from methodological shortcomings of many of the studies. Many studies fail to report on either or both the sampling procedure (e. g., McNaughton et al., 1990; Bolin & Klenow, 1982–83) and response rate (e. g., Gray & Calsyn, 1989; Kilijanek & Drabek, 1979; Poulshock & Cohen, 1975; Bell, 1978). Some do not use a control group (e. g., Melick & Logue, 1985–86; McNaughton et al., 1990). And some are based on data gathered by nonstandardized interviews or from impressions (e. g., Friedsman, 1961; Goenjian et al., 1994). All of these factors would make a consistent picture quite unlikely.

Another difficulty is that a very large range of events is involved, from robbery through accidents, natural disasters through wars. Some of the events are natural and others man-made; some affect individuals, others whole communities; while the victims themselves may experience varying degrees of exposure and destruction. Each and any one of these variables, as well as many others, can affect the psychological outcome.

Compounding the problem is that catastrophes often occur without warning and without pattern. They are thus not the sort of thing that a researcher can approach with a preplanned study design. Moreover, they happen to very different types of populations. Aged urbanites, rural folk, and villagers are likely to have different social, family, and economic structures, as well as different educational levels and income. All these resources may affect their psychological outcome.

Given these many variables, it is hardly surprising that the literature does not provide an unequivocal answer as to whether or how the age at which a person is exposed to trauma affects its psychological impact.

The Elderly Trauma Victim: The Israeli Perspective

Yet another factor that makes it difficult to obtain a clear picture is that old people are generally exposed to different types of stressful and traumatic events than younger people. Moreover, when the two groups are exposed to ostensibly the same event, it often impinges differently on their daily lives. The old and young tend to fulfill different functions and the event can have a different meaning for them. A salient example is war, where the elderly are rarely combatants and relatively shielded from the worst of the violence. On the other hand, they have little ability to affect their situation or assure their safety, or that of their loved ones, and their enforced helplessness and passivity can take its own toll.

Here we take a look at the differential responses of elderly and younger Israelis during two very different wars: the 1982 Lebanon War and the 1991 Gulf War.

The Lebanon War was a relatively contained military operation that lasted for several months over the summer of 1982. It took place on Lebanese soil. While Israeli soldiers were endangered on the front, the civilian population, including the elderly, were not directly threatened. Aside from their possible concern about their sons or grandsons on the front and their exposure to heavy TV and newspaper coverage of the war, civilians went about their daily lives as usual. The external experience of the elderly in this war did not differ in objective ways from that of younger civilians.

Information about their psychological experience is provided by a prospective nation-wide study that happened to be in process when the war broke out. Hobfoll, Lomranz, Eyal, Bridges, and Tzemach (1989) assessed the depressive mood of the Israeli population before, during and after the Lebanon War. They found a marked elevation in depressive mood at the onset of the war, followed by a decrease in depression when the war was at its height, suggesting adaptation to the stressful situation. Dividing the sample into four age groups (young adults – 18–22; mid-adults – 23–40; mid-lifers – 41–60; and older adults – 61 and over), they found that while the older adults exhibited the same pattern of increased depression and subsequent habituation as the young adults, their depressive mood had intensified more, indicating stronger reaction to war-stress.

The Gulf War, 10 years later, was quite different. In this war the entire population, again including the elderly, were in the line of fire. Thirty-nine Iraqi missiles struck Israel, most of them landing in densely populated neighborhoods in and around Tel Aviv. The missiles damaged or destroyed a considerable number of homes and caused a certain amount of bodily injury and even loss of life. Even where there was no direct damage, the threat of gas and biological attack, with unknown but terrifying consequences, hung over everyone's head.

The Gulf War was stressful for most Israelis, but it posed particular problems for Israel's elderly, who made up over 10% of the country's population at the time and happened to be highly concentrated in the targeted and stricken areas. While essential services were kept running, many "nonessential" services were radically curtailed. Among other things, the senior citizens' centers to which many elderly come for everything from company to instrumental services were shut. Since the missile danger tended to keep people indoors, close to gas-sealed rooms, the closure of the centers made the elderly even more housebound than they usually are and greatly exacerbated the isolation to which they are subjected at the best of times.

The emergency procedures that were adopted during the war also posed special problems for the elderly. Many older persons lacked the manual dexterity needed to fit the gas masks; some had trouble hearing the air raid sirens; yet others found it difficult to understand the emergency instructions broadcast over the radio and TV. On the whole, the elderly had more difficulty than their juniors in settling into their sealed room in the short time that was available between the air raid alarm and missile striking. Some dealt with the problem by sealing up their entire apartment, which meant that they spent long hours in sunless, airless confinement. For those with impaired vision or hearing, seclusion in the sealed room further aggravated their sense of isolation.

How they fared was examined by a comprehensive longitudinal survey conducted by the Israel Defense Force's Department of Behavioral Sciences (Carmeli, Mevorach, Leiberman, Taubman, Kahanovitz, & Navon, 1992). The study investigated the attitudes, behavior, coping, and morale of the entire population. It found that the elderly did not differ significantly from the rest of the population in their knowledge of the protective procedures, their satisfaction with the amount and clarity of the media information on the subject, or in actually carrying out the emergency instructions. That is, about the same proportion of elderly obeyed the instructions to seal rooms and wear gas masks as the rest of the population and about the same proportions did and did not hoard food and supplies. As the researchers explain it, Israel's elderly are well versed in wars and did not need a great deal of prompting to do what was required under the circumstances.

However, the study also revealed that in some ways the aged did differ from the rest of the adult population. One is that they found the war less disruptive of their daily routine and less damaging economically than their juniors. Only

16% of the aged reported that the disruption of their routine bothered them a great deal, in contrast to 35% of the younger subjects. Similarly, the impact on family relations was less salient among the elderly. Seventy percent of them reported that their family relations were not affected, in comparison to 50% of the younger subjects.

On the other hand, throughout most of the war the elderly felt that they managed less well than their juniors. As the self-report findings showed, at the start of the war, the aged coped only slightly less well than the rest of the population. However, while the rest of the population reported that they coped better as the war progressed, throughout much of that period the aged report-ed that they coped worse. It was only towards the very end of the war, when the missile strikes were few and far between and tended to be off target, that their coping improved and reached the level of that of the rest of the popula-tion.

In other words, the study suggests that while on a practical level the aged continued to function adequately during the war, obeying the emergency in-structions and going on with their lives, emotionally they found it harder to cope with the missile strikes and suffered greater distress than their juniors.

In another study conducted during the Gulf War, my colleagues and I (Prager & Solomon, 1995a,b) examined the relation between age and distress level on 164 persons between 50 and 91 years old. The subjects were divided into a "younger" group (age range 50–69; M = 64.8) and an "older" group (age range 70–91; M = 77.0). Their responses to the war were assessed via two indices: "affective distress," defined as a temporary, disturbing change in mood or feeling, and "social interaction distress," which is a temporary change in behavior vis-à-vis the social environment. Findings showed almost no differ-ence in the mean stress scores of the two age groups in either measure of distress. Nor did the two age groups differ in their perceived control of the situation or attribution of meaning to events and their outcomes.

The last study that we present in this connection was carried out by Lomranz and Ayal (1994). This was a longitudinal study of the Gulf War similar to one the authors had undertaken of the Lebanon war. It examined depressive mood in four age groups at four points of time: before the threat of war was on the horizon, under the threat of impending war, during the war, and after the end of the war. The findings indicate that during the war depressive mood rose in all the age groups, but while a significant age difference was found at the two points of time preceding the fighting, none was found during or after. Before the threat of war was in the air, the base depression rate of the aged and middle aged was higher than of the young age group; then when war was impending the level of depression among the aged rose strikingly, only to even out with that of the rest of the population during the war. In other words, while the aged were particularly disturbed by the anticipation of war, they felt much the same as younger Israelis during the war itself.

The findings of the four studies can be summarized as follows: during the Lebanon War, in which younger persons played an active fighting role but the rest of the population was not directly threatened, the elderly responded more strongly to the stress, with a sharper rise in depressive mood, than their juniors. During the Gulf War, however, when most of the population was exposed to the threat in similar measure, the elderly did not differ from the rest of the population in either depressive mood or distress and used similar cognitive coping strategies. Moreover, for all practical purposes, they handled the emergency orders and used the protective measures as well as their younger counterparts and reported being less bothered than their juniors by the disruption of their daily routine. The only notable difference was in their perceptions of their coping: the elderly perceived their coping as poorer than the rest of the population. This may be related to the generally lower sense of self-efficacy among the aged.

The Impact of Earlier Trauma on Coping with Current Traumas in Old Age

The Reawakening of Earlier Trauma in the Aging Process

Millions of today's elderly all over the world suffered traumatic events in their youth. The combatants, refugees, and POWs of the Second World War, along with the survivors of the Nazi Holocaust and atomic bomb, who are today in their seventies, eighties or nineties, are among the many examples. The literature suggests that many of them have been deeply scarred. Empirical studies conducted about forty years after the Second World War, when the victims were well into their sixties, have shown that former prisoners of war had high rates of PTSD, hovering between about 50% to 85% (White, 1983; Goldstein, Van Kammen, Shelly, Miller, & Van Kammen, 1987), as well as high levels of depression (Page, Engdahl, & Eberly, 1991) and anxiety (Goldstein et al., 1987). Similarly, studies of Holocaust survivors point to posttraumatic residues. For example, studies report that 30%–60% of the survivors show considerable emotional distress (Levav & Abramson, 1984; Carmil & Carel, 1986), manifested mainly in PTSD (Kuch & Cox, 1992) and especially in sleep disturbances (Rosen, Reynolds, Yaeger, Houck, & Horowitz, 1991). Although a number of studies have found recovery (Sperr, Sperr, Craft & Boudewyns, 1990; Kluznik, Speed, Van Valkenburg, & Magraw, 1986), the evidence thus far seems to point to lasting damage among a good proportion of these trauma victims.

Israel has a high proportion of trauma victims in its elderly population. The great majority of elderly Israelis are immigrants, most of them refugees, who came to Israel shortly after its founding, when it was a poor and struggling State, uncertain that it would survive the enmity of its neighbors. Those from Africa and the Middle East fled their countries, often following severe persecution or pogroms and braving many dangers to reach the country. Those from Europe had survived the Nazi Holocaust in hiding or in concentration or prison camps and had lost the better part of their families. Both groups arrived with little in the way of personal possessions; both had to make substantial adjustments in their way of life. Moreover, both they and the "old timers" who had arrived before the State was founded lived through at least several of the seven wars and countless terrorist attacks which the country has suffered in its short years of existence.

The question that interests us here is how the experience of trauma in their youth affects the response of the elderly to current trauma. Our knowledge of both the human response to traumatic events and of the aging process leads us to believe that such prior trauma would adversely effect elderly persons' coping with current adversity.

The Human Response to Traumatic Events

There is considerable variability in the human response to traumatic events (e. g., Solomon, Mikulincer, & Waysman, 1991). While many survivors are able to put the trauma behind them and resume their lives, others are detrimentally affected. They may suffer a deterioration of health and social functioning, along with a large variety of psychological disturbances, including anxiety, depression, somatization (Solomon, 1993), and Posttraumatic Stress Disorder (PTSD), the most common and conspicuous psychological sequelae of trauma (APA, 1994).

PTSD is often a chronic disturbance highly resistant to treatment. In many cases, the symptoms may subside, and the individual may be asymptomatic or suffer from only a sub-clinical level of symptoms for months or years. But these remissions are usually followed by sudden flare-ups, whether in the form of an exacerbation of the sub-clinical symptoms or of a full-blown reactivation. PTSD can also develop after a long latency period, sometimes with no apparent warning, but often following exposure to another stressful or traumatic stimulus that is reminiscent of the original traumatic event (APA, 1994), or even to a seemingly trivial event which has symbolic meaning for the survivor.

Two studies have shown that movies and television coverage of military violence can reactivate dormant PTSD in veterans (Brockway, 1988; Jones &

Lovell, 1987). Similarly, Long, Chamberlain and Vincent (1994) demonstrated that media coverage of the warfare in the Gulf revived memories of earlier combat among Vietnam veterans who had never presented combat related psychological problems, resulting in increased PTSD rates.

Similar evidence of reactivation following exposure to minor stressors was found among Holocaust survivors. Eaton, Sigal, and Weinfeld (1982) observed elevated levels of distress among Jewish Holocaust survivors when the Jewish community in Montreal was under strain due to local political issues. They concluded that the political stress awakened dormant feelings of insecurity among the survivors.

There is also empirical evidence that Holocaust survivors exhibit more distress than others when faced with a major stressor. Cancer patients with Holocaust background were found to manifest more psychological distress (Baider, Peretz, & De-Nour, 1992) and display lower level of coping potential (Baider & Sarell, 1984) than comparable cancer patients. It seems that the past trauma left them vulnerable and the new trauma they faced unmasked this vulnerability.

The Aging Process of Holocaust Survivors

Most trauma survivors try hard to put their past behind them. They put great effort into building new lives and invest considerable energy in their work and family. The Holocaust survivors who arrived in Israel were encouraged to make new lives for themselves and to participate actively in the building of the young state. They were discouraged from "dwelling on the past" and working through their experiences (Segev, 1991).

Much of this changed as they aged. Aging generally entails a reduction of activity and a shift from planning to reminiscing and from occupation with current events to the review and rethinking of one's life. As the Holocaust survivors aged, they naturally shifted their focus back to their past. At the same time, the society, which had previously ignored the survivors' emotional problems, has taken a new interest in their experience and encourages them to bear witness to the events. The combination of these psychological and social processes has resulted in the awakening of dormant memories among people who have not had a chance to work them through (Solomon, 1995).

In addition, aging inevitably entails many losses and exit events, from retirement through the death of a spouse, friends, and relatives. Painful in themselves, such losses may be particularly distressing for previously traumatized individuals, whom they often remind of the losses in the traumatic event. Several case reports have demonstrated the exacerbation of repressed memories and triggering of delayed PTSD following such events (e. g., Herman & Eryavec, 1994).

Retirement may be a special source of dread for elderly Holocaust survivors. Not only does it entail a loss of the routine, self-esteem, status, and social interaction that are vital to all of us, but it removes the structure and activity that had shield the trauma survivors against flooding by memories. Moreover, the fact that inability to work resulted in almost certain death in the concentration camps can only increase the survivors' anxiety about retiring.

The age-related deterioration of health may also pose special problems for Holocaust survivors. Findings show that aging Holocaust survivors (Hirschfield, 1977) and POWs (Beebe, 1975) tend to become more ill and more frequently so than comparable individuals without a traumatic past. The deterioration of health has been documented to trigger the outbreak of delayed PTSD (Hamner, 1994). Moreover, observations of Holocaust survivors suggest that many of them find hospitalization or entering a nursing home extremely traumatic since these echo and revive their former ordeal (Danieli, 1994; Hirschfield, 1977). They are again separated from their loved ones, confined, and sometimes required to share quarters with strangers; they are exposed to bodily smells and noises that remind them of their persecution, placed in a position of helplessness, and told what to do by authorities they had learned to mistrust. Clinical evidence (Hirschfield, 1977) indicates that in more than a few cases hospitalization brings about psychotic like delusions of being back in concentration camp, with the confined survivors accusing the doctors and nurses of Nazi-like experimentation.

Below I present a study carried out on Israeli elderly during the Gulf War that examined the implication of their Holocaust experience. Even though, as noted above, a very high proportion of Israel's aged population lived through extremely stressful events, the Holocaust survivors had probably endured the most, and might thus be expected to react differently from their non-Holocaust age mates.

Aged Holocaust Survivors in the Gulf War

As noted above, the Gulf War imposed special stresses on Israel's elderly population as a whole. In addition, it created even further stresses for Holocaust Survivors, for it bore disturbing resemblance to aspects of their Holocaust experience. These resemblance included the oft repeated threat of gas attack, the machinations of a megalomaniacal tyrant, and the targeting of unarmed civilians. Moreover, the Israeli government's policy of restraint, of neither striking back nor taking active measures to ward off the attacks, left the population passive in face of the threat, bore strong echoes of the survivors' helpless victimization.

My colleagues and I (Solomon & Prager, 1992; Hantman, Solomon, & Prager, 1994) addressed the question of whether elderly Holocaust survivors responded differently to the Gulf War than their non-Holocaust age-mates and, if so, how. Did they respond with more anxiety or less? Or was there no substantial difference? To put it differently, did the trials they endured during the Holocaust help them cope with the difficulties of the Gulf War or evoke old anxieties that impaired their ability to manage?

To answer these questions, we surveyed 192 senior citizens during the Gulf War. Sixty-one (31.8%) of the sample were Holocaust survivors (mean age = 68.3; SD = 7.2); 131 (68.2%) were not (Mean age = 72.9; SD = 7.5). Most of them (88%) lived in their own homes, the rest were residents of an urban community home for the aged. Utilizing standardized questionnaires, we measured perceptions of danger (level of personal safety during the war; e. g., "To what degree you feel that your life is in danger?" or "To what degree you assess that the country of Israel is in danger of being annihilated?"), wartime psychological distress (stress symptoms; e. g., nightmares, startle response), and state/trait anxiety.

The findings (Table 1) show that elderly Holocaust survivors responded to the Gulf War with greater distress than elderly nonsurvivors.

Holocaust survivors viewed the war as more dangerous, rating their own danger, the danger of Israel's being annihilated, and the danger of the war to their families higher than their nonsurvivor age-mates. They displayed both greater state anxiety and greater trait anxiety than nonsurvivors. And significantly more survivors than nonsurvivors reported more specific war-related distress, in the form of sleep disturbances (68.9% vs. 51.5%), concentration difficulties or memory impairment (54.1% as 36.6%), apprehension and tension (80.3% vs. 64%), nightmares (41% vs. 23.7%); loss of interest in significant activities (59% vs. 40.8%); sense of detachment from others (28.8% vs. 10.4%),

Table 1. Psychological ratings during the Gulf War for elderly Israeli survivors of the Holocaust and other elderly subjects[a].

	Holocaust survivors (N = 61)		Other subjects (N = 131)		
	Mean	SD	Mean	SD	$F(1,100)$
Perceptions of danger	−0.2	0.9	0.5	1.1	2.29
Psychological distress	42.9	11.9	33.0	10.1	6.20
State anxiety	47.4	13.2	36.5	13.0	6.27
Trait anxiety	50.3	10.4	41.5	7.4	7.53[b]

[a]A multivariate analysis of covariance was performed with age, sex, education, religiosity, health, and proximity to bomb sites as covariates. Overall $F = 2.43$, df = 4,97, $p < 0.05$.
[b]$p < .005$, with Bonferroni correction (Miller, 1981) for multiple comparisons.

as well as stronger feelings of panic and fear (37.7% vs. 16.9%), irritability (72% vs. 46.2%), excitability (65.6% vs. 48.1%), and feelings of hopelessness (42.6% vs. 11.6%).

In short, on all four of the measures Holocaust survivors showed greater vulnerability than nonsurvivors. Moreover, with the exception of the sense of danger, the differences remained significant when the background factors that might bias the findings, including the differences in mean age and gender in the two groups, were controlled for.

We also assessed the impact of other prior stressful experiences on the responses of the elderly to the Gulf War (Hantman et al., 1994). These included both the "objective" experiences such as losing a child and earlier exposure to war, and the "subjective" sense of having previously experienced an event similar to the Gulf War. The nature of the "similar" event was neither defined nor queried, since the aim of this question was to investigate the role of symbolic associations in the response to stress.

Surprisingly, none of the "objective" life events had any impact on how either the survivor or nonsurvivor group coped. But the "subjective" sense of having previously undergone a similar stressful experience had a significant impact on the coping of the survivors, though not on that of the nonsurvivors. Holocaust survivors who reported having had a prior experience similar to the Gulf War were even more vulnerable than other survivors. They reported a significantly greater sense of danger, lower sense of self-efficacy, and a higher level of trait, though not of state, anxiety. Among non-Holocaust survivors, no such differences were found. Neither their sense of danger, their self-efficacy, nor their level of anxiety was affected by whether or not they had a prior experience similar to the Gulf War.

The findings of this study clearly show that Holocaust survivors were more vulnerable during the Gulf War than nonsurvivors. The findings to the effect that the survivors felt more danger, had higher state anxiety, and reported more symptoms of war related stress than nonsurvivors show the residue of stress left by the Holocaust in the survivors' lives. So does the finding that they have higher trait anxiety than nonsurvivors. Together these findings suggest that the survivors retain from their Holocaust experience both a generalized sensitivity to stress and a more specific sensitivity to the stress of war.

The findings are consistent both with the abundant evidence that points to the long-lasting damage of exposure to traumatic events and with the evidence cited above to the effect that survivors suffer from psychological difficulties that can be traced back to their Holocaust ordeal (e. g., Eitinger, 1980; Niederland, 1968). They are also consistent with findings that the survivors are particularly susceptible to the resurgence of Holocaust related memories, anxieties, and stresses in old age (Dasberg, 1987; Lomranz, 1990;). They are consistent too with studies of Holocaust survivors that demonstrate their elevated sensitivity to issues of safety and security (Shanan & Shahar, 1983).

It seems that for many survivors the Gulf War exacerbated or reactivated the trauma of the Holocaust. Similar exacerbation or reactivation was found by Christenson, Walker, Ross, and Maltbie (1981) among aging World War II veterans. Presenting a case of a reactivation "precipitated by an event that simulated the original trauma," the authors went on to suggest that "losses associated with involution age, including parental loss, children leaving home, pending retirement, and increasing medical disability all serve as stressors that may reactivate a latent traumatic stress disorder" (p. 985).

Like the studies reported here, studies of reactivation of traumas in the civilian sphere have also shown that reactivation can occur after many years of dormancy and can be triggered by events only remotely reminiscent of the original trauma. For example, it has been shown that reactivation of unresolved grief reactions, in which the bereaved are suddenly reemerged in the mourning process – with all its attendant feelings of sadness, pining, and depression – can be triggered by a large range of events from deliberate recall through incidental reminders of the death (Lindemann, 1944). Similarly, Burgess, and Holmstrom (1974) and Notman and Nadelson (1976) report the unresolved feelings of rape victims emerging many years after the assault and giving rise to acute depression, anxiety, and phobic behaviors much like those commonly experienced in the period immediately following a rape. These findings suggest that it was indeed the associations of the Gulf War with the Holocaust (however remote the actual resemblance may have been), and their power to exacerbate or trigger reactivations of the survivors' Holocaust trauma that made that war such a potent stressor.

The current findings differ sharply from those of the only other systematic study of the effects of recurrent exposure on the elderly. Norris and Murrel (1988) found that elderly flood victims who had experienced prior floods fared emotionally better than those who had not. The difference probably stem from major differences in the nature of the traumatic events and in the populations studied. It is well known that man-made disasters wreck a great deal more psychological damage than natural ones (Beigel & Berren, 1985; Fredrick, 1980). Moreover, as suggested by the discussion above, Israel's Holocaust survivors probably experienced far more prior traumatic stress in their lives than Norris and Morrel's flood victims. Our findings suggest that even if life's "ordinary" stressors and natural disasters may strengthen a person's ability to cope, a massive catastrophe like the Holocaust depletes it.

The finding that survivors who reported having had an earlier experience similar to the Gulf War showed more distress than those who did not points to the ability of a similar earlier stressor – even if that similarity is purely subjective – to intensify the later stress it resembles. This finding is consistent with the results of a series of studies conducted on Israeli soldiers in the Lebanon War who had had acute or posttraumatic reactions to previous conflicts (Solomon, 1993). Those studies indicated that the more the Lebanon encounter reminded the soldier of his earlier traumatic experience, the more likely it was to exacerbate his residual symptoms or to trigger a reactivation of his previous stress reaction. Like the Gulf War, the later stressor did not have to be as intense as the first or even of objectively major dimensions; it was enough that it evoked memories and associations of the first in the soldier's mind.

Our finding that none of the objective stresses queried – neither participation in other wars nor the loss of loved ones – affected the survivors' coping with the Gulf War brings home the importance of the subjective meaning of an event in the reactivation of earlier traumas. Although it is common to speak of the survivors as a group, individual survivors undoubtedly differ in how well they worked through their experience. Their subjective feelings during and about the Gulf War may be one index of that working through. This interpretation suggests that it was the survivors who sustained the most serious and long lasting psychological injuries in the Holocaust who reported both previous experiences similar to the Gulf War and the strongest distress during it.

In conclusion, our study's results clearly show that Holocausts survivors are at high risk for survivors and persistent Pathologies. Furthermore they demonstrate that the enduring vulnerability is easily unmasked and exacerbated with the aging survivors are faced with current traumatic events. Yet not only survivors of labor and camps are at high risk as they age, but also other survivors of persecution and torture including refugees, combat veterans (Eitinger, 1980), freedom fighters (Op den Vede et al., 1993), and prisoners of war (Goldstein et al., 1987).

These findings have clear clinical implications. Clinicians are called to pay special attention to survivors of traumatic events as they age. Careful history of traumatic exposure over the life cycle and careful assessment of stress responses at various points of life during and after the traumatic exposure is called for. The more careful assessment could and should lead to a better psychiatric treatment for a very large cohort of today's elderly and hopefully to the development of specific mode of treatment of PTSD in the elderly. It is suggested that such intervention will include not only guided and supported life review but also setting attainable social cultural goals structuring of time and fostering meaningful activities.

References

American Psychiatric Association (1994). *Diagnostic and statistical manual of mental disorders, DSM-IV* .Washington, DC: Author.

Baider, L., Peretz, T., & Kaplan De-Nour, A. (1992). Effect of the Holocaust on coping with cancer. *Social Science and Medicine, 34,* 11–15.

Baider, L., & Sarell, M. (1984). Coping with cancer among Holocaust survivors in Israel: An exploratory study. *Journal of Human Stress,* 121–127.

Beebe, G.W. (1975). Follow up studies of World War II and Korea prisoners – II. Morbidity and maladjustment. *American Journal of Epidemiology, 101,* 400–422.

Beigel, A., & Berren, M.R. (1985). Human induced disasters. *Psychiatric Annals, 15,* 143–150.

Bell, B.D. (1978). Disaster impact and response: Overcoming the thousand natural shocks. *The Gerontologist, 18,* 531–540.

Bolin, R., & Klenow, D.J. (1982–83). Response of the elderly to disaster: An age-stratified analysis. *International Journal of Aging and Human Development, 16,* 283–296.

Bolin, R., & Klenow, D.J. (1988). Older people in disaster: A comparison of black and white victims. *International Journal of Aging and Human Development, 26,* 29–43.

Brockway, S. (1988). Case report: Flashback as a posttraumatic stress disorder (PTSD) symptom in a WWII veteran, *Military Medicine, 153,* 372–373.

Burgess, A.W., & Halmstrom, C.C. (1974). Rape trauma syndrome. *American Journal of Psychiatry, 131,* 981–986.

Carmeli, A., Mevorach, L., Leiberman, N., Taubman, A., Kahanovitz, S., & Navon, D. (1992). *The Gulf War: Home front in a test of crisis, Final report.* Department of Behavioral Sciences, IDF [in Hebrew].

Carmil, D., & Carel, R.S. (1986). Emotional distress and satisfaction in life among Holocaust survivors – A community study of survivors and controls. *Psychological Medicine, 16,* 141–149.

Christenson, R.M., Walker, J.L., Ross, D.R., & Maltbie, A.A. (1981). Reactivation of traumatic conflicts. *American Journal of Psychiatry, 138,* 984–985.

Danieli, Y. (1994). As survivors age: Part I. *Clinical Quarterly, 4,* 1–7.

Dasberg, H. (1987). Psychological distress of Holocaust survivors and their offspring in Israel, forty years later: A review. *Israel Journal of Psychiatry and Related Sciences, 24,* 243–256

Eaton, W.W., Sigal, J.J., & Weinfeld, M. (1982). Impairment in Holocaust survivors after 33 years: Data from an unbiased community sample. *American Journal of Psychiatry, 139,* 773–777.

Eitinger, L. (1980). The concentration camp syndrome and its late sequelae. In J. Dimsdale (Ed.), *Survivors, victims, and perpetrators.* Washington DC: Hemisphere.

Epstein, S. (1983). Natural healing processes of the mind: Graded stress inoculation as an inherent coping mechanism. In D. Michenbaum & M. Yarenko (Eds.), *Stress reduction and prevention.* New York: Plenum.

Frederick, C.J. (1980). Effects of natural vs. human-induced violence. *Evaluation and Change,* Special Issue, 71–75.

Friedsman, H.J. (1961). Reactions of older persons to disaster-caused losses: An hypothesis of relative deprivation. *The Gerontologist, 1,* 34–37.

Goenjian, A.K., Majarian, L.M., Pynoos, R.S., Steinberg, A.M., Manoukian, G., Tavosian,

A., & Fairbanks, L.A. (1994). Posttraumatic stress disorder in elderly and younger adults after the 1988 earthquake in Armenia. *American Journal of Psychiatry, 151*, 895–901.

Goldstein, G., Van Kammen, W., Shelly, C., Miller, D., & Van Kammen, D. (1987). Survivors of imprisonment in the Pacific theater during World War II. *American Journal of Psychiatry, 144*, 1210–1213.

Gray, D., & Calsyn, R.J. (1989). The relationship of stress and social support to life satisfaction: Age effects. *Journal of Community Psychology, 17*, 214–219.

Hagstrom, R. (1995). The acute psychological impact on survivors following a train accident. *Journal of Traumatic Stress, 8*, 391–402.

Hamner, M.B. (1994). Exacerbation of posttraumatic stress disorder symptoms with medical illness. *General Hospital Psychiatry, 16*, 135–137.

Hantman, S., Solomon, Z., & Prager, E. (1994). The effect of previous exposure to traumatic stress on the responses of elderly people to the Gulf War. In J. Lomranz & G. Naveh (Eds.), *Trauma and old age: Coping with the stress of the Gulf War* (pp. 59–72). Jerusalem: JDC [in Hebrew].

Herman, M.D., & Eryavec, G. (1994). Delayed onset post traumatic stress disorder in World War II veterans. *Canadian Journal of Psychiatry, 39*, 439–441.

Hirschfield, M.J. (1977). Care of the aging Holocaust survivors. *American Journal of Nursing, 77,* 1187–1189.

Hobfoll, S., Lomranz, J., Eyal, N., Bridges, A., & Tzemach, M. (1989). Pulse of a nation: Depressive mood reactions of Israelis to the Israel-Lebanon War. *Journal of Personality and Social Psychology, 56*, 1002–1012.

Huerta, F., & Horton, R. (1978). Coping behavior of elderly flood victims, *The Gerontologist, 18*, 541–546.

Jones, G.H., & Lovel, J.W.T. (1987). Delayed psychiatric sequelae among Falkland War veterans. *Journal of the Royal College of General Practitioners, 37*, 34–35.

Kilijanek, T.S., & Drabek, T.E. (1979). Assessing long-term impacts of a natural disaster: A focus on the elderly. *The Gerontologist, 19*, 555–566.

Kluznik, J.C., Speed, N.H., Van Valkenburg, C., & Magraw, R. (1986). Forty-year follow-up of United States prisoners of war. *American Journal of Psychiatry, 143*, 1443–1446.

Kuch, K., & Cox, B.J. (1992). Symptoms of PTSD in 124 survivors of the Holocaust. *American Journal of Psychiatry, 149*, 337–340.

Levav, I., & Abramson, J.H. (1984). Emotional distress among concentration camp survivors – A community study in Jerusalem. *Psychological Medicine, 14*, 215–218.

Lindeman, E. (1944). Symptomatology and management of acute grief. *American Journal of Psychiatry, 101*, 141–148.

Lomranz, J. (1990). Long-term adaptation to traumatic stress in light of adult development and aging perspectives. In M.A. Stephens, Crowther, S. Hobfoll, & Tennebaum (Eds.), *Stress and coping in later life families* (pp. 99–121). Washington, DC: Hemisphere.

Lomranz, J., & Eyal, N. (1994). A longitudinal study of depressive moods of men and women in several age groups during the Gulf War. In J. Lomranz & G. Naveh (Eds.), *Trauma and old age: Coping with the stress of the Gulf War* (pp. 13–29). Jerusalem: JDC [in Hebrew].

Long, N., Chamberlain, K., & Vincent, C. (1994). Effect of the Gulf War on reactivation of adverse combat-related memories in Vietnam veterans. *Journal of Clinical Psychology, 50*, 138–144.

McNaughton, M.E., Smith, L.W., Patterson, T.L., Grant, I. (1990). Stress, social support, coping resources, and immune status in elderly women. *Journal of Nervous and Mental Disease, 178*, 460–461.

Meichenbaum, D. (1985). *Stress inoculation training*. New York: Pergamon.

Melick, M.E., & Logue, J.N. (1985–86). The effect of disaster on the health and well-being of older women. *International Journal of Aging and Human Development, 21*, 27–38.

Miller, J.A., Turner, J.G., & Kimball, E. (1981). Big Thompson Flood victims: One year later. *Family Relations, 30*, 111–116.

Niederland, W.G. (1968). The problem of the survivor. In H. Krystal (Ed.), *Massive psychic trauma*. New York: International University Press.

Norris, F.H., & Murrel, S.A. (1988). Prior experience as a moderator of disaster impact on anxiety symptoms in older adults, *American Journal of Community Psychology, 16*, 665–683.

Notman, M., & Nadelson, C. (1976). The rape victim: Psychodynamic consideration. *American Journal of Psychiatry, 133*, 408–412.

Ollendick, D.G., & Hoffmann, M. (1982). Assessment of psychological reactions in disaster victims. *Journal of Community Psychology, 10*, 157–167.

Page, W.F., Engdahl, B.E., & Eberly, R.E. (1991). Prevalence and correlates of depressive symptoms among former prisoners of war. *Journal of Nervous and Mental Disease, 179*, 670–677.

Poulshock, S.W., & Cohen, E.S. (1975). The elderly in the aftermath of a disaster. *The Gerontologist, 15*, 357–361.

Prager, E., & Solomon, Z. (1995a). Cognitive control as a buffer of war induced stress in a middle-aged and older Israeli sample. *Aging and Society, 15*, 355–374.

Prager, E., & Solomon, Z. (1995b). Correlates of war induced stress responses among late middle aged and elderly Israelis. *International Journal of Aging and Human Development, 41*, 203–220.

Rosen, J., Reynolds, C.F., Yaeger, A.L., Houck, P.R., & Horowitz, L.F. (1991). Sleep disturbances in survivors of the Nazi Holocaust. *American Journal of Psychiatry, 148*, 62–66.

Segev, T. (1991). *The seventh million: The Israelis and the Holocaust*. Jerusalem: Mazwell-Macmillan-Keter Publishing House and Domino Press (in Hebrew).

Shanan, J., & Shahar, O. (1983). Cognitive and personality functioning of Jewish Holocaust survivors during mid-life transition in Israel. *Archives of Psychology, 135*, 275–294.

Solomon, Z. (1993). *Combat stress reaction: The enduring toll of war*. New York: Plenum.

Solomon, Z. (1995). From denial to recognition: Attitudes of therapists toward Holocaust survivors. *Journal of Traumatic Stress, 8*, 229–242.

Solomon, Z., Mikulincer, M., & Waysman, M. (1991). Delayed and immediate onset post-traumatic stress disorder: The role of life events and social resources. *Journal of Community Psychology, 19*, 231–236.

Solomon, Z., & Prager, E. (1992). Elderly Israeli Holocaust survivors during the Persian Gulf War: A study of psychological distress. *American Journal of Psychiatry, 149*, 1707–1710.

Sperr, E.V., Sperr, S.J., Craft, R.S., & Boudewyns, P.A. (1990). MMPI profiles and post-traumatic symptomatology in former prisoners of war. *Journal of Traumatic Stress, 3*, 369–378.

White, N.S. (1983). Post-traumatic stress disorder. Letter to the editor. *Hospital and Community Psychiatry, 34*, 1061–1062.

Reminiscence of Traumatic Experiences in (Former) Jewish Emigrants and Extermination Camp Survivors

Andreas Kruse and Eric Schmitt

Introduction

Medical and psychological studies on the effects of persecution suffered in National Socialist Germany have concentrated largely on the survivors of the National Socialist extermination camps (see v. Baeyer, Häfner, & Kisker, 1964; Friedmann, 1948; Matussek, 1971; Niederland, 1980). In the so-called *"survivor syndrome,"* Krystal and Niederland (1968, 1971) described a posttraumatic stress disorder whose clinical features include acute anxiety states, nightmares, depression, hypochondriac reactions, and a lifelong increased probability of confrontation with and awareness of threatening and frightening situations (see also Eitinger, 1990; Porter, 1981; Rustin, 1983). The concern with the physical, mental, and social damage caused to humans and the possibilities of treating these have understandably dominated psychological and medical research for a long time. However, there are no unequivocal findings on the question of how far the survivor syndrome as a form of reaction to injuries and stress can be overcome or "treated" in the long term, or whether the stresses suffered gain in importance (again) in old age (see Brainin, Ligeti, & Teicher, 1994; Leon, Butcher, Klanmon, Goldberg, & Almager, 1982; Luel & Marcus, 1984).

In a research project we try to explore in which way subjective perceptions of current life situation in Jewish people formerly imprisoned in extermination camps or forced to escape from National Socialist Germany are influenced by Holocaust experiences and how those people try to cope with stressful Holocaust reminiscence (see Kruse & Schmitt, 1994; Schmitt & Kruse, 1998). An essential part of our methodological approach in this project are semi-structured interviews (see Kruse, 1987a; Kruse & Schmitt, in press; Undeutsch, 1983). It is the aim of these interviews to explore how specific life situations, events, and developments are represented in subjective life space (see Thomae, 1996), and to describe the significance of specific life situations, events, and developments as complete and authentic as possible from the perspective of the participants. For this reason, no preexisting standard questionnaire is applied. Instead, researchers only possess a number of prototypical questions representing the central issues of our study. In which manner concrete questions are applied to the study participants depends on former discourse (Which questions have already been answered? Which comments should be further explicated?) and the frame of reference offered by our subjects (How do participants reconstruct personal development? Which connections between different stages of the life-span exist from the participants' perspective?). Issues of interest in our study are perceptions of Jewish decent, personal and societal development, personal and social identity, perceived stress and coping, social relationships, reminiscence, life review and future time perspective.

Semi-structured interviews with 248 subjects indicate that for most people Holocaust reminiscence increased in old age. In later life, traumatic memories do not only occur spontaneously and unexpectedly. Moreover they are an essential part of the people's frame of reference for questions about personal identity, perceptions of social relationships, society and societal development, and coping with specific themes. All of our subjects report that they cannot protect themselves against stressful reminiscence. But people greatly differ in coping with such stressful reminiscence. Some study participants react with depression, anxiety, feelings of survivor guilt, and withdrawal from social relationships. Others, however, are highly engaged in social relationships, especially with the following generations. They want to give a contribution to the educational work of their society and to prevent discrimination, racism, and xenophobia.

Conducting interviews with Holocaust survivors raises an important ethical question: Are we allowed to confront people with traumatic memories? Since people cannot protect themselves against spontaneously occurring traumatic memories and since supportive networks decrease in old age, there is a need for opportunities to talk about their personal experiences and fate (see also Betten & Du-nor, 1996). Most of the study participants were convinced that they are obliged to witness the significance of the Holocaust for personal and societal development so that it will not happen again – even if the Holocaust might be a historical aberration beyond comprehension. Given this need for conversation we should not ignore traumatic reminiscence in Holocaust survivors but we should keep in mind that often the true response is silence (see Berger, 1983; Rosenberg, 1983).

Obtaining Study Participants

In constituting our sample we were supported by Jewish communities and organizations, by universities, homes for the elderly, and residential foundations. Without this support, the interviews could not have been organized and carried out. In *Israel* we cooperated with researchers from the Hebrew University in Jerusalem and the Technion in Haifa. In the *United States* we cooperated with researchers of Northwestern University at Chicago and the International Psychogeriatric Association. Further support could be received from the staff of the Self Help home in Chicago, a residence for Jewish elderly which was founded to improve the situation of aged emigrants from National Socialist Germany. Our research in *Argentina* was carried out in close cooperation with representatives of the Delegación de Asociaciónes Israelitas Argentinas (DAIA), the Asociación Cultural Israelita de Buenos Aires (ACIBA) the Asociación Filantrópica Israelita (AFI), and the staff of San Miguel, a residence for Jewish elderly founded in 1933 by Jewish emigrants from Germany. In *Germany* we cooperated with the Jewish Communities in Frankfurt and Aachen. Further support could be received here by representatives of homes for the elderly and residential foundations in Bad Kissingen, Bad Soden, Frankfurt, Konstanz, Stuttgart, and Überlingen.

Our research in Germany in particular benefited from the fact that the interest of the study participants in our research project was extremely high, which gained expression in the fact that other study participants were acquired from private contacts. The institutions mentioned above were informed about the aims of our study and asked to approach people whom they believed to be eligible for participation in the study and to notify us of their address if they consented. Study participants in Germany then received a letter. This letter gave some details about our research project. They were also informed that they would be contacted by telephone, which happened about a fortnight later. For the actual interview the subjects were visited in their apartments. Following the interview they were asked to help us to find other study participants. In the case of the interviews in the three institutions selected, a personal letter to the study participants was not possible for organizational reasons. In these cases most of the interview times were organized by our partners. For this reason a more detailed explanation of our research project was necessary before the actual interview. In addition, private contacts were less important in obtaining additional study participants as a) our partners were informed about the intended number of interviews and b) for organizational reasons only a small amount of time remained available for additional interview sessions.

Sample

248 people participated in our study. These were divided into one subsample of (former) Jewish emigrants who decided to return to Germany in their old age or who preferred to stay in three destination countries of emigration (Argentina, Israel, United States) and one subsample of Jewish extermination camp survivors living in Germany or Israel. Both subsamples are described below.

Subsample of (Former) Jewish Emigrants

This subsample consists of 180 people who had to escape from National Socialist Germany because of their Jewish descent (see Lacina, 1982; Strauss & Röder, 1980–1983). These subjects were divided equally between three destination countries of Jewish emigration: 60 people finally settled in Argentina, Israel (Palestine) and the United States. In each of these groups 30 people decided to return to Germany in their old age and 30 people continued to stay abroad. 55 of the 180 people escaped from Germany in the period between the *National Socialist Takeover* and the *Nuremberg Laws*, 74 in the period between the *Nuremberg Laws* and the *Night of Broken Glass*, 58 between the *Night of Broken Glass* and the *Outbreak of World War II*, 3 in the period from the *beginning of World War II* to *German Surrender*. At the time of emigration, 163 of the subjects were under 30 years of age, 51 under 20 years of age. 91 subjects emigrated directly to the subsequent destination country of emigration. In the case of 49 subjects the emigration involved two, and in the case of 40 subjects three or more stops (in these data a later return to Germany is not recognized as a further stop of emigration).

Only those subjects were included in the subsample of (former) Jewish emigrants who
– at the time of the *National Socialist Takeover* were at least 10 years old,
– lived in Germany during the period of National Socialist Germany,
– possessed German citizenship before 1933.

The first two criteria were intended to ensure that the subjects could remember the time of National Socialist Germany, could report personal experiences and, in particular, could provide information about the stages in their decision to leave Germany and the detailed circumstances of the emigration. As the question about the development of social identity constituted an important part of our study, the limitation to people possessing German citizenship before 1933 took account of the fact that Jewish people emigrating from Eastern

European countries differed considerably from German Jewry, not only in their understanding as citizens, but also in their social structure and self-concept and their integration in the Weimar Republic.

In addition, one further criterion was introduced: the subjects had to have taken the decision to return to Germany after the completion of their working life at an advanced age. We assumed here that the problems of reintegration were more marked for this group of people than for those who had already lived in Germany for long periods of their working life and therefore had probably collected experiences with Christian members of their age group who were not forced to escape from National Socialist Germany and who might have supported or at least tolerated German racism in National Socialist Germany.

Subsample of Jewish Extermination Camp Survivors

Of the 68 Jewish extermination camp survivors who participated in our study 48 lived in Israel and 20 lived in Germany. In contrast to the subjects in the subsample of (former) Jewish emigrants, these people stemmed in a very great majority of cases from families who had lived in Eastern European countries and therefore did not possess German citizenship (see Sofsky, 1993). In 1933, 32 of the 68 subjects lived in Germany, 36 in Poland, Hungary, or the Soviet Union. After 1941 our subjects were deported to Auschwitz-Birkenau, Sobibór, and Treblinka. The people now living in Israel left Germany after the end of World War II as so called *Displaced Persons* (see Jacobmeyer, 1992; Zertal, 1989). The people now living in Germany did not return to their Eastern-European homelands primarily for two reasons: on the one hand, no close relatives or friends were alive any more and their former property had been stolen or destroyed. On the other hand, persecution of European Jewry did not end with German surrender. Especially in Poland fear of antisemitic pogroms was totally realistic. All those extermination camp survivors now living in Germany intended to leave Germany later. The planned departure (namely to the United States and Israel/Palestine) was delayed, however, partly because of organizational difficulties of the Allies and partly also for health and family reasons. For some people the restoration of their own state of health and the search for relatives and friends who had "disappeared" took several years. For occupational reasons also (the subjects had taken on work to support themselves and wanted first to create a "financial basis" for the subsequent new start) and out of fear of not being able to adapt to yet another new culture, the departure was repeatedly postponed – a phenomenon that other authors have described by the metaphor of "packed bags" (see Fleischmann, 1981; Heenen-Wolff, 1992). In the belief of democratic progress in the Federal Republic of Germany, some of the subjects had also consciously decided to continue living in Germany so that the fate of the persecuted remained alive there and a new (old) antisemitism did not develop in the new generation.

Table 1 describes some details for interpreting the results of our research.

Table 1. Sample.

	(former) Jewish emigrants (n = 180)	Jewish extermination camp survivors (n = 68)	total (n = 248)
Recruitment of participants			
– Jewish communities and organizations	78 (43.3%)	23 (33.8%)	101 (40.7%)
– Universities	19 (10.6%)	28 (41.2%)	47 (19.0%)
– Homes for the elderly	50 (27.8%)	3 (4.4%)	53 (21.4%)
– private contact	33 (18.3%)	14 (20.6%)	47 (19.0%)
Sex			
– Men	85 (47.2%)	27 (39.7%)	112 (45.2%)
– Women	95 (52.8%)	41 (60.3%)	136 (54.8%)
Age			
– 70–79 years	64 (35.6%)	21 (30.9%)	85 (34.3%)
– 80–89 years	106 (58.9%)	42 (61.8%)	148 (59.7%)
– 90 years and older	10 (5.6%)	5 (7.4%)	15 (6,0%)
School-leaving qualification			
– university education	33 (18.3%)	6 (8.8%)	39 (15.7%)
– A levels (Abitur)	81 (45.0%)	27 (39.7%)	108 (43.5%)
– school leaving certificate at Realschule	28 (15.6%)	17 (25.0%)	45 (18.1%)
– primary school (Volksschule)	16 (8.9%)	2 (2.9%)	18 (7.3%)
– none	22 (12.2%)	16 (23.5%)	38 (40.7%)
Family status			
– Single	14 (7.8%)	4 (5.9%)	18 (7.3%)
– Married	73 (40.6%)	28 (41.2%)	101 (40.7%)
– Widowed	80 (44.4%)	35 (51.5%)	115 (46.4%)
– Divorced	13 (7.2%)	1 (1.5%)	14 (5.6%)
Number of children			
– none	80 (44.4%)	31 (45.6%)	111 (44.8%)
– 1	55 (30.6%)	18 (26.5%)	73 (29.4%)
– 2	33 (18.3%)	13 (19.1%)	46 (18.5%)
– 3 or more	12 (6.7%)	6 (8.8%)	18 (7.3%)
Citizenship			
– German	71 (39.4%)	20 (29.4%)	91 (36.7%)
– US-American	47 (26.1%)	–	47 (19.0%)
– Israeli	53 (29.4%)	48 (70.6%)	101 (40.7%)
– Argentinean	40 (22.2%)	–	40 (16.1%)

Research Perspective on Reminiscence of Traumatic Experiences

It is not our aim here to examine the extent to which the primary psychopathological symptoms of the much described and well documented survivor syndrome were found in our study participants. The aim of our analyses was much more to describe as concretely as possible *everyday contexts* in which the subjects' experience and behavior were influenced by their memories. The stressful memories may either occur spontaneously by imposing themselves on the subjects to a certain extent, or may be consciously activated by the subject in processes of life review (see Butler, 1963; Coleman, 1997; Haight, 1991; Thornton & Brotchie, 1987). Preference was given to an analysis of this kind for the question about the presence of symptoms such as anxiety states, feelings of "survivor guilt," and feelings of inadequacy for three reasons:

1) The Jews who had emigrated since 1933 represented an important factor in the economic, scientific, and cultural development of numerous emigrant destination countries. A purely psychopathological perspective runs the risk of neglecting the significant achievements of the people in the emigration.

2) The majority of German Jews were largely assimilated before 1933. The self-concept of these people may be described as "German citizens of Jewish religion," the identification with Germany and the German language and culture was in general very high. We assumed that the period of emigration for many was and is characterized to a large extent by problems of identification which cannot be adequately classified in purely psychopathological categories.

3) Finally, a psychopathological perspective conceals the risk of seeking the causes for the continuing effect of the traumas "in the person," in other words it is the person who has failed to adapt to their environment.

It is not a simple matter to assess individual reactions to the Holocaust in terms of an – albeit implicit – standard. Possibly a "pathological" social reality does not allow "normal" forms of coping or "processing." Frequently recurring memories of the period of persecution and a preoccupation with them are therefore not per se any more pathological than "forgetting" or the view that that period of history is finished and need no longer be a subject of discussion today.

Identifying General Contexts of Traumatic Reminiscence: Method of Analysis

The analysis of the semistructured interviews was divided into four stages.

In the *first stage*, three qualified psychologists working independently of one another selected passages from 90 transcribed interviews in which the interviewees (a) referred explicitly to the fact that their way of life or behavior should be understood against the background of their experiences, (b) referred to personal experiences when explaining the significance which they attributed to specific situations, events, and developments, or (c) made spontaneous comparisons between the present political situation and their personal past. In this way 755 relevant passages were identified initially. Where individual passages were not chosen unanimously by all three qualified psychologists – there was agreement about 692 passages – possible interpretations were discussed. On the basis of the mutual exchanges, the three psychologists agreed on a further 49 passages which were included in the subsequent analyses; 38 of these passages had been chosen previously by two psychologists and 11 by only one psychologist; 14 passages were not included in the subsequent analysis as the psychologists had either agreed to incorporate them in a larger area of text or rejected the interpretation of a spontaneous reference.

In the *second stage*, each of the psychologists had the task of defining broader areas on the basis of the 741 (692 + 49) passages. Here too there was a high degree of agreement between the three psychologists. There was total agreement on the selection of 15 areas, while 4 areas were merged into 2 following a joint discussion as a distinction appeared difficult in individual cases (the question as to how far one may feel German and the question of to what extent one may now live in Germany, and the involvement in clubs and organizations and involvement in understanding between natives and foreigners). Finally, it was agreed in the discussion to treat the reunification of Germany as a separate area (and not as a constituent part of the political development in Germany). On the basis of the discussion, the psychologists therefore agreed on 18 areas.

In the *third stage*, the three psychologists independently assigned the 741 passages to these 18 areas. In so doing, the individual areas could only be categorized once per person. Repetitions or thematically related statements were not included. The categorization of the three psychologists agreed completely in 83 of the 90 study participants. There was disagreement about the categorization of one thematic area in 5 people and the psychologists differed in their categorization of two areas in two people. In these cases the disagreements were resolved on the basis of a joint discussion.

In the *fourth stage*, the transcriptions that had not previously been considered in establishing the coding system were each coded by two psychologists on the basis of the established coding system. There was a high degree of agreement for this assessment stage also. Differences in individual categories only occurred in the categorization of three cases. These were eliminated on the basis of a joint case conference.

Contexts in which Stressful Memories Occur: Results of the Analysis

Table 2 gives an overview of the distribution of the 18 established everyday memory contexts for the subsamples of (former) Jewish emigrants and extermination camp survivors. As can be seen from this overview, traumatic memories occurred in areas of widely differing content: spontaneously as in conjunction with questions about one's own identity and the life review or in coping with specific themes.

Spontaneously and Unexpectedly Occurring Memories

Spontaneously and unexpectedly occurring memories were reported in 143 of the 248 interviews. Despite considerable effort, the majority of people were unable to separate swastikas, stars of David, SS symbols or xenophobic slogans as the "scrawling of some reprobates and scatterbrains" from the public opinion prevailing in the country concerned. Even if these people in general were convinced that they were not exposed to any "real threat," the sight of signs, emblems or slogans *awoke stressful memories which inevitably resulted in anxiety states* despite all the efforts made in the concrete situation "to follow one's own senses." Spontaneous memories also occurred frequently in situations in which at first sight no reference to xenophobic or antisemitic tendencies could be found. Thus, the consequences of dispossession and persecution are still visible today, either because previous stores and banks continue to exist under new management and a new name, or because places associated with memories of a familiar picture of the city in their youth had disappeared. Finally, situations were also mentioned in which the subjects themselves could find no cause for the intruding memories. These situations in particular were frequently felt to be particularly stressful because of the impression of having no control over one's own feelings and hence of being exposed helplessly to the situation.

Search for Personal Identity

Three other very frequently described everyday contexts of memories are associated with questions of their personal identity, particularly the signifi-

Table 2. Everyday contexts conditioned by stressful memories.

01.	Spontaneously and unexpectedly occurring memories	143 (57.7%)
02.	The question of whether in view of the past one may feel a German to-day and whether one has the right to live in Germany today	113 (45.6%)
03.	The preoccupation with the losses suffered, constantly recurring thoughts of the fate of relatives and friends	111 (44.8%)
04.	The question of what one had in common with "the Germans" and how one differed from them	110 (44.4%)
05.	The question of how far people of one's own generation have grown distant from National Socialist ideology	109 (44.0%)
06.	The awareness of political developments in Germany – particularly of xenophobia and antisemitism – similar to those in the late Weimar Republic	104 (41.9%)
07.	The avoidance of situations which one believes will revive memories or confront with tendencies of antisemitism	99 (39.9%)
08.	Integration of German Jewry before 1933	80 (32.3%)
09.	Concern with one's own mortality, associated with the effort to organize one's own life	78 (31.5%)
10.	Search for a personal definition of Jewish religion and Jewish people	75 (30.2%)
11.	Personal confrontations with xenophobia and antisemitism	72 (29.0%)
12.	Anniversaries, remembrance days, commemorations, etc.	62 (25.0%)
13.	Involvement in schools and clubs with the aim of broadening the knowledge of the younger generation about German history	62 (25.0%)
14.	Political conflicts in the Near East	59 (23.8%)
15.	The question of the future of relatives, particularly the grandchildren's generation	50 (20.2%)
16.	Personal involvement for the relationship between Christians and Jews, involvement in Jewish communities, clubs, and organizations	36 (14.5%)
17.	German re-unification	21 (8.5%)
18.	Racist and xenophobic tendencies in other countries	15 (6.0%)

cance of their own origin. 113 of the study participants were intensely concerned with the moral dimension of a self-definition as "German." These people were frequently tormented by doubts as to whether they should not have decided against assuming German nationality or against returning to Germany. Feelings of shame and guilt alternated with "rational" efforts at justification. These important moral dimensions in the experience of the study participants also came out in the question of how far the members of their own generation who were not obliged to emigrate had grown distant (n = 109). Like the questions describing the significance of their origin, the search reported by 75 people for their own personal definition of Jewish religion and Jewry is connected with the question of personal identity. For 110 of our study participants, the question of what they had in common with "the Germans" and how they differed from them was a central concern in their present life situation. 104 of our subjects reported that the actual political situation in Germany would be quite similar to those in the last years of the Weimar Republic when the importance of the racist Nazi ideology increased dramatically. The discussion that was being held at the time of the interview about a change in the right to asylum in the Federal Republic of Germany and a series of proposals and attacks directed against foreign citizens, which, moreover, in the opinion of our study participants, frequently had not been countered with the necessary vigour by the authorities, contributed in particular to this impression. This development had contributed to a recurrence of stressful memories of past traumas. The historical developments in National Socialist Germany throw up the question for a considerable number (80 subjects) of whether they had correctly perceived the relationship between Jewish and non-Jewish Germans, whether there had not been a degree of hostility even beforehand which had shown the previous patriotism of German Jewry as a tragic misunderstanding. In this connection, our interviewees were also concerned with possible reasons as to why they had not previously been faced with greater hostility.

Fate of Acquaintances, Survivor Guilt, and Avoidance of Social Contexts

A total of 111 people also reported constantly recurring thoughts about the fate of relatives and friends, victims of the racist Nazi ideology who did not survive. Some of them specifically emphasized that they felt morally obliged to safeguard the memory of their dead relatives and bear witness to their fate. They had to fulfill a task which had to take precedence over personal interests and preference. For others among the study participants, the fact that they belonged to the few "remaining" members of their family caused pronounced feelings of "survival guilt." These people were frequently tormented by the thought that it would have been better if others had survived instead of them or if they themselves had met the same fate as their relatives. 99 avoided certain situations in order not to be constantly reminded of the fate of relatives and friends or to be exposed to xenophobic and antisemitic tendencies. In particular, there was a tendency among these study participants to avoid public premises, celebrations, and festivities as it was assumed that it was precisely on

such occasions that they would be confronted with a large number of people
not known to them personally in an environment in which xenophobia is openly expressed. Public places (particularly regulars' tables in pubs) were associated to a high degree with stressful memories by some of the people. They refer
to the fact that excesses, particularly those occurring spontaneously as a result
of the disinhibitory effect of alcohol, produced a mutual "infection" and
"build-up". The fear of stressful memories at celebrations or festivities is not
due solely to those people who may be present at these events or the conflicts
arising in certain circumstances in conjunction with xenophobia. At happy
celebrations also they might spontaneously remember someone with whom
they had celebrated in the past or with whom they would have liked to celebrate. For some people it was a problem to celebrate with others as a result of
a perceived duty to those no longer alive. A further tendency to avoidance was
expressed in the organization of social relationships or in the way in which
people approached others whom they did not (yet) know personally. For many
people it was important to inform others as soon as possible about their personal fate. They not only introduced themselves to others by name, but also
added immediately that they were Jewish, that they had had to emigrate or
that they were imprisoned in Auschwitz, Sobibór, or Treblinka. They hoped
they would be able to protect themselves from antisemitic hostility in the belief
that whoever rejected them personally would also avoid their company.

Encounters with Antisemitic Hostility and Joint Responsibility

Personal encounters with antisemitic hostility were reported by 72 subjects. It
became apparent in a series of interviews that efforts were being made to offer
other interpretations for antisemitic hostility, such as intolerance, ignorance or
stupidity. In our opinion, however, this expresses precisely the extent to which
these people are affected in that they could not permit the existence of socially
unsanctioned incursions upon their environment because of their personal
memories.

It is also apparent from Table 2 that some of the people attempted to communicate and make use of their own memories beyond the immediate family
environment. 62 people were involved in schools and clubs with the aim of
broadening the knowledge of the younger generation about German history
and 36 people were involved in Jewish communities, clubs, and organizations
or for understanding between Christians and Jews. This context of reminiscence is strongly associated with participants efforts to cope with traumatic
memories. Since the meaning of personal development in the period of the
Holocaust is a dominant concern for the people, there is a need for discourse
with others who might not have enough knowledge about history. To inform

about traumatic experiences also means to contribute to the education of members of society and (hopefully) to the prevention of xenophobia and antisemitism. Therefore, in our perspective information and discourse are a kind of active coping. People try to change societal contexts that are responsible for anxiety and threat caused by traumatic reminiscence.

Does the Intensity of Stressful Memories Increase in Old Age?

In our research project, subjects were asked firstly about their life story and secondly about the preoccupation with stressful experiences at various times in their subsequent personal development. We deal below with the second question, the preoccupation with stressful experiences. The study participants were asked to indicate how intense the memories had been in seven stages of their personal development:

1) phase of restoration of health,

2) phase of establishing an existence and gaining a living,

3) phase of family and occupational development,

4) retirement (or retirement of partner) from work,

5) entry of grandchildren into adolescence,

6) death of partner,

7) the last 2–4 years.

In a *pilot study* which we conducted ourselves on the question of how (former) emigrants and extermination camp survivors reconstruct their personal history, in other words which periods they referred to when spontaneously describing their life course, the different phases of personal development mentioned above had proved to be useful dividing points. 15 people had participated in this pilot study, 8 extermination camp survivors and 7 former emigrants. The inclusion of other dividing points recognizable for emigrants' individual destination countries (see the Junta in Argentina or Wars in the Near East) was omitted to provide greater opportunities for generalization. For each of the seven periods mentioned, the study participants had to rate on a five-point scale how intense the memories had been (from very slight to very strong). It is important to note that a division of the life span following the Holocaust into 7 stages of post-Holocaust development is not valid for all of the study participants. For 65 (former) Jewish emigrants a phase of restoration of health could not be distinguished, 7 participants did not retire from work, 132 participants had no grandchildren, 133 of the participants had not experienced the

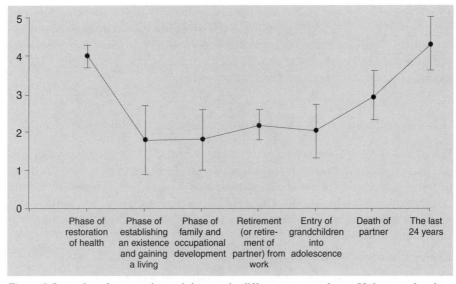

Figure 1. Intensity of traumatic reminiscence in different stages of post-Holocaust development (mean, standard deviation).

death of a spouse. Since these people could not be asked about intensity of reminiscence in stages of development that did not exist in their biography, the number of informants differs between the 7 stages of post-Holocaust development.

In Figure 1 participants' ratings for intensity of traumatic reminiscence in the seven stages of post-Holocaust development are reported.

In the first stage of personal development following the traumatic experiences suffered during the period of National Socialist Germany (= phase of restoration of health) intensity of stressful reminiscence was very high. This result is attributable to the fact that health problems as well as psychosocial problems in this phase of development are strongly associated with persecution and deportation. New challenges in a new culture might have contributed to the decreasing of traumatic reminiscence in middle adulthood. People had to concentrate on establishing an existence and gaining a living, on familial and occupational development. Moreover, they might have established supporting social relationships that protected at least in part against re-occurrence of anxiety and depression. Our data suggest that when occupational roles get lost and close relatives died, social integration and supportive networks decreased. As a consequence, states of anxiety, feelings of isolation, survivor guilt, and depression increased. Obviously, a further dramatic increase in intensity of traumatic reminiscence occurred in the last 2–4 years. Our results indicate that intensity of traumatic reminiscence in this period is as high as immediately after the breakdown of National Socialist Germany. Several findings of gerontological research can be hypothesized as an explanation for this dramatic increase:

1) Because of changes in social roles there are fewer personal tasks and challenges in old age. In later stages of life it can become difficult for people to engage in social activities so that they might be forced to concentrate on "personal affairs".

2) Losses of close acquaintances in former stages of personal development gain higher importance in old age. When social networks decline, many people might realize that there personal situation would could be much better if close relatives were still alive.

3) There is a need for giving meaning to one's own life in old age. Processes of life review become more frequent when people realize that there is not much time left. In processes of life review experiences of discrimination, persecution, and deportation become salient and cannot be ignored or denied.

4) The balance of long-term memory and short-term memory changes with increasing age. In old age processes of long-term memory are more important. A reappearance of traumatic memories might be a consequence of this development.

In interpreting our results it should be considered that participant's reports on intensity in different stages of post-Holocaust development are *retrospective*. For this reason it might be argued, that our data are not valid for assessing *questions of development*. Maybe they simply reflect an actual impression of change that is highly influenced by errors in memory and psychodynamic (partly "unconscious") motives and needs. Obviously we have no opportunity to compare participants' ratings with "objective" data. However, ratings for the last stage of post-Holocaust development do not reflect personal reconstruction. At least our data confirm *that the actual intensity of traumatic Holocaust reminiscence is extremely high*, and therefore discrimination, persecution, and deportation suffered in the past are an integral part of the present life situation in (former) Jewish emigrants and extermination camp survivors.

Further analysis of our data show that ratings of intensity of traumatic experiences in Jewish extermination camp survivors are systematically higher than in (former) Jewish emigrants. We attribute this difference to the generally much greater threat to people belonging to the former subsample.

Coping with Memories of Traumatic Experiences

Subjects' coping efforts with reminiscence of traumatic experiences are a dominant concern of our research project. Our approach to this topic is based on a taxonomy of possible individual reactions to challenging situations and stress developed by Hans Thomae which inspired numerous empirical studies in psychological and gerontological research since the early 1960s (for a detailed description, see Kruse, 1987b; Kruse & Lehr, 1989; Thomae, 1996; Thomae & Lehr, 1986). In this taxonomy 20 alternative coping techniques are distin-

---

Table 3. Patterns of coping with reminiscence of traumatic experiences.

I. Efforts to maintain a positive approach to life (n = 80)

Dominant techniques:
* Positive interpretation of personal development and achievements,
* Objective achievement in the form of adaptation to the concrete requirements and tasks of the current life situation,
* Acceptance of the situation in the sense of the resolution of previous traumatic experiences

II. Efforts to subordinate own situation and to deal more intensely with the development of own children (n = 47)

Dominant techniques:
* Identification with the aims and fates of others, particularly own children,
* Subordination of own needs by refraining from bringing up their personal history in conversations with other people

III. Experience of joint responsibility (n = 61)

Dominant techniques:
* Establishment and maintenance of social contacts, particularly of people from the following generations,
* Hope relating primarily to the responsibility of subsequent generations for tolerance,
* Objective achievement in the form of a desire for communication with people from the following generations

IV. Depression, bemoaning one's fate, withdrawal from other people (n = 39)

Dominant techniques:
* Depression,
* Bemoaning one's fate,
* Search for help from other people

V. Efforts to avoid memories of previous events under all circumstances (n = 21)

Dominant techniques:
* Evasive reaction,
* Objective achievement in the form of adaptation to the concrete requirements and tasks of the current life situation,
* Establishment and maintenance of social contacts solely with people who do not remind one of one's previous fate

guished. In analyzing the transcriptions of the 248 interviews each of these techniques was rated independently by two psychologists on a 5-point rating scale (interraterreliability: Kendall's $\tau = .87$). In a second step a cluster analysis (Ward) was calculated to identify more global, trans-situational valid patterns of coping which differentiate between subgroups of our study participants (for a more detailed description see Kruse & Schmitt, 1995). As a result of this analysis, five dominant coping patterns could be distinguished. These coping patterns are described below.

Only about a quarter of the people interviewed (see coping patterns 4 and 5) reacted with depression and bemoaning their fate to the stressful events or attempted to escape these memories. In about one third (see coping method 1), the attempt to accept one's personal life history – despite the traumatic events – and to find a positive approach to the current situation and the future on this basis was a dominant feature.

108 of the interviewees were intensely concerned with the fate of the subsequent generation (see coping pattern 2) or sought opportunities for involvement in relationships with members of the following generations (see coping pattern 3). It is apparent from the characterization of this third coping method that the processing of stressful events can also find expression in an experience of joint responsibility for the future of a society and a culture. In view of the fact that during the course of their life the subjects had suffered in some cases extreme injuries, social involvement is a remarkable form of personally creative and socially constructive coping.

If, as characteristics of "successful processing," one adopts (a) cognitive restructuring in the form of greater accentuation of positively viewed experiences in the past and present, but above all (b) a high degree of involvement in relationships with other people, the great majority of subjects had to a certain extent been able to process the traumas they had suffered. Those coping methods for which the above characteristics constitute the core occurred most frequently in the sample.

Once again it should be pointed out here that involvement with other people, particularly for the subsequent generations, was especially apparent in Israel. As mentioned elsewhere (Kruse & Schmitt, 1995), we interpret this finding again as a sign of a more intense public exposure with the period of German National Socialist Germany. This exposure is far less intense in Germany which reduces the possibilities of personal processing.

Psychological Requirements on Conversations and Intense Memories of Traumatic Events

One of the great fears which the subjects mentioned spontaneously concerns the denial of the discrimination to which they were exposed. They also expressed the concern that other people were indifferent to their story. The first requirement of conversations may be deduced from these fears and concerns: this relates to the openness and sensitivity to the particular history and the resultant psychological vulnerability of these people. It was apparent in all the interviews that the interviewees attempted first of all to assess the extent to which the members of our research team were capable and prepared to approach the statements about their personal history sympathetically. Most people have experienced situations in which others have behaved "indifferently" to their remarks about their personal history. In addition, they complained of the lack of sensitivity of these people to their uncertainties in contact with others and to their fears of social discrimination. This indifference which they experienced has a highly hurtful and disconcerting effect.

The fact that memories of past traumas in many people increase in intensity with age points to the need for these people to find the opportunity to speak with others about these memories. It should also be borne in mind that in the last few years many have lost close acquaintances who themselves either suffered persecution or had developed a high degree of sensitivity to the psychological situation of refugees: the social network has shrunk. The mere fact of no longer being able to speak about their memories with other people contributes to the increasing intensity of these memories.

> *"When there is no longer anyone who knows everything that happened to me, who takes me just as I am, what went before now becomes all the stronger and I can no longer protect myself against memories of before. That happens particularly in the evening. Then the experiences are there once more and I can't do anything about it. There is no-one there any more to whom I can say it. Just think how helpless you then become."*

Two things are apparent from these comments by a 79-year-old woman in the United States: Firstly, the fact that memories of traumas which one has experienced also occur with great intensity in old age, "suddenly stand before one" – a comment which was made in a similar way by most of the interviewees; and, secondly, the fact that the loss of close acquaintances considerably reduces the possibilities of being able to protect oneself at least a little from the effects of these memories. This produces the need to provide (former) Jewish emigrants and extermination camp survivors with new opportunities for conversation to relieve their stress. Another reason for the great readiness of many persecuted people to talk about their personal situation in our study lies also in the need to communicate memories of suffered traumas; at the end of the interview, all the interviewees emphasized that the discussion about their personal history had been a help to them in their current attempt to cope with their memories. As these memories constantly recur, the subjects are in need of continuous opportunities for conversation.

An important question which arose in the conversations concerns the expression of the traumatic experiences. If it is said that many took up the opportunity of talking about their stressful memories, this does not imply any comment about the "depth" of the conversations: how far can one go in these conversations, which experiences should one try to have expressed and which not? It became apparent in the interviews that all the subjects were confronted with experiences which they did not wish to discuss and the expression of which was associated with major trauma.

In extermination camp survivors in particular we felt the desire not to have to talk about highly traumatic experiences. Even if they mentioned experiences which still had an effect into old age, they did not go into individual experiences in detail. According to the comments of the study participants, the reason for this lies in the urge to protect themselves to at least some extent from the highly traumatic experiences and their aftereffects. Thus, in the conversations one gains no more than a vague impression of the terrible experiences that confronted them. Only occasionally did we come upon a detailed description of these experiences. If we summarize our findings from the interviews, it may be said that these people would not have been served by a detailed description; in fact just the experience of being able to indicate to another human being what one has experienced has a relieving effect. (It should also be borne in mind here that these experiences are almost incapable of being expressed in words.)

The same applies to the group of (former) Jewish emigrants: among these too we constantly came up against stages in their reported life story which they could not and would not describe in detail. Sensitivity to the "depth" of the conversations permitted by the subjects is a precondition for these conversations to be seen as providing relief.

We observed that in many of the people whom we asked to participate in the study there was a recognizable readiness to speak about the course of their life and their personal situation. We had attributed this readiness to their desire to relieve the severe psychological pressure associated with the memories of the traumas they had experienced by conversations with other people. However, this is to mention only one reason for their readiness – and it is not the essential reason. The crucial reason for participating according to the interviewees lies in the fact that they wanted to warn the following generations to take particular care against all forms of political radicalism and against all forms of discrimination along the way.

"Why I am telling you this, why I am spending so much time with you, why I am talking about the terrible things from the past? It is good that I can see that there is someone who is interested in what used to be. But there are other things that are also important. Beware of bad political developments. Perhaps it will happen again. And if you have learnt now – I can use that word, can't I – if you have learnt where it all can lead, then good. Then there has also been a meaning to the conversation."

This comment by a 77-year-old woman in Israel points clearly to the "warning" aspect. It is apparent from this statement what many see as a significant task: communicating the traumas they have experienced with the aim of making the subsequent generations particularly aware of radical political currents and the risk of discrimination.

References

Baeyer, W.v., Häfner, H., & Kisker, H.P. (1964). *Psychiatrie der Verfolgten* [Psychiatry of the victims of persecution]. Heidelberg: Springer.

Berger, L. (1983). A psychological perspective of the Holocaust: Is mass murder part of human behavior? In R. L. Braham (Ed.), *Perspectives on the Holocaust*. Dordrecht: Kluwer-Nijhoff Publishing.

Betten, A., & Du-nor, M. (1996). *Wir sind die Letzten. Fragt uns aus. Gespräche mit den Emigranten der dreißiger Jahre in Israel* [We are the last ones. Ask us. Discourses with emigrants of the 30's in Israel]. Gerlingen: Bleicher Verlag.

Brainin, E., Ligeti, V., & Teicher, S. (1994). Die Zeit heilt keine Wunden. Pathologie zweier Generationen oder Pathologie der Wirklichkeit? [Time does not heal wounds. Pathology of two generations or pathology of reality?] In J. Wiesse & E. Olbrich (Eds.), *Ein Ast bei Nacht kein Ast: seelische Folgen der Menschenvernichtung für Kinder und Kindeskinder* [A bough in the night no bough: Psychological consequences of mass murder in children and grandchildren] (pp. 21–51). Göttingen: Vandenhoeck & Ruprecht.

Butler, R.N. (1963). The life review: An interpretation of reminiscence in the aged. *Psychiatry, 26*, 65–76.

Coleman, P.G. (1997). Erinnerung und Lebensrückblick im höheren Lebensalter [Reminiscence and life review in old age]. *Zeitschrift für Gerontologie und Geriatrie, 30*, 362–367.

Eitinger, L. (1990). KZ-Haft und psychische Traumatisierung [Imprisonment in concentration camps and mental traumatization]. *Psyche, 2*, 118–132.

Fleischmann, L. (1981). *Dies ist nicht mein Land. Eine Jüdin verläßt die Bundesrepublik* [This is not my country. A Jewish woman leaves the Federal Republic of Germany]. Hamburg: Heine.

Friedmann, P. (1948). Some aspects of concentration camp psychology. *American Journal of Psychiatry, 105*, 601–605.

Haight, B.K. (1991). Reminiscing: The state of the art as a basis for praxis. *International Journal of Ageing and Human Development, 33*, 1–32.

Heenen-Wolff, S. (1992). *Im Haus des Henkers. Gespräche in Deutschland* [In the house of the hangman. Discourses in Germany]. Frankfurt/Main: Dvorah Verlag.

Jacobmeyer, W. (1992). Ortlos am Ende des Grauens: "Displaced Persons" in der Nachkriegszeit [No where to go at the end of horror: "Displaced Persons" in post-war Germany]. In W. Bade (Ed.), *Deutsche im Ausland – Fremde in Deutschland. Migration in Geschichte und Gegenwart* [Germans in foreign countries – foreigners in Germany. Migration in past and present]. München: Beck.

Kruse, A. (1987a). Biographische Methode und Exploration [Biographical method and exploration]. In G. Jüttemann & H. Thomae (Eds.), *Biographie und Psychologie* [Biography and psychology] (pp. 119–137). Heidelberg: Springer.

Kruse, A. (1987b). Coping with chronic disease, dying, and death. *Comprehensive Gerontology, 1,* 1–11.

Kruse, A., & Lehr, U. (1989). Longitudinal analysis of the developmental processes in chronically ill and healthy persons. Empirical findings from the Bonn Longitudinal Study on Aging. *International Psychogeriatrics, 1,* 73–86.

Kruse, A., & Schmitt, E. (in press). Halbstrukturiertes Interview [Semi-structured interview]. In G. Jüttemann (Ed.), *Biographie und Psychologie* [Biography and psychology]. Berlin: Springer-Verlag.

Kruse, A., & Schmitt, E. (1995). Wurden die in der Lagerhaft erlittenen Traumatisierungen wirklich verarbeitet? Ergebnisse aus einem Forschungsprojekt zu psychischen Nachwirkungen des Holocaust [Did people succeed in coping with trauma suffered in extermination camps? Results from a research project on psychological consequences of the holocaust]. In G. Heuft, A. Kruse, H.G. Nehen, & H. Radebold (Eds.), *Interdisziplinäre Gerontopsychosomatik* [Interdisciplinary gerontopsychosomatics] (pp. 31–42). München: MMV Medizin Verlag.

Kruse, A., & Schmitt, E. (1994). Rückkehr nach Deutschland – persönliche Motive und Merkmale des subjektiven Lebensraums jüdischer Emigranten [Returning to Germany – personal motives and aspects of subjective living space of Jewish emigrants]. *Zeitschrift für Gerontologie, 27,* 129–139.

Krystal, H., & Niederland, W. (1971). *Psychic traumatization.* Boston: Little Brown.

Krystal, H., & Niederland, W. (1968). Clinical observations on the survivor syndrome. In H. Krystal (Ed.), *Massive psychic trauma* (pp. 327–348). New York: International Universities Press.

Lacina, E. (1982). *Emigration. Sozialhistorische Darstellung der deutschsprachigen Emigration und einiger ihrer Asylländer aufgrund ausgewählter Selbstzeugnisse* [Emigration. Portrayal of the social history of the German-speaking emigration and some destination countries on the basis of selected self-reports]. Stuttgart: Quell-Verlag.

Leon, G.R., Butcher, J.N., Klanmon, M., Goldberg, A., & Almager, M. (1982). Survivors of the Holocaust and their children: current status and adjustment. *Journal of Personality and Social Psychology, 41,* 503–516.

Luel, S., & Marcus, P. (Eds.). (1984). *Psychoanalytic reflexions on the Holocaust.* New York: Springer.

Matussek, P. (1971). *Die Konzentrationslagerhaft und ihre Folgen* [Imprisonment in concentration camps and its consequences]. Heidelberg: Springer.

Niederland, W. (1980). *Folgen der Verfolgung. Das Überlebenden-Syndrom* [Consequences of persecution. The survivor syndrom]. Frankfurt/Main: Suhrkamp.

Porter, J.N. (1981). Is there a survivor syndrom? Psychological and socio-political implications. *Journal of Personality and Judaism, 6*(1), 33–52.

Rosenberg, A. (1983). The philosophical implications of the Holocaust. In R.L. Braham (Ed.), *Perspectives on the Holocaust* (pp. 1–18). Dordrecht: Kluwer-Nijhoff.

Rustin, S.L. (1983). The post-Holocaust generations: A psychological perspective. In R.L. Braham (Ed.), *Perspectives on the Holocaust* (pp. 33–40). Dordrecht: Kluwer-Nijhoff.

Schmitt, E., Kruse, A. (1998). Die Gegenwart des Holocaust im Erleben zurückgekehrter jüdischer Emigranten [The importance of the Holocaust in former Jewish emigrant's perceptions of present life situation in Germany]. In A. Kruse (Ed.), *Psychosoziale Gerontologie. Band 1. Grundlagen* [Psychosocial gerontology. Vol. 1. Basics] (pp. 276–298). Göttingen: Hogrefe.

Sofsky, W. (1993). *Die Ordnung des Terrors: Das Konzentrationslager* [The order of terror. The concentration camp]. Frankfurt/Main: Fischer.

Strauss, H.A., & Röder, W. (1980–1983). *International biographical dictionary of Central European emigres. 1933–1945*. München: Saur Verlag.

Thomae, H. (1996). *Das Individuum und seine Welt* [The individual and his world]. Göttingen: Hogrefe.

Thomae, H., Lehr, U. (1986). Stages, crisis, and life-span development. In A.B. Sorensen, F.E. Weinert, & L.R. Sherrod (Eds.), *Human development and the life course* (pp. 429–444). Hillsdale, NJ: Erlbaum.

Thornton, S., Brotchie, L. (1987). Reminiscence: A critical review of the empirical literature. *British Journal of Clinical Psychology, 26*, 93–111.

Undeutsch, U. (1983). Exploration. In H. Feger & J. Bredenkamp (Eds.), *Datenerhebung. Enzyklopädie der Psychologie, 1* [Data selection. Encyclopedia of Psychology] (pp. 321–361). Göttingen: Hogrefe.

Zertal, I. (1989). Verlorene Seelen. Die jüdischen DP's und die israelische Staatsführung. Babylon. *Beiträge zur jüdischen Gegenwart.* [Lost souls. The Jewish DP's and the Israeli government.] *Babylon, 5.* Frankfurt/Main: Verlag Neue Kritik.

Victimization in Old Age: Consequences for Mental Health and Protective Conditions*

Daniela Hosser and Werner Greve

As people age, many of them feel that the quality of their lives is threatened by losses and crises and the subjective result comparing gains and losses becomes increasingly unfavorable (Heckhausen, Dixon, & Baltes, 1987). In the field of criminology above all the high fear of crime and greater vulnerabilities are considered a handicap accompanied with age (see for example Fattah & Sacco, 1989; Kawelowski, 1985). On the other hand, a large number of results indicates that the subjective well-being of old people is not threatened in general. Recent research in developmental psychology has convincingly shown that adaptive resources of the aging self normally enables a stable well-being and a stable, positive self-image well into old age when health, psychic and social crises become increasingly more likely (Baltes & Baltes, 1990; Brandtstädter & Greve, 1994; Brandtstädter, Wentura, & Greve, 1993; Staudinger, Marsiske, & P. Baltes, 1994). For example people obviously maintain, in relevant areas of life, the feeling of being in control well into old age (M. Baltes & Silberberg, 1994; Brandtstädter & Rothermund, 1994). Resources and capacities of resilience in old age, especially greater experience in dealing with crisis and illness (Eysenck, 1983), are considered the reason why elderly people face even unexpected crises and traumatic experiences in a competent manner (Norris & Murrell, 1988; Norris, Phifer, & Kaniasty, 1994; Ursano & McCarroll, 1994).

However, experiences of real violence and criminal victimization of elderly people as well as their fear of such have rarely been discussed from a geronto-psychological point of view apart from occasional remarks in textbooks or some specialist papers (e. g., Cutler, 1987; Doyle, 1990; Fattah & Sacco, 1989; Norris, 1992). Furthermore, though this subject has been investigated from a criminological perspective for some time (Aday, 1988), a systematic connec-

* The data discussed in this paper were obtained in a large research project supported by two grants from the German Federal Ministry for Family, Seniors, Women, and Youth (BMFSFJ). For valuable help with the translation we would like to thank Ute Amaning.

tion between gerontological theories and results of criminological research still has to be drawn in this field (Greve & Niederfranke, 1998; Yin, 1985).

However, there are good reasons to take the threat of violence and crime in old age seriously. Elderly people, due to their vulnerability, are subjectively and objectively threatened in a special way. In particular, reduced physical resistance and vulnerability in old age as well as an increased multimorbidity (e. g., Steinhagen-Thiessen & Borchelt, 1993) forces the danger at least of all those offences that result in physical injury and damage to health (Eve, 1985; Yin, 1980, 1985). Even smaller injuries can, in elderly people, lead to serious damage or cause increased strain and distress because the process of recovering and healing is delayed and more difficult (Smith, Enderson, & Maull, 1990). In addition, a longer lasting loss of bodily functions, for example, fractures, can be accompanied by loss of autonomy and dependence on the care of others (Killias, 1990). Furthermore, it is probable that as a result of losses due to age related losses of the sensory system, a corresponding injury is experienced as an additional handicap and therefore experienced as a greater burden. Furthermore, many losses or injuries in old age are experienced as being a threat due to the fact that the time available for compensation or healing becomes increasingly shorter and the thought of many changes as remaining permanent becomes a dominant perspective (Brandstädter & Wentura, 1994). In addition, in old age the social net is diminished which reduces the potential for social support (Arling, 1987; Vaux, 1985).

Additionally, the strain put on elderly people by crime and violence is a current topic from a criminal policy perspective, not least because the elderly become an increasingly relevant section of the population. In the Federal Republic of Germany, the number of people aged sixty years and over is rising steadily. At the moment they make up about 22%, in the year 2010 they could, according to actual projections, amount to 37% (Höhn & Roloff, 1994, p. 50). Nevertheless, exact figures and information regarding the volume of the threat of violence in old age are missing. All the more a closer analysis of psychic and social consequences of criminal victimization – and the fear of such – in old age is still needed.

In this chapter we discuss the psychic consequences of criminal victimization in old age by means of data from a representative victimization survey in Germany. First, the extent of criminal victimization of old people is described. Second the psychic consequences of victimization (especially with respect to depressiveness and fear of crime) are discussed. Third, the (moderating) influence of coping resources and social support is investigated. Finally, conclusions for future research and intervention are outlined.

The results presented in the following are based on a victim survey in the Federal Republic of Germany carried out by the *Criminological Research In-*

stitute of Lower Saxony (KFN) in 1992 on behalf of the Federal Ministry for Family and Senior Citizens. In this study a representative sample of 15,771 persons in the old and new Federal States was obtained by means of a personal verbal interview. Priority was given to personal experience of victimization (a total of 16 types of offences was included) and the feeling of personal safety (for general results, see e. g., Bilsky & Wetzels, 1993, 1994; Wetzels et al., 1995). A systematic oversampling of elderly persons (over 60 years of age) takes into account the special questioning of strain caused by crime in old age (for details of the procedure and the description of sampling see Bilsky, Pfeiffer, & Wetzels, 1993; Wetzels et al., 1995). However, due to a modular fashion of the questionnaire, information concerning the psychic consequences of and coping with victimization are available only for part of the sampling. This implies varied and in all cases considerably lower case numbers (degrees of freedom).

Victimization Experience of Elderly Persons: Empirical Size of the Problem

In the early seventies, with reference mainly to the increase of vulnerability with age, criminologists had suspected that elderly people were especially affected by crime. However, it soon began to emerge that, compared to younger people, they become victims of crime less frequently (Yin, 1985; for a short review see Fattah & Sacco, 1989). This has been shown consistently over a long period in official statistics (with respect to the FRG see Ahlf, 1994; Kawelowski, 1995). Even data from victimization surveys which allow to estimate parts of the dark figure of crime beyond the crimes registered by the police show that the prevalence rates for almost all crimes with personal victims are falling considerably with age (Table 1; see Wetzels et al., 1995). Official statistics currently obtainable indicate that even the notorious exception of purse snatching has a falling tendency (Pfeiffer, Brettfeld, & Delzer, 1997).

However, this perspective for the estimate of victimization experience of elderly persons falls short for at least three reasons. The scope of perspective with respect to the temporal horizon as well as to the types of offences taken into account could prove to be too restricted. In addition, it is very important – especially with respect to older people – not to exclude indirect victims.

The Temporal Scope of Examination: The Problem of Life-Span Prevalence Rates

Calculating the risk of criminal victimization relating to short reference periods ignores the fact that elderly people were more likely to have ever made

Table 1. Prevalence (victims per 1,000 interviewees) and incidence rates (victimizations per 1,000 interviewees) in a five-year period (1987–1991) for younger and elderly people (for former West Germany; see Wetzels et al., 1995, p. 54f.).

age cohort	offence	preva-lence	inci-dence	offence	preva-lence	inci-dence
<60 yr.	break-in residence	40.7	46.9	theft of handbag	25.0	29.9
≥60 yr.		34.7	39.9		35.4	38.8
<60 yr.	break-in other	79.5	93.9	other robbery	21.1	25.5
≥60 yr.		77.7	97.7		12.4	13.8
<60 yr.	car theft	23.2	25.8	assault w/weapon	19.5	32.2
≥60 yr.		9.6	10.4		4.5	7.9
<60 yr.	theft from car	157.9	204.5	assault w/o weapon	52.6	121.0
≥60 yr.		73.3	90.1		8.8	16.5
<60 yr.	wilful damage of car	192.7	257.6	threat/coercion	30.4	58.0
≥60 yr.		95.5	122.2		15.2	20.0
<60 yr.	theft of motorcycle	20.6	22.8	sexual harassment	79.1	231.1
≥60 yr.		12.2	17.8		10.3	26.6
<60 yr.	theft of bicycle	177.4	234.4	rape/sexual assault	13.7	50.6
≥60 yr.		67.8	86.9		1.7	3.1
<60 yr.	other theft	109.7	156.4	fraud	61.8	113.1
≥60 yr.		81.9	138.2		46.9	64.7

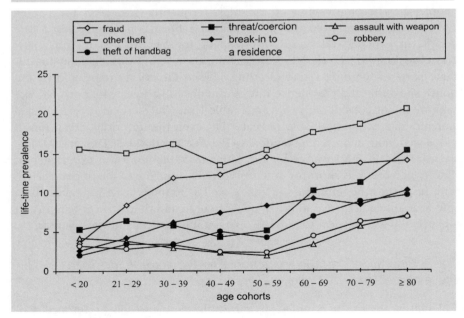

Figure 1. Life-span prevalence of threatening areas of crime.

victimization experiences during the total course of their lives. *Ceteris paribus*, the victimization risk rises with age. In fact, this has been corroborated in the KFN Survey. In areas of crime relevant to threats, i. e., burglary, robbery or bodily harm the rate of life-span prevalence increases through the age groups. For example people of the age of eighty state twice as often as twenty-year-olds, that they have become victims of a burglary (Figure 1, see Greve, Hosser, & Wetzels, 1996).

However, the argument of a life-span prevalence increasing with age is rather complex. For example, its plausibility differs for various areas of crime. In contrast to burglary, the probability to become the victim of rape is, beyond a certain age, of little significance. Rather, in this case the victimization risk concentrates on the stage of life of young and middle-aged adulthood. Secondly, as longitudinal studies are lacking, it has to be considered that historical effects can present a distorted picture of some of the crimes. It can be assumed that a war generation does not only connote violent crimes in a different way, but has different probabilities of experience at their disposal. On the other hand one has to take into account the increasing effects of forgetting due to the decline of memory capabilities in old age. As a consequence, retrospective estimation may tend to underestimate incidents rates of crime, especially with respect to more frequent but less threatening offences (a simple theft, especially if several have been experienced in a life-span, is more easily forgotten than serious bodily harm) (see Norris, 1992).

Empirical invalidity of this kind affects the validity of general estimates of psychological consequences of experiences of crime victims. The consequences of possible distortions, however, depend mainly on the effects of such experience on the process of coping with victimization at a later date. If the process of coping with criminal victimization would become *easier* with increasing experience of crime, for example because one can look back on to a successful adaptation to such an event and therefore acquired strategies to solve problems are already available, then an under-estimate of prevalence and incidence rates would imply an *over*-estimate of capabilities of coping of "inexperienced" victims (and, accordingly, an *under*-estimate of consequences of victimization). If, however, repeated victimization experience has a traumatic effect (e. g., if coping subjectively fails), and if prevalence rates are fixed at a level that is too low, this would result in an *over*-estimate of the consequences of "actual" victimization experience. The danger of a misinterpretation of life-time related victimization rises with age for the reasons mentioned which makes the demand for research from life-span perspective even more urgent.

Shifting the Risk: Dark Figures of Violence Within the Family

Furthermore, the relatively low strain on elderly people as victims of "public" violence must not be taken as an all-clear. On the contrary, there is reason to fear that a part of the experience of violence and victimization simply drifts into a different context, i. e., in the area of close social relationships. The social withdrawal of older people into the social, especially intrafamily proximity may reduce the risk of victimization in public. However, it also increases the probability of conflicts in the social and intrafamily milieu. Unfortunately, little is still known about the risk of what happens behind these closed doors. In particular, the violent results of the escalation of such conflicts, especially in the area of private and professional care, are seldom recorded in the crime statistics of the police. There is reason to assume that this lies not only in the lack of willingness to report crimes on behalf of the victims. Additionally, intra- and interpersonal dynamics support this tendency which is shown in the fact that, up until the recent past, this area was also hardly noted by criminological research of criminal dark figures. Apart from the fact that shame, consideration towards others or fear are a hindrance to the readiness of giving information even outside the police station, in this case an often very variable categorization of corresponding experiences plays a part. A violation from one's partner is not considered as "assault," neither is being locked into a room regarded as "restriction of personal freedom." Moreover it is necessary to distinguish between different forms (chronic or episodic) violence (Estman, 1991), which reach from neglect to abuse and can include psychic mal-treatment (verbal abuse, intimidation or threats) and other forms of aggression which are less obvious (e. g., financial exploitation). Family violence remains to a major part in a "double dark field" (Wetzels, 1993; see Glendenning, 1993; Pillemer, 1993; Pillemer & Finkelhor, 1988; Pillemer & Suitor, 1992; Pillemer & Wolf, 1986; Wolf, 1992; for Germany: Wetzels et al., 1995; Wetzels & Greve, 1995).

These problems of social threshold and subjective perception and categorization make an exact estimate of the size of this problem area considerably more difficult. An additional survey with a written questionnaire carried out with part sampling of the KFN Survey, shows that the area of experience of violence within close social relationships is important. By carefully ensuring the anonymity of the questionnaire ("drop-off"; "sealed envelope technique"; Wetzels et al., 1995) and explicitly asking for specific ways of behavior in the close social network, the total prevalence rate of victims of bodily harm rises as opposed to the personal verbal interview to a four-fold figure (from 4.2% to 15.6% with reference to a five-year period of reference; Wetzels et al., 1995, p. 180). Regarding the group of 60- to 75-year-old persons living independently in private households, it is known that, even though the absolute frequency of corresponding experience of violence is lower than that of very young persons, the *relative* share rises with age (Greve, Hosser, & Wetzels, 1996). On the basis of these data it can be estimated (conservatively) that in the Federal Republic of Germany in the year 1991 340,000 persons aged between 60 and 70 years have, at least once, been the victim of physical violence within close social relationships or the family, whereby in more than half the cases (ca. 172,000) serious forms of violence were reported (see Wetzels & Greve, 1996). Moreover about two thirds of the cases are cases of repeated victimization which will have especially serious psychic consequences for the victims (Wetzels et al., 1995, p. 178).

Indirect Victims: The Scope of Threat

However, the threat by violence and criminality reaches obviously beyond personal victimization. Especially with reference to possible reactions to stress, also indirect or vicarious victims have to be taken into account, i. e., persons who have either become witnesses of violence or whose family members or close acquaintances have become victims. Results of the KFN Survey show for example, that although "only" 6% of the over 60s became direct victims of crime with personal contact (1987–1991), the part of indirect victims (family members or close acquaintance becoming victim of a corresponding crime during the same period) in this age group amounted to 38.2%.

This aspect is important for two reasons. First, indirect victims can be restricted in their well-being at a comparable level; accordingly these experiences are included in the criteria of diagnosis of posttraumatic stress disorder (Kilpatrick & Resnick, 1993; Saigh, 1995). Even in less serious cases, the confidence of the members of the social network can be shaken by doubts and fears to an extent that fears of personal safety arise. Figley (1985) speaks of "infection" of the related person with the negative results of victimization. In addition, the worry for the well-being of the victim is a considerable stress factor which can have negative effects on the psychic health of the indirect victim. This in turn can result in the total loss or restricted availability of some source of support for the direct victim. It can be assumed that this has a special negative effect on old people, who are increasingly dependent on help and support (Figley & Kleber, 1996; Harris, 1991; Sorenson & Golding, 1990).

Second, the discussion of criminologists concerning the threat of crime in old age has centered less around experiences of crime victims but rather around the problem of fear of crime in elderly people. Since the first studies in this area, the result has been replicated several times, that elderly people, in spite of their objectively relatively low risk of victimization in a public context, are more afraid of crime than younger people. Already in 1976 Clemente and

Kleimann wrote, in a much cited paper, that for elderly people apparently fear of crime poses a greater problem than crime itself. In fact, this so-called "fear–victimization paradox" can be considered being almost *common sense* in criminology (Fattah & Sacco, 1989; Hale, 1996, Yin, 1985). A closer look reveals, however, that several basic points of this claim cannot be maintained; relating to both their empirical basis as well as their theoretical coherence (Greve, 1997; see also Eve, 1985; Ferraro & LaGrange, 1992). Recent data especially prove that if fear of crime is recorded in a more differentiated manner, only behavioral indicators show an increase of fear related to age (Greve, 1997; Greve, Hosser, & Wetzels, 1996; see Frieze, Hymer, & Greenberg, 1987). With respect to affective or cognitive aspects of fear, however, elderly people do not differ significantly from younger ones. The fact that elderly people behave more cautiously, however, is based on a number of factors. Increased vulnerability certainly explains cautious behavior, but also a general tendency of social withdrawal in old age, reduced mobility and increased morbidity of elderly people, as mentioned above, are likely to play an important role. From this follows that a more differently assessed fear of crime, taking into account behavioral aspects as well as cognitive and affective facets of fear, should gain importance as an indicator of unusual grades of threat and stress and as an indication of deficits of coping in elderly people.

Psychological Consequences of Victimization in Old Age

Now, what are the consequences if elderly people, despite an objectively reduced risk of victimization (in public areas) and increased cautions, become victims of criminal victimization? The vulnerability of elderly people mentioned makes it plausible that the psychic consequences of victimization have, especially in this age group, objectively and subjectively, a stronger effect on quality of life, physical and psychic well-being. On the other hand, however, it has to be considered that resources and capacities typical at that age can support the process of coping with victimization, part of this is the increased experience of life which can facilitate the handling of crisis and reduce the suffering and losses resulting from it.

In the following, results of the KFN Victim Survey are described which relate to the area of public crime. However, two points restricting the interpretation have to be made in advance. First, the reduced availability of psychological and especially clinical indicators has to be pointed out. This results from the fact that originally a criminological purpose governed the survey. As a consequence, the information available therefore leaves a lot to be desired from a gerontological and clinical-psychological point of view. Secondly, the results shown refer exclusively to cross-sectional data. Therefore the interpretations offered cannot be covered against cohort effects.

Indicators of Psychic Stress

The psychic consequences of experiences of crime victims are various. Apart from posttraumatic stress disorder (PTSD), anxieties, depression, fear of crime as well as somatic disorders, substance abuse and social withdrawal are observed (Kilpatrick et al., 1985; Saigh, 1995; Sorenson & Golding, 1990). Depression and fear of crime as examples of the more frequent and long-lasting consequences (Frieze, Hymer, & Greenberg, 1987; Meichenbaum, 1994; Norris & Kaniasty, 1994), are considered in the following as indicators (general and more specific crime-related) of the psychic well-being.

Depressiveness

Because of the lack of a clinical scale in the survey questionnaire a scale "depressiveness" (Table 2) was constructed from 7 items of a scale of trait-anxiety (STAI; Laux et al., 1981). Based on the criteria of content validity the collection of items chosen can reasonably be regarded a scale of depressiveness (the internal consistency of this scale is satisfactory: Cronbach's $\alpha = .81$). Also based on criteria on convergent validity this indicator may be viewed as valid. The correlation with loneliness (UCLA-loneliness scale: Russel, Peplau, & Cutrona, 1980; see Bilsky, Pfeiffer, & Wetzels, 1992) is significant and practically important ($r = .57, p < .01$). Accordingly, the correlation with actual well-being (single-item measure: "How satisfied with your life are you currently?"; seven-point-rating-scale) is significant ($r = -.55; p < .01$). Also the correlation with the age variable, as expected (see Brandtstädter, Wentura, & Greve, 1993), is not very high, but still significant ($r = .18, p < .05$).

Item		Item-Total-Corr.
(A)	I think that I am worse off than other people	.59
(B)	I am happy [–]	.58
(C)	I tend to take things harder	.57
(D)	I feel safe [–]	.57
(F)	I am satisfied [–]	.61
(G)	Unimportant thoughts inflict my mind and are weighing me	.48
(H)	I take disappointments hard in a way that I cannot forget them	.48

Table 2. Depressiveness scale: Items and consistencies.

Cronbach's $\alpha = .81$

Fear of Crime

Methodical and theoretical criticism towards usual ways of assessing fear of crime in the field of criminology (Eve, 1985; Ferraro & LaGrange, 1992; Greve, 1997) indicates a need to construct an indicator for fear of crime following a component approach, taking into account affective, cognitive, and behavioral facets of fear (Greve, 1997; Greve, Hosser, & Wetzels, 1996). In the KFN Survey, each of these aspects was assessed separately. The affective facet ("How often are you afraid that you could be …?") as well as the cognitive aspect of fear ("How probable you think it is that … will happen to you within the next 12 months?") are questioned with reference to four areas of crime (being burgled, being beaten and injured, being mugged and robbed, being sexually assaulted or raped). Concerning the behavioral aspect of fear, the frequency of a total of eight types of behavior was questioned (e. g., avoid certain places or streets; carry something to defend oneself; get out of the way of strangers, if possible, etc.) All three scales show a satisfactory internal consistency (cog: $\alpha = .83$; aff: $\alpha = .84$; beh: $\alpha = .85$) The z-standardized sum scores were added up to a total score "fear of crime." The data show that the often reported age-related increase of fear of crime could not be replicated without restrictions. The correlation with the age variable is significant ($r = .12$, $p < .05$), but with an amount of two percent variance explained not practically important. Furthermore, comparison of means for eight age cohorts (10-year intervals) clearly show stability of fear of crime beyond an age of 60 years and even a falling tendency beyond 70 (Greve, Hosser, & Wetzels, 1996, p. 60 ff.).

Suspicion and Fright

Finally, consequences of the most serious criminal victimization reported by the participant were assessed using a questionnaire of eight items combined into two subscales (see Wetzels et al., 1995, p. 105 f.): (a) suspicion and fright (5 items, Cronbach's $\alpha = .74$) and (b) (loss of) self confidence (3 items, Cronbach's $\alpha = .79$).

Relationships Between Victimization and Well-Being

Using multiple regression analysis the findings reveal that with respect to a reference period of one year (1991) victimization (across all areas of crime questioned) is accompanied with a significant higher level of depressiveness and fear of crime (Table 3). Elderly people show a lower level of well-being in general.

Table 3. Multiple regression on depressiveness and fear of crime.

	depressiveness		fear of crime	
	β	p	β	p
age	.19	p < .001	.13	p < .001
victimization[1]	.04	p < .001	.12	p < .001
age * victimization	−.09	p < .01	−.06	p > .05
R²	.04		.03	

[1] 0 = nonvictim, 1 = victim

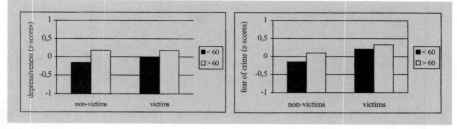

Figure 2. Depressiveness and fear of crime relating to age and victim experience (1991).

Hence, if interaction effects between age and victimization were not considered, this could result in an overestimation of the psychic consequences of victimization in age (Figure 2).

Therefore, in addition to the main effects the interaction term (product term: age * victimization) is introduced in the model in the final step to test the moderating effects of age. The product term reaches significance with respect to depressiveness. One-way ANOVA also shows that in the group of the elderly (60 years and over) there are no differences between victims and nonvictims whereas depressiveness is higher in younger (less than 60 years) victims than in younger nonvictims.

These results seem to confirm the assumption that elderly victims are not more affected by victimization than younger victims. However, the effects noted above could be due to differences in victimization experiences with younger people becoming more frequently victims of serious crime (robbery, bodily harm).

If victims are studied separately according to different categories of crime, younger people react more depressively to burglary than older people $(F_{age*vic}[1;9199] = 5.42; p = .020)$.* Surprisingly however, no age differences are shown in the reaction to violence (robbery, bodily harm, sexual violence)

---

* Because of the low numbers of victims in the separated delict categories victimization refers here to a five-year period (1987–1991).

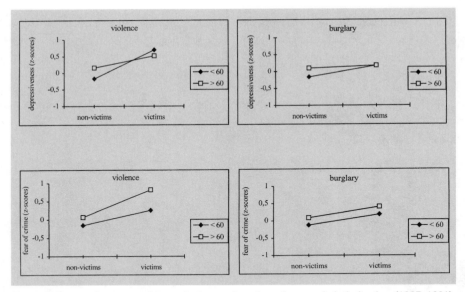

Figure 3. Depressiveness and fear of crime as function of age and victimization (1987–1991).

($F_{age*vic}[1;9200] = 2.80; p = .094$).* In contrast if fear of crime is chosen as dependent variable results are opposite. In case of burglary young and old people are affected in the same way ($F_{age*vic}[1;7694] = .01; p = .981$), whilst in case of violent crimes elderly people are more affected than younger ones ($F_{age*vic}[1;7698] = 15.89; p < .001$) (Figure 3).

With the view to increased vulnerability and dependency it can be assumed, that, for elderly people repeated victimization have more serious effects (Tomb, 1994; Sorenson & Golding, 1990). If, instead of prevalence rates, incidence rates are included in a multiple regression analysis as a criterion, it is found that victimization has a more serious effect with increased age. With reference to depressiveness ($t[9194] = 2.85; p = .004$) as well as fear of crime ($t[7693] = 5.97; p < .001$) the age by victimization interaction is significant.

If in addition to direct victims, indirect victims (whose relatives or related persons have been victimized) are included in the analysis, it becomes apparent that indirect victims are less affected than the victims themselves but still show significantly higher depressiveness and fear of crime than nonvictims. However, there are no interaction effects, younger and older people do not differ significantly in their reaction to indirect victimization.

---

*   Same results are shown for intrafamily violence ($F[1;4456] = .88; p = .349$), which indicates that older people in spite of their rising dependency are not more concerned than the younger ones.

Subjective Consequences of Victimization

With reference to restrictions which the victims themselves attribute to their most serious experience of victimization it becomes clear that older people subjectively are more affected by crime. Of those persons who became victims of a crime with personal contact or robbery within the last five years (1987–1991), 41% of the elderly persons state that they had suffered from fear which for 16.2% lasted until the time of questioning. 18.9% of the persons over 60 years did not feel safe at home, in 7.6% permanently. Opposed to that physical consequences of victimization (in the public context) generally appear to be lower (Table 4).

Table 4. Psychic and physiological consequences of victimization with respect to contact crimes and burglary (1987–1991).

	< 60 years			≥ 60 years		
	over longer period, but not now	up to today	not relevant	over longer period, but not now	up to today	not relevant
feels unsafe at home	11.7%	4.1%	84.2%	11.3%	7.6%	81.1%
suffers from anxiety	21.9%	9.6%	68.5%	24.8%	16.2%	59.0%
suffers from physiological consequences	10.6%	2.3%	87.1%	8.1%	1.5%	90.4%

ANOVA's reveal that older persons reported higher suspicion and fright ($F[1;1956] = 85.18; p < .001$) and lower self confidence ($F[1;1958] = 28.95; p < .001$) as long-lasting reactions to victimization.

These results have to be assured against the aforementioned argument of an overestimation of the consequences of victimization due to the general lower well-being of older persons. However, if the amount of depressiveness which is predicted by age (using regression analysis) is controlled as a covariate in a one-way ANOVA, the effects described above become less but remain significant. However, if only victims of burglary are analyzed in the same procedure no differences between younger and older victims are found. In contrast to that, older victims of violence have higher scores of suspicion and fright ($F[1;690] = 4.87; p = .028$) and lower self confidence ($F[1;689] = 10.01; p = .002$) even when the age related depressiveness is controlled.

Coping Strategies and Social Support as Palliative Factors

The data indicate that elderly people, despite restrictions due to age, at least partially have the resources to react in the right manner towards critical events in their lives. This corresponds with gerontological results mentioned in the beginning which draw a picture of surprising resilience and stability in general well-being well into high age (Baltes & Baltes, 1990; Brandstädter, Wentura, & Greve, 1993; Staudinger & Fleeson, 1996; Staudinger, Marsiske, & Baltes, 1994; see above). It poses the question, with reference to the experience of crime victims, which strategies and mechanism the individuals use in order to "neutralize" the consequences of a direct or indirect victimization (Agnew, 1985). Especially the concepts of coping and social support are central to understanding the psychological consequences of traumatic life events (Jones, & Barlow, 1990).

Personal Resources of Coping

Experience of crime in public areas usually have the character of the uncontrollable and noncorrectable. They cannot be coped with in an active assimilative way. Even though the careful behavior of elderly people already mentioned can be interpreted as an assimilative way of coping with the threat of crime, it necessarily only relates to experience of victimization. These in turn have to be handled through the adaptation of preferences, i. e., plans for life and goals have to be adjusted to the new situation. Characteristic here is a flexible accommodation of personal goals and norms to losses and restrictions experienced. It is shown that older people prefer accommodative ways of coping whereas assimilative problem focused coping strategies decrease with age (Brandtstädter & Wentura, 1995). In handling with the consequences of criminal victimization it is to be expected that people with high accommodative coping would be more successful.

In the KFN study the tendency towards accommodative coping in the original approach of the survey was not considered. But various items of a stress-response-scale which was administered in the survey could theoretically be plausibly arranged to a scale of accommodative coping tendency (ACT) (sample items: "I say to myself, it's not as bad as all that"; "I take my mind off things somehow"; "I say to myself, pull yourself together"; see Greve, Hosser, & Wetzels, 1996). The scale resulting from this is replicated by factor analysis and proves to be sufficiently reliable ($\alpha = .65$). The validity of this scale is supported by the result that the increase of depression with age is enlarged by adaptive coping which is compatible to the findings of Brandtstädter (see for example Brandtstädter, Wentura, & Greve, 1993).

The results show that the impact of victimization (one-year reference) on fear of crime is moderated by accommodative coping tendency (ACT). Victims with low ACT reveal higher fear of crime whereas victims with high ACT do not differ from nonvictims ($F_{akko*vic}[1;2364] = 8.54; p = .004$). With reference to depression there is a main effect that persons with low ACT have higher depressiveness scores ($F_{akko}[1;2709] = 144.90; p < .001$). No direct correlation between age and ACT was found ($r = -.01$).

Again the findings do not hold when burglary and violent crimes are analyzed separately. Victims of burglary can profit by ACT with respect to depressiveness especially in old age. The reported interaction between age and victimization does not reach significance when ACT is used as a covariate in a one-way ANOVA ($F_{age*vic}[1;3024] = .74; p = .390$). In contrast, after controlling for adaptive coping, younger victims of violence show higher depressiveness ($F_{age*vic}[1;3025] = 4.62; p = .022$) and fear of crime ($F_{age*vic}[1;2635] = 3.79; p = .052$) than older victims. Hence, older victims of violence do not seem to profit from accommodation with respect to this kind of offence.

Social Resources of Coping

Beside personal resources social support is discussed as a further moderator of the consequences of victimization (Frieze, Hymer, & Greenberg, 1987; Norris & Feldmann-Summers 1981; Ruch & Henessy, 1982). Support from relatives and friends goes along with less pronounced symptoms of victims, especially regarding depression, somatic disorders, and alcoholism; (Ruch & Henessy, 1982). However, social support is not always helpful, but could be perceived as an additional stressor especially in crisis if expected help is lacking or support is considered to be inappropriate (Herbert & Dunckel-Schetter, 1994; Hosser 1997). Thus, not only quantity but also quality of social support obviously determines the effects of social support. Only aid fitting to the victims needs and expectations can contribute to its relief and support coping processes (Solomon, 1985; Solomon & Smith, 1994)

In old age various factors become effective, which can change the influence of social support on ways of coping with victimization. Due to their increased vulnerability elderly people depend on help from their social environment to a greater degree. However, the social network usually becomes weaker and starts to crumble with increasing age. Death and illness amongst members of the social network leave gaps, which can be filled only with difficulty, and sometimes not at all. Moreover, restricted mobility of elderly people sometimes leads to a reduction of social integration. It can be assumed that this restriction of sources for social support especially in old age increases importance of the remaining social contacts and even greater appreciation of the help still available.

Furthermore, due to the reduced number of members of the social security network, exchange of support is shifted increasingly from the circle of friends and acquaintances to the kinship, especially a partner or one's own children.

The latter above all increases the risk that the recipient begins to feel helpless and dependant or feelings of guilt arise, due to lack of reciprocity when support is exchanged. On the other hand it can be assumed that with age the stigmatizing reactions to victimization (e. g., blaming the victim) decreases. This heterogeneity of possible outcomes makes it difficult to formulate *general* hypotheses about the effects of social support on elderly victims of crime.

Social support was assessed in the KFN Survey in two variations. With respect to the extent of support *available* it was asked how many persons (close members of family, relatives, friends, neighbors) would probably lend support if needed; thus, this measure estimates mainly *anticipated* support. The social support *perceived* was measured by a questionnaire (SOZU: Sommer & Fydrich, 1989; 22 items, $\alpha = .94$; see Hosser, 1997). In accordance with current results of research (Ruch & Hennessy, 1982) the KFN results confirm that social support goes along with lower depression and fear (Table 5). The perceived support ($t$ps[3706] = 8.53; $p < .001$) as well as the support available ($t$as[4337] = 5.94; $p < .001$) decline with age.

A separate analysis of different categories of criminal victimization reveals that for victims of violence as well as for victims of burglary high *perceived* support covariates with low depressiveness (violence: $F_{ps*vic}[1;2543] = 9.66$; $p = .002$; burglary: $F_{ps*vic}[1;2543] = 3.73$; $p = .053$). *Available* support however predicts low depressiveness only for victims of burglary ($F_{as*vic}[1;2448] = 14.56$; $p < .001$). No differences have been found between elderly and younger victims.

With respect to fear of crime, no moderation effect of perceived support was observed for victims of violence. In contrast, victims of burglary with high perceived support show higher fear of crime ($F_{ps*vic}[1;3781] = 7.75$; $p = .005$). Similarly, with respect to available support victims of violence show a higher fear of crime with increasing size of the social network. ($F_{as*vic}[1;2067] = 11.75$; $p = .001$).

Table 5. Correlations between social support and other variables.

	depressiveness	fear of crime	age
available support	–.17	–.04	–.08
perceived support	–.40	–.13	–.14

Experience of Violence in Old Age.
The Necessity of a Geronto-Victimological Perspective

The results presented support mainly the assumption that elderly people are affected by crime in a different way and would react to victimization in a way which differs from that of young people. This supports the necessity to discuss psychic consequences of victimization of elderly people in view of the special conditions of old age. Some of the data indicate that elderly people can compensate increased vulnerability with increased adaptive resources of coping. This holds especially for coping with criminal victimization which is a paradigmatic example for uncontrollable threat.

Furthermore the results presented prove that a differentiation of the categories of criminal victimization is useful and even necessary. Victims of violence react differently as compared with victims of burglary. In addition, the perceived and available support may have ambivalent effects as the results concerning fear of crime demonstrates. Finally, whereas social support does not interact with age, coping resources work differently for different age cohorts.

An area which has been largely neglected by research is indirect victimization, especially since it seems to be more relevant for elderly people than direct victimization from a quantity point of view. The increase of cautious behavior co-related with age (Greve, 1997) gives an initial indication to strain caused by indirect threat of crime. Especially the social withdrawal increased in this way can again have a negative influence on quality of life and well-being. In addition, the danger of shifting the risk into the double dark field of intrafamily violence mentioned beforehand is increased.

In this connection one has to recall the selectivity of the sampling of the KFN study. Old persons, who had been exposed to experience of violence in public, are mainly persons who, up until the date of victimization were sufficiently mobile and active to move about in public independently. Opposed to that mainly persons who have no longer the possibility to defend themselves or leave the situation will be affected by intrafamily violence. For that reason it can be assumed that the consequences of victimization for those persons affected are especially serious, but in many cases different in nature. At the same time in this area, obtaining serious data is rather a problem for many reasons. For example, elderly people especially those in (permanent) need of nursing, in many cases cannot be questioned themselves or only with restrictions. Relatives or the persons involved in the care, however, could possibly include offenders. This does not only carry implications for further scientific research but also for intervention.

The quality of future research will depend largely on improvements in the area of surveys and diagnosis. First of all the need should be mentioned to include systematically selected groups with respect to age and victimization. Insights into causal relations, however, can only be obtained from longitudinal studies. Furthermore the use of instruments which avoid age-related artifacts in the measurement of the dependent variables (e. g., with reference to depressiveness: geriatric depression scale; Sheik, & Yesavage, 1986) seems fruitful and even necessary. Referring to the aspects of coping and social support mentioned beforehand, above all differentiated and more extensive assessment of coping appears to be promising. This should also include ways of coping which are considered less functional in other stages of life (e. g., denial and repression). When assessing social support the size and homogeneity of the network as well as subjective expectations of corresponding assistance have to be taken into account.

From a clinical perspective the results presented have shown that some victims of crime, even years after the event still suffer from its results and are affected in the quality of their lives. In spite of that there are very few institutions in Germany which specifically address crime victims and offer help which is specifically tailored to their needs (Wetzels, 1996). Therefore demands have to be made to extend help offers for victims, not only in financial terms. In therapeutic work, accommodative ways of coping should be promoted especially for elderly victims. In addition the competence of the members of the social network must also be improved. However, the problem of violence in close relationships has to be appropriately taken into account. Here new strategies of social engagement are needed. Above all the training of sensibility and social competence for primary contact persons, e. g., doctors, nursing staff, and physiotherapists, is necessary.

References

Aday, R.H. (1988). *Crime and the elderly. An annotated bibliography*. New York: Greenwood.

Agnew, R.S. (1985). Neutralizing the impact of crime. *Criminal Justice and Behavior, 12,* 221–239.

Ahlf, E.-H. (1994). Alte Menschen als Opfer von Gewaltkriminalität [Elderly as victims of violent crime]. *Zeitschrift für Gerontologie, 27,* 289–298.

Arling, G. (1987). Strain, social support, and distress in old age. *Journal of Gerontology, 42,* 107–113.

Baltes, M.M., & Silverberg, S.B. (1994). The dynamics between dependency and autonomy: Illustrations across the life span. In D.L. Featherman, R.M. Lerner, & M. Perlmutter (Eds.), *Life-span development and behavior* (Vol. 12, pp. 41–90). Hillsdale, NJ: Erlbaum.

Baltes, P.B., & Baltes, M.M. (1990). Psychological perspectives on successful aging: The model of selective optimization with compensation. In P.B. Baltes, & M.M. Baltes (Eds.),

Successful aging: Perspectives from the behavioral sciences (pp. 1–34). New York: Cambridge University Press.

Bilsky, W., Pfeiffer, C., & Wetzels, P. (1993). Feelings of personal safety, fear of crime and violence, and the experience of victimization amongst elderly people: Research instrument and survey design. In W. Bilsky, C. Pfeiffer, & P. Wetzels (Eds.), *Fear of crime and criminal victimization* (pp. 245–267). Stuttgart: Enke.

Bilsky, W., & Wetzels, P. (1993). Wellbeing, feelings of personal safety, and fear of crime: Towards a conceptual integration. *Proceedings of the Fourth International Facet Theory Conference* (pp. 11–19). Prague, Czech Republic: Facet Theory Association.

Bilsky, W., & Wetzels, P. (1994). Victimization and crime. *International Annals of Criminology, 32,* 135–154.

Brandtstädter, J., & Greve, W. (1994). The aging self: Stabilizing and protective processes. *Developmental Review, 14,* 52–80.

Brandtstädter, J., & Renner, G. (1990). Tenacious goal pursuit and flexible goal adjustment: Explication and age-related analysis of assimilative and accommodative strategies of coping. *Psychology and Aging, 5,* 58–67.

Brandtstädter, J., & Rothermund, K. (1994). Self-percepts of control in middle and later adulthood: Buffering losses by rescaling goals. *Psychology and Aging, 9,* 265–273.

Brandtstädter, J., & Wentura, D. (1994). Veränderungen der Zeit- und Zukunftsperspektive im Übergang zum höheren Erwachsenenalter: Entwicklungspsychologische und differentielle Aspekte [Changes of perspective toward time and the future during the transition to late adulthood: Developmental and interindividual aspects]. *Zeitschrift für Entwicklungspsychologie u. Pädagogische Psychologie, 26,* 2–21.

Brandtstädter, J., Wentura, D., & Greve, W. (1993). Adaptive resources of the aging self: Outlines of an emergent perspective. *International Journal of Behavioral Development, 16,* 323–349.

Clemente, F., & Kleiman, M.J. (1982). Fear of crime among the elderly, *British Journal of Criminology, 22,* 49–62.

Cutler, S.J. (1987). Crime (against and by elderly). In G.L. Maddox (Ed.), *The encyclopedia of aging* (pp. 155–156). New York: Springer-Verlag.

Doyle, D.P. (1990). Aging and crime. In K.F. Ferraro (Ed.), *Gerontology: Perspectives and issues* (pp. 294–315). New York: Springer-Verlag.

Eastman, M. (1984). *Old age abuse.* Mitcham: Age Concern England.

Eve, S.B. (1985). Criminal victimization and fear of crime among the noninstitutionalized elderly in the United States: A critique of the empirical research literature. *Victimology, 10,* 397–408.

Eysenck, H. (1983). Stress, disease, and personality: the inoculation effect. In C.J. Cooper (Ed.), *Stress research* (pp. 121–146). New York: Wiley.

Fattah, E.A., & Sacco, V.F. (1989). *Crime and victimization of the elderly.* New York: Springer-Verlag.

Ferraro, K.F., & LaGrange, R.L. (1992). Are older people most afraid of crime? Reconsidering age differences in fear of victimization. *Journal of Gerontology: Social Sciences, 47,* S233–S244.

Figley, C.F. (1985). *Trauma and its wake: The study and treatment of posttraumatic stress disorder.* New York: Brunner/Mazel.

Figley, C.R., & Kleber, R.J. (1996). Beyond the "victim." Secondary traumatic stress. In R.J. Kleber, C.R. Figley, & B.P. Gersons (Eds.), *Beyond trauma: Cultural and societal dynamics* (pp. 75–98). New York: Plenum.

Frieze, I.H., Hymer, S., & Greenberg, M.S. (1987). Describing the crime victim: Psychological reactions to victimization. *Professional Psychology: Research and Practice, 18,* 299–315.

Glendenning, F. (1993). What is elder abuse and neglect? In P. Decalmer & F. Glendenning (Eds.), *The mistreatment of elderly people* (p. 1–34). Newbury Park: Sage.

Greve, W. (1997). *Fear of crime among the elderly: Beyond simplifying paradoxes.* KFN-Forschungsberichte, No. 65. Hannover: Kriminologisches Forschungsinstitut Niedersachsen.

Greve, W., Hosser, D., & Wetzels, P. (1996). *Bedrohung durch Kriminalität im Alter: Kriminalitätsfurcht älterer Menschen als Brennpunkt einer Gerontoviktimologie* [Threat by criminality in old age. Fear of crime as focus for a geronto-victimology]. Baden-Baden: Nomos.

Greve, W., & Niederfranke, A. (1998). Bedrohung durch Gewalt und Kriminalität im Alter [Threat by violence and criminality in old age]. *Zeitschrift für Klinische Psychologie, 27,* 130–135.

Greve, W., & Wetzels, P. (1995). Opfererfahrungen und Kriminalitätsfurcht älterer Menschen [Victimization and fear of crime among the elderly]. *Report Psychologie, 20,* 24–35.

Hale, C. (1996). Fear of crime: A review of the literature. *International Review of Victimology, 4,* 79–150.

Harris, C.J. (1991). A family crisis-intervention model for the treatment of post-traumatic stress reaction. *Journal of Traumatic Stress, 4,* 195–207.

Heckhausen, J., Dixon, R.A., & Baltes, P.B. (1989). Gains and losses in development throughout adulthood as perceived by different adult age groups. *Developmental Psychology, 25,* 109–121.

Herbert, T.B., & Dunckel-Schetter, C. (1992). Negative social reactions to victims: An overview of responses and their determinants. In L. Montada, S.-H. Filipp, & M.J. Lerner (Eds.), *Life crises and experiences of loss in adulthood* (pp. 497–518). Hillsdale, NJ: Erlbaum.

Höhn,C., & Roloff, J. (1994). *Die Alten der Zukunft – Bevölkerungsstatistische Datenanalyse* (unter Mitarbeit von U. Schneekloth und B. Störtzbach) [Elderly people in the future]. Stuttgart: Kohlhammer.

Hosser, D. (1997). Hilfe oder Hindernis? Die Bedeutung sozialer Unterstützung für Opfer krimineller Gewalt [Help or hindrance: The significance of social support for victims of crime]. *Monatsschrift für Kriminologie und Strafrechtsreform, 80,* 388–403.

Jones, J.C., & Barlow, D.H. (1990). The etiology of posttraumatic stress disorder. *Clinical Psychology Review, 10,* 299–328.

Kawelowski, F. (1995). *Ältere Menschen als Kriminalitätsopfer* [Older persons as victims of crime]. Wiesbaden: Bundeskriminalamt.

Killias, M. (1990). Vulnerability: Towards a better understanding of a key variable in the genesis of fear of crime. *Violence and Victims, 5,* 97–108.

Kilpatrick, D.G., & Resnick, H.S. (1993). Posttraumatic stress disorder associated with exposure to criminal victimization in clinical and community populations. In J.R.T. Davidson & E.B. Foa (Eds.), *Posttraumatic stress disorder: DSM-IV and beyond* (pp. 113–143). Washington: American Psychiatric Press.

Kilpatrick, D.G., Best, C.L., Veronen, L.J., Amick, A.E., Villeponteaux, L.A., & Ruff, G.A. (1985). Mental health correlates of criminal victimization: A random community survey. *Journal of Consulting and Clinical Psychology, 53,* 866–873.

Laux, L., Glanzmann, P., Schaffner, P., & Spielberger, C.D. (1981). *Das State-Trait-Angst-Inventar (STAI)* [State trait fear inventory] . Weinheim: Beltz.

Meichenbaum, D. (1994). *A clinical handbook / Practical therapist manual for assessing and treating adults with post-traumatic stress disorder (PTSD)*. University of Waterloo: Institute Press.

Norris, F.H. (1992). Epidemiology of trauma: Frequency and impact of different potentially traumatic events on different demographic groups. *Journal of Consulting and Clinical Psychology, 60,* 409–418.

Norris, J., & Feldman-Summers, S. (1981). Factors related to the psychological impact of rape on the victim. *Journal of Abnormal Psychology, 90,* 562–567.

Norris, F.H., & Kaniasty, K. (1994). Psychological distress following criminal victimization in the general population: Cross-sectional, longitudinal, and prospective analyses. *Journal of Consulting and Clinical Psychology, 62,* 11–123.

Norris, F.H., & Murrell, S.A. (1988). Prior experience as a moderator of disaster impact on anxiety symptoms in older adults. *American Journal of Community Psychology, 16,* 665–683.

Norris, F.H., Phifer, J.F., & Kaniasty, K. (1994). Individual and community reactions to the Kentucky floods: Findings from a longitudinal study of older adults. In R.J. Ursano, B.M. McCaughey, & C.S. Fullerton (Eds.), *Individual and community responses to trauma and disaster: The structure of human chaos* (pp. 378–400). Cambridge: Cambridge University Press.

Pfeiffer, C., Brettfeld, K., & Delzer, I. (1997). *Kriminalität in Niedersachsen 1985 bis 1996. Eine Analyse auf der Basis der Polizeilichen Kriminalstatistik* [Criminality in Lower Saxony from 1985 to 1996. An analysis on the basis of the police statistics]. KFN-Forschungsberichte, Nr. 60. Hannover: Kriminologisches Forschungsinstitut Niedersachsen.

Pillemer, K.A. (1993). The abused offspring are dependent. Abuse is caused by the deviance and dependence of abusive caregivers. In R.J. Gelles & D.R. Loseke (Eds.), *Current controversies on family violence* (pp. 237–249). Newbury Park: Sage.

Pillemer, K.A., & Finkelhor, D. (1988). The prevalence of elder abuse: A random sample survey. *The Gerontologist, 28,* 51–57.

Pillemer, K.A., & Suitor, J. (1992). Violence and violent feelings: What causes them among family caregivers? *Journal of Gerontology, 47,* 165–172.

Pillemer, K.A., & Wolf, R.S. (Eds.). (1986). *Elder abuse: Conflict in the family*. Dover, MA: Auburn House Publishing Co.

Ruch, L. O., & Henessy, M. (1982). Sexual assault: Victim and attack dimensions. *Journal of Victimology, 7,* 94–105.

Russel, D., Peplau, L.A., & Cutrona, C. (1980). The revised UCLA loneliness scale: Concurrent and discriminant validity evidence. *Journal of Personality and Social Psychology, 39,* 472–480.

Saigh, P. (1992). History, current nosology and epidemiology. In P.A. Saigh (Ed.), *Posttraumatic Stress Disorder: A behavioral approach to assessment and treatment* (pp. 1–27). Boston: Allyn & Bacon.

Sheik, J.I, & Yesavage, J.A. (1986). Geriatric depression scale (GDS): Recent evidence and development of a shorter version. *Clinical Gerontology, 5,* 165–173.

Smith, D.P., Enderson, B.L., & Maull, K.I. (1990). Trauma in the elderly: Determinants of outcome. *Southern Medical Journal, 82,* 171–177.

Solomon, S.D. (1985). Enhancing Social Support For Disaster Victims. In B.J. Sowder (Ed.), *Disasters and mental health: Selected contemporary perspectives* (pp. 107–121). Bethesda: National Institute of Mental Health.

Solomon, S.D., & Smith, E.M. (1994). Social Support and perceived control as moderators of responses to dioxin and flood exposure. In R.J. Ursano, B.M. McCaughey, & C.S. Fullerton (Eds.), *Individual and community responses to trauma and disaster: The structure of human chaos* (pp. 179–200). Cambridge: Cambridge University Press.

Sommer, G., & Fydrich, T. (1989). *Soziale Unterstützung. Diagnostik, Konzepte, F-SOZU* [Social support: Diagnostics, concepts, F-SOZU]. Tübingen: Deutsche Gesellschaft für Verhaltenstherapie.

Sorenson, S.B., & Golding, J.M. (1990). Depressiv sequelae of recent criminal victimization. *Journal of Traumatic Stress, 3,* 337–350.

Staudinger, U.M., & Fleeson, W. (1996). Self and personality in old and very old age: A sample case of resilience? *Development and Psychopathology, 8,* 867–885.

Staudinger, U., Marsiske, M., & Baltes, P.B. (1995). Resilience and reserve capacity in later adulthood: Potentials and limits of development across the life-span. In D. Cicchetti & D. Cohen (Eds.), *Developmental psychopathology. Vol. 2: Risk, disorder, and adaptation* (pp. 801–847). New York: Wiley.

Steinhagen-Thiessen, E., & Borchelt, M. (1993). Health differences in advanced old age. *Ageing and Society, 13,* 619–655.

Tomb, D.A. (1994). The phenomenology of post-traumatic stress disorder. *Post-Traumatic Stress Disorder, 17,* 237–250.

Ursano, R.J., & McCarroll, J.E. (1994). Exposure to traumatic death: The nature of the stressor. In R.J. Ursano, B.M. McCaughey, & C.S. Fullerton (Eds.), *Individual and community responses to trauma and disaster: The structure of human chaos* (pp. 46–71). Cambridge: Cambridge University Press.

Vaux, A. (1985). Variations in social support associated with gender, ethnicity, and age. *Journal of Social Issues, 41,* 89–110.

Wetzels, P. (1993). Victimization experiences in close relationships: Another blank in victim surveys. In W. Bilsky, C. Pfeiffer, & P. Wetzels (Eds.), *Fear of crime an criminal victimization* (pp. 21–41). Stuttgart: Enke.

Wetzels, P., & Greve, W. (1996). Alte Menschen als Opfer innerfamiliärer Gewalt Ergebnisse einer kriminologischen Dunkelfeldstudie [Older people as victims of family violence. Results of a German victimization survey]. *Zeitschrift für Gerontologie und Geriatrie, 29,* 191–200.

Wetzels, P., Greve, W., Mecklenburg, E., Bilsky, W., & Pfeiffer, C. (1995). *Kriminalität im Leben alter Menschen* [Crime in the life of the elderly]. Stuttgart: Kohlhammer.

Wolf, R.S. (1992). Victimization and the elderly: Elder abuse and neglect. *Reviews in Clinical Gerontology, 2,* 269–276.

Yin, P. (1980). Fear of crime among the elderly: Some issues and suggestions. *Social Problems, 27,* 492–504.

Yin, P. (1985). *Victimization and the aged.* Springfield, IL: Thomas.

PART IV:
COPING, SOCIAL SUPPORT, MEANING, AND GROWTH

Long-Term Posttraumatic Stress Reactions, Coping, and Social Support: A Structural Equation Model in a Group of Former Political Prisoners*

Matthias Schützwohl, Andreas Maercker, and Rolf Manz

In this chapter assumptions about the relationship between chronically persistent posttraumatic stress reactions, coping strategies, and social support will be investigated. Data derived from a study on the psychological aftereffects of political imprisonment in the former East Germany will be used to develop a structural equation model, which presents detailed information of the interrelationship between coping, social support, and PTSD. Finally, we will discuss this detailed pattern of results with regard to some possible implications for the treatment of PTSD.

Long-Term Persistence of Posttraumatic Stress Reactions

A number of empirical investigations have provided evidence showing that posttraumatic stress reactions often persist over extended periods of time, from years to decades. For example, in the most recent epidemiological study on PTSD about 35% of persons with an index episode of PTSD did not recover even after 10 years, irrespective of whether they had been on treatment or not (Kessler, Sonnega, Bromet, & Nelson, 1995). In Vietnam veterans, Kulka and colleagues (1990) found a lifetime prevalence of 30% and, on average approximately 19 years postwar, a current prevalence rate of 15%. Thus, 50% of Vietnam veterans who had met PTSD criteria at any one point in time during the Vietnam war still suffered from a manifest PTSD disorder many years later. Further, in a sample of former prisoners of war from World War II, 50% had PTSD during the year following repatriation and 29% still qualified for the

* The research on which this article is based was supported by a grant from the German Ministry of Education and Research (Forschungsverbund Public Health Sachsen DLR01EG9410,A3). We gratefully acknowledge the assistance in translation by Michael Mangold, M.Sc.

diagnosis of PTSD 40 years later (Speed, Engdahl, & Schwartz, 1989). Likewise, in a 40-year follow up of former prisoners of World War II, 67% had PTSD, of whom 29% had fully recovered, 39% still reported mild symptoms, 24% had moderate residual symptoms, and 8% showed no recovery or had even worsened (Kluznik, Speed, van Valkenburg, & Margraw, 1986).

In view of such variability the question arises as to which factors determine the course and the maintenance of posttraumatic stress reactions. Even though the degree of an individual's exposure to a traumatic event was repeatedly found to be an important factor affecting the likelihood of developing posttraumatic stress reactions (e. g., Fontana & Rosenheck, 1994; McFarlane, 1989; Resnick, Kilpatrick, Best, & Kramer, 1992) its relevance to the development of posttraumatic stress reactions appears to diminish with time (e. g., McFarlane, Davidson, & Fairbaink, 1993).

Traumatic events of a lower level of traumatization, in particular, have long term psychological effects that appear to be increasingly determined by a number of factors such as cognitive factors (Ehlers & Steil, 1995) and, above all, coping behavior and the extent of social support (Jones & Barlow, 1990).

Symptom Structure of Posttraumatic Stress Reactions

What do we know about the symptom structure of posttraumatic stress reactions and the interactions of the individual symptom groups? The coherence of the specific posttraumatic stress syndrome of re-experiencing, avoidance, numbing, and hyperarousal reactions is empirically well established (Davidson & Foa, 1993). Previously held concepts according to which avoidance behavior precedes intrusive recollections thereby creating a circular alternating pattern of intrusions and avoidance behavior (Horowitz, 1993) could yet not be empirically verified. According to a hypothetical model by Creamer and colleagues (1990, 1992), for example, intrusions precede avoidance, with the latter being perceived as maladaptive coping strategies in response to the resulting discomfort. Likewise, McFarlane (1992) found that avoidance behavior was not directly related to exposure to a traumatic event but could instead be well predicted by the intensity of intrusive memories. It therefore appears that avoidance behavior constitutes a defensive strategy, the purpose of which is to cope with the distress generated by the re-experiencing of the traumatic event. Foa and colleagues (Foa, Riggs, & Gershuny, 1995), too, consider intrusion and arousal symptoms as aversive events exacerbating avoidance and numbing, with avoidance and numbing representing distinct phenomena that both prevent adequate processing of the trauma.

However, there are studies indicating that stress caused by intrusions and hyperarousal do not always lead to avoidance behavior and emotional numbness. In fact, individuals can suffer from intrusions and hyperarousal symptoms following a traumatic event and yet show relatively little avoidance behavior and numbing (e. g., Maercker & Schützwohl, 1997; Kilpatrick & Resnick, 1993; Schützwohl & Maercker, 1996).

On the other hand, a number of medical studies found that intrusion symptoms substantially improved or decreased in number, whereas avoidance symptoms did not (Burstein, 1984; Frank, Kosten, Giller, & Dan, 1988). This points to the fact that meaningful factors other than intrusion and hyperarousal contribute to the development and maintenance of posttraumatic avoidance behavior (Burstein, 1989).

It may well be that coping styles influence the avoidance level and that individuals who tend to use avoidance as a strategy of coping with stressful situations will presumably continue to do so in coping with a traumatic event and the resulting psychological effects (Creamer et al., 1992; Myrtek, Itte, Zimmermann, & Brügner, 1994). We have already assumed that coping behavior, including the extent of avoidance, varies with social conditions, without influencing the degree of intrusion and hyperarousal (Maercker & Schützwohl, 1997).

In this regard it appears to make sense to differentiate between intrusions and hyperarousal as primary factors indicating the severity of PTSD and posttraumatic avoidance as a secondary factor.

Posttraumatic Stress Reactions, Coping Strategies, and Their Interaction

Studies on long-term coping point to the fact that the efforts to cope with the psychological aftereffects of traumatic events increase with the extent of the posttraumatic stress reactions (see Aldwin, 1993). For example, former prisoners from World War II suffering from PTSD made use of a greater variety of coping behavior and employed these coping strategies more frequently in their efforts to cope with posttraumatic memories than did individuals not suffering from PTSD (Fairbank, Hansen, & Fitterling, 1991). Likewise, in a study on long-term coping with stressful memories or reminders of war, external ratings and self-ratings of posttraumatic stress reactions correlated positively with the majority of coping factors (Green, Lindy, & Grace, 1988). In a sample of train drivers who had encountered fatal accidents, those suffering from posttraumatic stress reactions had significantly higher mean scores in all coping items (Myrtek et al., 1994).

In accordance with Aldwin (1993) one can assume that coping effort rather than coping efficacy is being reflected in these studies. The data can therefore be interpreted to mean that individuals with posttraumatic stress reactions by all means try to overcome the emotional stress which leads to a considerable increase in their coping efforts. On the other hand, in accordance with the transactional stress model by Lazarus those not suffering from posttraumatic stress reactions after a lengthy period of time following trauma have little reason to employ coping strategies (Lazarus & Folkman, 1984).

At the same time, however, these investigations indicate that coping strategies are not essential for the success of long-term coping with posttraumatic stress reactions. The fact that largely positive correlations were found between the extent of posttraumatic psychological stress and coping efforts suggests that there may, in fact, be no qualitative differences between coping strategies (Myrtek et al., 1994). The observed negative correlation between the extent of psychological stress and the specific coping strategy of putting traumatic events into relative terms and re-evaluation (Maercker, 1998), can be interpreted in such a way that individuals with rather minor psychological stress can more readily perform cognitive re-evaluations of the trauma and the resulting psychological aftereffects. The causal relationship between long-term posttraumatic stress reactions on the one hand and coping strategies on the other may therefore be such that while coping behavior is essentially determined by the extent of intrusive and hyperarousal stress reactions, coping behavior has no significant impact on the individual's well-being.

Posttraumatic Stress Reactions, Social Support, and Their Interaction

A number of cross-sectional studies found that posttraumatic stress reactions correlate with a variety of dimensions of social support at different points in time after traumatization occurred (e. g., Boscarino, 1995; Schützwohl & Maercker, 1997; Solomon, Mikulincer, & Avitzur, 1988). Within the framework of such cross-sectional studies the causality of the relationship between social support and posttraumatic stress reactions remains unclear. A fundamental tenet of social support research purports that social support contributes to an increase of well-being and health as well as to a reduction of psychological and physical disorders. One explanatory assumption made in this regard is that social support has a beneficial effect on well-being irrespective of whether a traumatic event had been experienced or not ("main effect model"). Moreover, it is assumed that social support has a generally positive influence on the individual's ability to cope with a traumatic event ("stress-buffer-model"; Sommer & Fydrich, 1989).

Conversely, there has been increasing recognition of the fact that victimization as well as the resulting posttraumatic stress reactions can influence the extent of social support (Norris & Kaniassty, 1996). It can be assumed that victimization and the resulting posttraumatic stress reactions mobilize social support and that traumatized individuals actively seek social support in attempts to cope with their traumatic experiences. On the other hand, however, social contact with traumatized persons can cause feelings of discomfort and embarrassment that can eventually lead to a decrease in social support. It is also conceivable that efforts of traumatized individuals at avoiding conversations associated with the trauma as well as their tendency to avoid people who arouse recollections of the trauma can both lead to a reduction in received social support whereas feelings of detachment or estrangement from others may be concomitant with a lessening of perceived social support.

There are, in fact, longitudinal studies on the relationship between social support and posttraumatic stress reactions that suggest that the extent of perceived social support decreases with an increase of the severity of the trauma (Norris & Kaniasty, 1996) and that individuals diagnosed with posttraumatic stress disorders following traumatization perceive increasingly less social support (Keane, Scott, Chavoya, Lamparski, & Fairbank, 1985). Findings in other longitudinal studies, however, support the opposite in as much as they indicate that social support influences the development of posttraumatic stress reactions (Fontana & Rosenheck, 1994; Solomon et al., 1988).

Overall one can assume an interaction, i. e., during the time following a traumatic experience social support affects the development and the maintenance of posttraumatic stress reactions, while victimization and the resulting posttraumatic stress reactions determine the extent of social support.

Coping Strategies and Social Support

In social support research it is hypothesized that social support has a beneficial effect on the individual's ability to cope with stress ("stress-buffer model"). With regard to the transactional stress model by Lazarus (Lazarus & Folkman, 1984) it is assumed that the perception of social support influences the process of primary and secondary cognitive appraisal of person-environment encounters, i. e., the evaluation of situations and personal coping abilities. More specifically it is assumed that persons who perceive themselves as receiving strong social support experience less emotional stress as a result of person-environment encounters. This is being attributed to the potential fact that they have a greater number of potential or de facto coping strategies at their disposal (Sommer & Fydrich, 1989). Thus, according to the transactional stress model, social support has an influence on coping behavior as coping behavior is determined by cognitive appraisals and their resulting emotions.

A number of studies support this assumed relationship. One study, for instance, found that the likelihood that a traumatized individual actively seeks the support of others in coping with the aftereffects of trauma increases with the perceived extent of perceived social support (Pierce & Contey, 1992, as cited by Pierce et al., 1996). According to Holahan and Moos (1987) the extent of family support largely determines the extent to which individuals use "active coping" and "avoidance coping" in dealing with stressful situations.

On the other hand, however, there is empirical evidence indicating that coping behavior can have an influence on the extent of social support. Thus, Billings and Moos (1981), for example, report that people who use avoidance coping have fewer social resources. Again these findings point to an interaction between social support and coping strategies, i. e., social support affects the ways in which individuals cope with traumatic events and the resulting posttraumatic stress reactions and vice versa (Pierce, Sarason, & Sarason, 1996).

Proposed Model for the Relationship between PTSD, Coping, and Social Support

The proposed model is based on the above-mentioned theoretical considerations and empirical findings. The model does not include all elements that influence posttraumatic stress reactions, coping behavior, and social support; as noted, such factors as the degree of an individual's exposure to a traumatic event and cognitive factors are likely to contribute to psychopathology as well as to coping behavior and social support.

Within a cross sectional design a research model was employed based on the following general assumptions:
- posttraumatic intrusion and hyperarousal symptoms have an impact on posttraumatic avoidance symptoms, coping strategies, and social support
- posttraumatic avoidance symptoms and coping strategies have no impact on posttraumatic intrusion and hyperarousal, while social support has an impact
- coping strategies and social support as well as social support and posttraumatic avoidance symptoms influence each other reciprocally.

The corresponding preliminary functional model is shown in Figure 1.

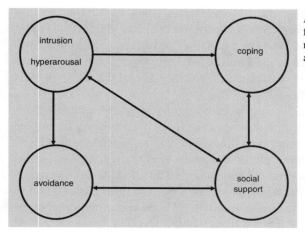

Figure 1. Model assumptions for the interaction of posttraumatic stress reactions, coping, and social support.

The Dresden Study on Long-Term Psychological Effects of Political Imprisonment

The data referred to below were collected within a study on the long-term psychological effects of political imprisonment in the German Democratic Republic (Maercker & Schützwohl, 1997). In this study, a nontreatment seeking group of 146 former political prisoners was investigated. For the present analyses, data from 123 participants were available. The remaining 23 had to be excluded due to missing data. The sample analyzed included 103 men and 20 women. Their average age was 53.4 years (range 27–82, SD = 11.8). The average time the participants spent in prison was 34.8 months (range 1–216, SD = 36.0). On average 24.2 years (range 5–42, SD = 11.4) had elapsed since the participants were released from prison.

Data on current posttraumatic stress reactions were collected using the *Diagnostic Interview for Psychological Symptoms* (DIPS; Margraf, Schneider, & Ehlers, 1991) and the German version of the Impact of Event Scale – Revised (IES-R; Weiss & Marmar, 1996; Maercker & Schützwohl, 1998). The DIPS is an extended German version of the Anxiety Disorders Interview Schedule – Revised (ADIS-R; DiNardo & Barlow, 1988). The interview allows for the assessment of those 17 symptom criteria of PTSD that define the disorder according to DSM standards. In accordance with their allocation to criteria B, C, and D of the DSM-III-R (American Psychiatric Association, 1987) the number of existing symptoms was added up, resulting in the sum values of intrusion (DSM-I), avoidance (DSM-A) and hyperarousal (DSM-H). On the basis of the participant's self-ratings on the IES-R the subscales of intrusion (IES-I), avoidance (IES-A) and hyperarousal (IES-H) were calculated. Expert ratings and self-ratings of posttraumatic stress-reactions constitute those measurable variables to be explained by the latent variables of intrusion, avoidance and hyperarousal. In other words, DSM-I and IES-I are to be explained by "intrusion," DSM-A and IES-A by "avoidance," and DSM-H and IES-H by "hyperarousal."

Data on the coping strategies employed by the participants in dealing with the aftereffects of political imprisonment at the time of the investigation were collected using a modified version of the Stress Coping Questionnaire (Reicherts & Perrez, 1993). Factor analyses and analyses of the resulting subscales allowed for the calculation of three sum scores. The subscale Interpersonal Mastery (INTMAST) includes 5 items, such as "I want to find comfort, advice, and help from people who are close to me" or "I blame other people or curse the circumstances." The subscale Blunting (BLUNTING) includes 5 items indicating avoidance and distraction, such as "I try to switch off, divert myself, and avoid the situation altogether." Finally, the subscale Pallation (PALLIAT) includes 4 items indicating efforts to reduce emotional distress, such as "I persuade my inner self (e. g., encourage myself, tell myself: 'keep calm')." Coping efforts can refer to both, the environment and the self (Lazarus & Folkman, 1984). In accordance with this differentiation the subscales are presented as "environment-focused coping" where the subscale INTMAST is concerned and "self-focused coping" where those of BLUNTING and PALLIAT are referred to.

Two dimensions of social support were measured using the *Social Support Questionnaire* (F-SOZU; Sommer & Fydrich, 1989): the extent of presently perceived emotional support (ES) and the extent of presently perceived social integration (SI). The ES-scale includes 16 items, such as "Whenever I feel low I know whom I can go to." The SI-scale includes 13 items, such as "Oftentimes I meet friends whom I first of all have a chat with." The subscales ES and SI are the subscales of the latent variable "perceived social support."

Psychopathological Description of the Sample*

Being imprisoned in the former German Democratic Republic for political reasons always involved extreme hardship. Whereas physical torture was common until 1953 (Werkentin, 1995), psychological torture was frequently used until 1989 (amnesty international, 1989). Accordingly, criterion A of the DSM-III-R is met by all participants. Within the sub-sample of this analysis, 85% (*n*

---

* Diagnostic findings have been presented in detail elsewhere (Maercker & Schützwohl, 1997).

= 105) of the participants met the reexperiencing criterion, 34% (n = 42) the avoidance criterion, and 60% (n = 74) met the hyperarousal criterion. The full set of diagnostic criteria for PTSD was met by 29% (n = 36). The sum score of the external rating of intrusive symptoms (DSM-I) is $M \pm SD$ = 2.1 ± 1.3, the sum score of the external rating of avoidance symptoms (DSM-A) $M \pm SD$ = 1.8 ± 1.7 and the sum score of external ratings of hyperarousal symptoms (DSM-H) $M \pm SD$ = 2.6 ± 1.9. In self-ratings of posttraumatic stress reactions a mean value of $M \pm SD$ = 18.7 ± 10.7 was found on the IES-R subscale for intrusion (IES-I). A mean value of $M \pm SD$ = 13.4 ± 9.2 was found on the IES-R subscale for avoidance (IES-A), and a mean value of $M \pm SD$ = 16.7 ± 11.1 was found on the IES-R subscale for hyperarousal (IES-H).

First Order Correlations of Model Parameters

Table 1 shows the correlation-coefficients between the variables. As expected the measurable variables that are to be explained by the corresponding latent variables correlate highly with one another. Moreover, most correlations among the measurable variables of the six latent variables are statistically significant.

Structural Equation Model

Structural equation modelling is a way to investigate complex variable structures (Jöreskog & Sörbom, 1979; Bentler & Weeks, 1980; Faulbaum & Bentler, 1994). A structural equation model tests the interplay (i. e., direct and indirect effects) of measured constructs and their indicators. It is helpful to distinguish between the structural model (i. e., the constructs) and the measurement model (i. e., the observed variables or indicators). Several tests and computer programs have been developed to study structural equation models. EQS (Bentler, 1993, 1996) provides the most commonly used test statistics in structural equation modelling (goodness of fit statistics) and also tests for adding or dropping parameters like the Wald Test and the multivariate Lagrange Multiplier Test which offers the opportunity to compare different models or groups. The program also enables the use of more general elliptical and arbitrarily distributed variables. This is very important as normal distributions of variables is usually an unreasonable assumption in social and behavioral sciences.

We used EQS to identify and test functional correspondences between posttraumatic stress reactions, coping strategies, and social support within a cross sectional study. The proposed model shown in Figure 1 served as a guideline for our analyses. Using EQS (Wald-Test, Lagrange Multiplier Test) led to the

Matthias Schützwohl, Andreas Maercker, & Rolf Manz

Table 1. First order correlations.

	1	2	3	4	5	6	7	8	9	10
1 Expert-rating of intrusions (DSM-I)										
2 Self-rating of intrusions (IES-I)	.60***									
3 Expert-rating of hyperarousal (DSM-H)	.63***	.52***								
4 Self-rating of hyperarousal (IES-H)	.59***	.78***	.71***							
5 Expert-rating of avoidance (DSM-A)	.53***	.44***	.68***	.58***						
6 Self-rating of avoidance (IES-A)	.41***	.61***	.43***	.65***	.52***					
7 Perceived Emotional Support (EU)	-.09	-.08	-.22*	-.20*	-.40***	-.14				
8 Perceived Social Integration (SI)	-.05	-.07	-.25**	-.23**	-.40***	-.12	.75***			
9 Interpersonal Mastery (INTMAST)	.26**	.38***	.25**	.35***	.16*	.19*	.21**	.11		
10 BLUNTING	.19*	.14	.07	.15*	.09	.33***	.19*	.24**	.26**	
11 PALLIATion	.29**	.30***	.20*	.29**	.26**	.42***	.06	.15	.31***	.51***

*p < .05, **p < .01, ***p < .001

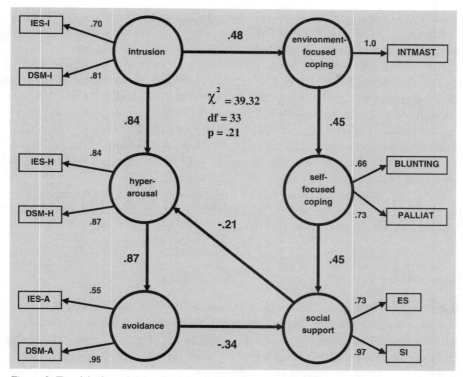

Figure 2. Empirical model for the interaction of posttraumatic stress reactions, coping, and social support.

empirical model shown in Figure 2. This model shows good characteristics ($\chi^2(33, N = 123) = 39.3$, $p = .21$, and adjusted goodness of fit = .96), i. e., the model corresponds well with the empirically acquired data*.

The model includes 5 constructs ("intrusion," "hyperarousal," "avoidance," "social support," "self-focused coping") each measured by use of two variables and the construct "environment-focused coping" which is measured by only one variable. The measurement variables show loadings on the constructs ranging from .55 to 1.0 with a mean of .80 indicating good reliability of the model.

---

* To reduce complexity, we present the model without measurement errors. In structural equation models measurement errors with high magnitude usually represent constructs that are not
recognized within the model. However, in our case only few measurement errors with low
magnitude have been identified. Thus errors could be interpreted as instrument-specific
variances not declared within the model. For a complete version of the model including this
error terms please call the first author.

All PTSD constructs show good correspondence to self and expert ratings which underlines the validity of the constructs. The correspondence between the PTSD constructs is very high. In line with theoretical assumptions intrusion and hyperarousal seem to indicate the severity of PTSD with intrusion effecting hyperarousal (directly: .84). The extent of avoidance is significantly determined by hyperarousal (directly: .87) and intrusion (indirectly: .73).

Coping constructs depend directly (environment focused coping: .48) and indirectly (self-focused coping: .24) from the PTSD construct intrusion. In accordance with theoretical assumptions there is no substantial effect of coping on any PTSD construct. The strongest indirect effect, from self-focused coping on hyperarousal, is –.09.

Social support is affected directly by avoidance (–.34) and self-focused coping (.45). In line with theoretical assumptions social support directly effects symptomatology, namely hyperarousal (–.21).

Discussion

The results of the Dresden study impressively confirm once more that the psychological stress felt by many former political prisoners can be substantial even many years or even decades after a traumatic event occurred. The majority of the study's participants who had been imprisoned under extremely stressful conditions for political reasons still suffer from intrusive recollections and chronic hyperarousal, on average, even 25 years after imprisonment in the former East Germany. The diagnostic criteria of PTSD are still met by approximately 30% of the study's participants.

The relationships between posttraumatic stress reactions and maintenance factors as outlined above show that there are long term causal relationships between the investigated constructs. Thus, intrusion symptoms related to the traumatic event are closely related to the posttraumatic hyperarousal symptoms and are not directly related to posttraumatic avoidance. In other words, someone who still suffers emotionally as well as mentally from memories of the traumatic experience, even many years after the event occurred, develops hyperarousal that leads to exaggerated startle reactions and heightened alertness as well as to insomnia and physical reactions such as constant trembling.

Obviously, avoidance reactions result in an attempt to protect oneself from stress reactions resulting from this chronic hyperarousal. Trauma victims continuously try to suppress and avoid thoughts and ideas that remind them of the event.

The variance in intrusion and hyperarousal, however, cannot fully account for the variance found in avoidance behavior (and emotional numbness)*. The proportion of unexplained variance shows that factors other than intrusion and hyperarousal contribute to the development and maintenance of posttraumatic avoidance behavior. In accordance with other empirical findings such factors may be coping styles (Creamer, Burgess, & Pattison, 1992; Myrtek et al., 1994) and social conditions (Maercker & Schützwohl, 1997) which significantly contribute to the explanation of the observed variance in posttraumatic avoidance.

In order to empirically investigate the role of coping strategies in the persistence of posttraumatic stress reactions we divided the coping construct into two meaningful subconstructs: "environment-focused coping" and "self-focused coping." A third factor introduced was "perceived social support."

The extent of perceived social support appears to be lessened by posttraumatic avoidance behavior. Individuals who try to avoid thoughts or situations related to the traumatic event, show little interest in important activities, or experience feelings of estrangement towards others have reported to experience rather scant emotional support and little social integration. It is conceivable that these people do in fact receive relatively little emotional support as a result of their avoidance behavior since they deny themselves the opportunity to talk to relatives and friends about their experiences and their current psychological problems. Moreover, feelings of estrangement towards others may result in the fact that support provided by existing social networks is not fully perceived. Consequently, those afflicted with this symptomology perceive themselves as having nobody to share their values and interests with and as socially marginalized.

On the other hand, the extent of perceived social support leads to less posttraumatic hyperarousal and thus has a positive effect on well-being. People who feel emotionally supported and socially integrated are likely to suffer less from posttraumatic hyperarousal symptoms. Those, on the other hand, suffering from recurrent memories of the trauma feel particularly irritable, frightful, and overly alert, when they feel emotionally unsupported and not socially integrated.

With regard to coping strategies, stressful intrusions of the trauma appear to act as catalyzers in the victims' motivation to cope with them. Six years after the breakdown of the former East Germany, those who were imprisoned in

---

*   Within the structural equation model presented in this study, numbing symptoms too are brought on chronic hyperarousal. The assumption that those afflicted with posttraumatic stress reactions develop emotional numbness when failing to suppress or to avoid recurring recollections (Foa et al., 1993) can unfortunately not be verified with the constructs used in the Dresden study.

this country between the years of 1949 and 1989 still direct their coping efforts towards their environment – at a time when the general public hardly pays any attention anymore to the ordeals suffered by them. With an increase in stress caused by intrusive recollections of imprisonment there appears to be primarily a need for environment-focused coping, e. g., a need for comfort, advice, and support as well as a desire to report to other people about their experiences in prison including to blame perpetrators responsible for their suffering.

Trauma victims trying to deal with stressful recurring recollections by directing their coping efforts towards their human environment seem to subsequently try harder at calming down and suppressing those memories. Such self-focused coping strategies increase the extent of perceived social support. We consider that the attempt to calm down mobilizes social support and thus increases the degree of really existing support.

In summary, the empirical model largely supports published clinical observations of the relationship between posttraumatic stress reactions, coping behavior and perceived social support. We therefore believe that implications can be drawn from the presented structural equation model that can be of relevance to psychological long-term aftereffects following various traumatizations, although the participants in the study were former political prisoners, i. e., victims of prolonged, repeated interpersonal violence.*

Possible Implications for Treatment

What does the study come up with regard to practical or treatment implications? First, we discuss the posttraumatic core symptomatology (intrusion, hyperarousal) and its suitable intervention. Second, the role of perceived social support and its intervention possibilities will be focused on. Third, we discuss the ambivalent role of coping efforts in overcoming posttraumatic stress reactions.

Interventions for Posttraumatic Intrusions and Hyperarousal as Core Symptoms

Chronic hyperarousal as well as avoidance and numbing appear to be largely determined by the maintenance of stressful intrusions. With regard to the treatment of individuals suffering from chronic posttraumatic stress disorders one may therefore consider whether or not that treatment should be primarily

---

*   This is important to note as various authors have pointed to the fact that the sequelae of prolonged and repeated trauma differ from those of brief single events (Herman, 1993).

aimed at reducing stress caused by intrusions or recurrent recollections. Here, our point of view is that behavioral therapeutic exposure techniques and especially flooding in sensu should be the preferred therapeutic techniques. Both have proved particularly successful in numerous efficacy studies (Foa, Rothbaum, & Molnar, 1997).

Studies in therapy research have shown that exposure techniques not only decrease intrusions but also lead to a reduction of startle reactions, concentration difficulties, and irritability (Foa et al., 1997). This finding is in accordance with the functional relationship that exists between stressful intrusions on the one hand and posttraumatic hyperarousal on the other, as described in the above model. Individuals who as a result of confrontation treatment and the ensuing habituation no longer suffer from intrusions and recurrent recollections following habituation also show less psychological hyperarousal. Efforts to put outside or suppress memories, i. e., posttraumatic avoidance, are then no longer necessary. Instead memories can be tolerated and processed, i. e., they can be integrated into existing cognitive structures or they can lead to an accommodation of these cognitive structures. This appears to be of central importance in recovering from posttraumatic stress reactions (Greenberg, 1995).

One restriction of our structural equation model is that there is no clue as to what factors determine the frequency of intrusions themselves. As noted by cognitive therapists (e. g., Ehlers & Steil, 1995), dysfunctional cognitions appear to be important factors involved in the development and maintenance of intrusions. We therefore propose that exposure techniques should be supplemented by cognitive techniques (Maercker, 1997). So far there are hardly any studies on the efficacy of pure cognitive techniques for posttraumatic stress reactions (Foa et al., 1997). Cognitive therapeutic techniques, however, appear to be a promising treatment method with regard to symptoms of emotional numbness (i. e., loss of interest in activities, detachment from others, sense of a foreshortened future).

Role of Perceived Social Support

The perception of social support has a beneficial effect on degrees of posttraumatic hyperarousal and consequently on well-being. Working on the patient's perception of social support or increasing existing degrees of social support may therefore be essential treatment goals. Thus, the therapy of posttraumatic stress reactions can be effectively supplemented by social skill training. Here, particular emphasis should be placed on the improvement of social skills involved in establishing social contacts and interpersonal relationships (Hollin & Trower, 1986).

However, one should keep in mind that an increase of the perceived social support may possibly be achieved indirectly by virtue of the fact that as a result of exposure treatment PTSD victims may less frequently attempt to avoid memories of the trauma and more often reach out for support from others. It appears sensible in this context to train PTSD victims in their ability to share their memories and to advise their relatives.

Ambivalent Role of Coping Efforts

As reported and in accordance with other studies (Fairbainks et al., 1991; Green et al., 1988; Myrtek et al., 1994), coping strategies studied have little influence on posttraumatic stress reactions years after a traumatic event. This finding points to the fact that at least the majority of coping strategies seem to be not essential in overcoming long-term trauma effects. Thus, the training of coping strategies does not seem to constitute a prerequisite for the treatment of posttraumatic stress reactions.

Yet, we believe that the improvement of coping skills is a goal in the treatment of traumatized individuals. Of course, the EQS-model presented cannot encompass the entire range of psychological and social factors influenced by coping behavior. We believe that coping behavior impacts on the development of other psychopathological symptoms and disorders such as alcohol addiction and psychosocial problems such as unemployment and family problems. In line with the current literature we therefore recommend that coping behavior and the resulting consequences (e. g., reactions to the environment) need to be recorded and coping skills improved (Hankin, 1997; Schützwohl, 1997). Even though such treatment modalities will not, as we believe, bring about reductions in posttraumatic stress reactions we are convinced that they are effective in reducing and avoiding secondary disorders.

With regard to the importance of coping behavior we should like to direct attention to the finding that the course and maintenance of posttraumatic stress reactions may be determined to a great extent by primary and secondary cognitive appraisals preceding coping behavior (Ehlers & Steil, 1995). With this in mind, it may well be another therapist's task to determine diagnostically the cognitive appraisals related to the traumatization and the resulting psychological reactions.

References

American Psychiatric Association (1987). *Diagnostic and statistical manual of mental disorders, DSM-III-R* (3rd ed., revised). Washington, DC: Author.

Aldwin, C.M. (1993). Coping with traumatic stress. *PTSD Research Quarterly, 4,* 1–3.

Amnesty International (1989). *German Democratic Republic – Sweeping laws – Secret justice.* London: Amnesty International Publication.

Bentler, P.M. (1993). *EQS. Structural equations program manual.* Los Angeles: BMDP Statistical Software.

Bentler, P.M. (1996). *EQS. Structural equations program manual.* Los Angeles: BMDP Statistical Software.

Bentler, P. M., & Weeks, D.G. (1980). Linear structural equations with latent variables. *Psychometrika, 45,* 289–308.

Billings, A., & Moos, R. (1981). The role of coping responses and social resources in attenuating the stress of life events. *Journal of Behavioral Medicine, 4,* 139–157.

Boscarino, J.A. (1995). Posttraumatic stress and associated disorders among Vietnam veterans: The significance of combat exposure and social support. *Journal of Traumatic Stress, 8,* 317–336.

Burstein, A. (1984). Treatment of posttraumatic stress disorder with imipramine. *Psychosomatics, 25,* 683–687.

Burstein, A. (1989). Intrusion and avoidance symptoms in PTSD. *American Journal of Psychiatry, 146,* 1518.

Creamer, M., Burgess, P., & Pattison, P. (1990). Cognitive processing in posttrauma reactions: Some preliminary findings. *Psychological Medicine, 20,* 597–604.

Creamer, M., Burgess, P., & Pattison, P. (1992). Reaction to trauma: A cognitive processing model. *Journal of Abnormal Psychology, 101,* 452–459.

Davidson, J.R.T., & Fairbank, J.A. (1993). The epidemiology of posttraumatic stress disorder. In J.R.T. Davidson & E.B. Foa (Eds.), *Posttraumatic stress disorder. DSM-IV and beyond* (pp. 147–172). Washington: American Psychiatric Press.

Davidson, J.R.T., & Foa E.B. (1993). (Eds.). *Posttraumatic stress-disorder. DSM-IV and beyond.* Washington: American Psychiatric Press.

DiNardo, P.A., & Barlow, D.H. (1988). *Anxiety Disorders Interview Schedule – Revised (ADIS-R).* Albany: State University of New York at Albany.

Ehlers, A., & Steil, R. (1995). Maintenance of intrusive memories in Posttraumatic Stress Disorder: A cognitive approach. *Behavioral and Cognitive Psychotherapy, 23,* 217–249.

Fairbank, J.A., Hansen, D.J., & Fitterling, J.M. (1991). Patterns of appraisal and coping across different stressor conditions among former prisoners of war with and without posttraumatic stress disorder. *Journal of Consulting and Clinical Psychology, 59,* 274–281.

Faulbaum, F., Bentler, P.M. (1994). Causal Modeling: Some Trends and Perspectives. In I. Borg & Ph. Mohler (Eds.), *Trends and perspectives in empirical social research* (pp. 224–249). Berlin: de Gruyter.

Foa, E.B., Riggs, D.S., & Gershuny, B.S. (1995). Arousal, numbing, and intrusion: Symptom structure of PTSD following assault. *American Journal of Psychiatry, 152,* 116–120.

Foa, E.B., Rothbaum, B.O., & Molnar, C. (1997). Cognitive-behavioral treatment of PTSD. In M.J. Friedman, D.S. Charney & Y. Deutch (Eds.), *Neurobiological and clinical correspondence of stress: From normal adaptation to PTSD.* New York: Raven Press.

Fontana, A., & Rosenheck, R. (1994). Posttraumatic stress disorder among Vietnam theater veterans. A causal model of etiology in a community sample. *Journal of Nervous and Mental Disease, 182,* 677–684.

Frank, J.B., Kosten, T.R., Giller, E.L., & Dan, E. (1988). A randomized clinical trial of phenelzine and imipramine for posttraumatic stress disorder. *American Journal of Psychiatry, 145,* 1289–1291.

Green, B.L., Lindy, J.D., & Grace, M.C. (1988). Long-term coping with combat stress. *Journal of Traumatic Stress, 1*, 399–412.

Greenberg, M. (1995). Cognitive processing of traumas: The role of intrusive thoughts and reappraisals. *Journal of Applied Social Psychology, 25*, 1262–1296.

Hankin, C.S. (1997). Chronische posttraumatische Belastungsstörungen im Alter [Chronic posttraumatic stress disorder among elderly]. In A. Maercker (Ed.), *Therapie der posttraumatischen Belastungsstörungen* [Treatment of posttraumatic stress disorder]. Berlin: Springer-Verlag.

Herman, J.L. (1993). Sequelae of prolonged and repeated trauma: Evidence for a complex posttraumatic syndrome (DESNOS). In J.R.T. Davidson & E.B. Foa (Eds.), *Posttraumatic stress disorder. DSM-IV and beyond* (pp. 213–228). Washington: American Psychiatric Press.

Holahan, C.J., & Moos, R.H. (1987). Personal and contextual determinants of coping strategies. *Journal of Personality and Social Psychology, 52*, 946–955

Hollin, C.R., & Trower, P. (Eds.). (1986). *Handbook of social skills training.* New York: Pergamon.

Horowitz, M.J. (1993). Stress-response syndromes. A review of posttraumatic stress and adjustment disorders. In J.P. Wilson & B. Raphael (Eds.), *International handbook of traumatic stress syndromes* (pp. 49–60). New York, London: Plenum.

Jöreskog, K.G., & Sörbom, D. (1979). *Advances in factor analysis and structural equation models.* Cambridge, MA: Abt Books.

Jones, J.C., & Barlow, D.H. (1990). The etiology of posttraumatic stress disorder. *Clinical Psychology Review, 10*, 299–328.

Keane, T.M., Scott, W.O., Chavoya, G.A., Lamparski, D.M., & Fairbank, J.A. (1985). Social support in Vietnam veterans with posttraumatic stress disorder: A comparative analysis. *Journal of Consulting and Clinical Psychology, 53*, 95–102.

Kessler, R.C., Sonnega, A., Bromet, E., Hughes, M., & Nelson, C.B. (1995). Posttraumatic stress disorder in the National Comorbidity Survey. *Archives of General Psychiatry, 52*, 1048–1060.

Kilpatrick, D.G., & Resnick, H.S. (1993). Posttraumatic stress disorder associated with exposure to criminal victimization in clinical and community populations. In J.R.T. Davidson & E.B. Foa (Eds.), *Posttraumatic stress disorder. DSM-IV and beyond* (pp. 113–143). Washington: American Academic Press.

Kluznik, J.C., Speed, N., Van Valkenburg, C., & Magraw, R. (1986). Forty-year follow-up of United States prisoners of war. *American Journal of Psychiatry, 143*, 1443–1446.

Kulka, R.A., Schlenger, W.E., Fairbank, J.A., Hough, R.L., Jordan, B.K., Marmar, C.R., & Weiss, D.S. (1990). Trauma and the Vietnam War generation: Report of findings from the National Vietnam Veterans Readjustment Study [Abstract]. *PTSD Research Quarterly, 1*, 5.

Lazarus, R.S., & Folkman, S. (1984). *Stress, appraisal, and coping.* New York: Springer-Verlag.

Maercker, A. (1997). *Therapie der Posttraumatischen Belastungsstörung* [Treatment of posttraumatic stress disorder]. Berlin: Springer-Verlag.

Maercker, A. (1998). *Posttraumatische Belastungsstörungen: Psychologie der Extrembelastungsfolgen bei ehemals politisch Inhaftierten* [Posttraumatic stress disorders: Psychology of the effects of extreme psychological stress among former political prisoners]. Technische Universität Dresden, Unveröffentlichte Habilitationsschrift.

Maercker, A., & Schützwohl, M. (1997). Long-term effects of political imprisonment: A group comparison study. *Social Psychiatry and Psychiatric Epidemiology, 32*, 435–442.

Maercker, A., & Schützwohl, M. (1998). *Erfassung von psychischen Belastungsfolgen: Die Impact of Event Skala – revidierte Version (IES-R)* [Assessment of posttraumatic stress reactions: The Impact of Event Scale – Revised]. *Diagnostica, 44*, 130–141.

Margraf, J., Schneider, S., & Ehlers, A. (1991). *Diagnostisches Interview bei psychischen Störungen: DIPS* [Diagnostical Interview for Mental Disorders: DIPS]. Berlin: Springer-Verlag.

McFarlane, A.C. (1989). The etiology of posttraumatic morbidity: Predisposing, precipitating, and perpetuating factors. *British Journal of Psychiatry, 154*, 221–228.

McFarlane, A.C. (1992). Avoidance and intrusion in posttraumatic stress disorder. *Journal of Nervous and Mental Disease, 180*, 439–445.

Myrtek, M., Itte, H., Zimmermann, W., & Brügner, G. (1994). Psychische Bewältigung von Unfällen bei Lokomotivführern: Die Relevanz von Copingfragebogen zur Erfassung von funktionalen und dysfunktionalen Copingprozessen [Coping with fatal accidents in train drivers: The relevance of coping questionnaires for the differentiation of functional and dysfunctional coping processes]. *Zeitschrift für Klinische Psychologie, 23*, 293–304.

Norris, F.H., & Kaniasty, K. (1996). Received and perceived social support in times of stress: A test of the social support deterioration deterrence model. *Journal of Personality and Social Psychology, 71*, 498–511.

Pierce, G.R., & Contey, C. (1992). *An experimental study of stress, social support, and coping.* Unpublished manuscript.

Pierce, G.R., Sarason, I.G., & Sarason, B.R. (1996). Coping and social support. In M. Zeidner & N.S. Endler (Eds.), *Handbook of coping. Theory, research, applications* (pp. 434–451). New York: Wiley.

Reicherts, M., & Perrez, M. (1993). *Fragebogen zum Umgang mit Belastungen im Verlauf.* [Coping with the Course of Stress Questionnaire]. Bern: Huber.

Resnick, H.S., Kilpatrick, D.G., Best, C.L., & Kramer, T.L. (1992). Vulnerability-stress factors in development of posttraumatic stress disorder. *Journal of Nervous and Mental Disease, 180*, 424–430.

Schützwohl, M. (1997). Diagnostik und Differentialdiagnostik [Diagnosis and differential diagnosis]. In A. Maercker (Ed.), *Therapie der Posttraumatischen Belastungsstörung* [Treatment of posttraumatic stress disorder] (pp. 75–101). Berlin: Springer-Verlag.

Schützwohl, M., & Maercker, A. (1996, November). *Effects of varying diagnostic criteria for PTSD.* Paper presented at the 12th Annual Meeting of the International Society for Traumatic Stress Studies, San Francisco, CA.

Schützwohl, M., & Maercker, A. (1997). Posttraumatische Belastungsreaktionen nach kriminellen Gewaltdelikten [Posttraumatic stress reactions due to criminal victimization]. *Zeitschrift für Klinische Psychologie, 26*, 258–268.

Solomon, Z., Mikulincer, M., & Avitzur, A. (1988). Coping, locus of control, social support, and combat-related posttraumatic stress disorder: A prospective study. *Journal of Personality and Social Psychology, 55*, 279–285.

Sommer, G., & Fydrich, T. (1989). *Soziale Unterstützung: Diagnostik, Konzepte, F-SOZU* [Social support: Diagnostics, concepts, F-SOZU]. Tübingen: Deutsche Gesellschaft für Verhaltenstherapie.

Speed, N., Engdahl, B.E., & Schwartz, J. (1989). Post-traumatic stress disorder as a consequence of the prisoners of war experience. *Journal of Nervous and Mental Disease, 177*, 147–153.

Weiss, D.S., & Marmar, C.R. (1996). The Impact of Event Scale – Revised. In J.P. Wilson & T.M. Keane (Eds.), *Assessing psychological trauma and PTSD* (pp. 399–411). New York: Guilford.

Werkentin, F. (1995). *Politische Strafjustiz in der Ära Ulbricht* [Political criminal justice in the Ulbricht era]. Berlin: Ch. Links.

The Concept of Working Through Loss: A Critical Evaluation of the Cultural, Historical, and Empirical Evidence

George A. Bonanno

The death of a loved one is typically ranked among the most difficult stressor events a person might endure (Holmes & Rahe, 1967). Depending upon the study, between 16% and 38% of bereaved samples have evidenced elevated symptoms and distress into the second year of the loss (Bornstein, 1973; Vachon et al., 1982; Zisook & Shuchter, 1991). Decrements in functioning in bereaved individuals relative to matched controls have been observed as long as 4 to 7 years after a loss (Lehman, Wortman, & Williams, 1987). Nonetheless, considerable individual variation in grief responses are commonly observed and, in most studies, the majority of bereaved individuals continue to function normally and to evidence only minor changes in functioning (Shuchter & Zisook, 1993; Wortman & Silver, 1989).

A number of predisposing factors have been implicated as moderators of grief severity, including prior history of emotional difficulties (Jacobs et al., 1990; Zisook & Shuchter, 1991), previous losses (Raphael, Middleton, Martinek, & Misso, 1993),or stressful live events (Parkes, 1970), specific types of personality disposition (Horowitz, Bonanno, & Holen, 1993; Sanders, 1993; Stroebe & Stroebe, 1987), features of the death event, e. g., type of death, degree of forewarning, etc. (Parkes & Weiss, 1983), and the quality of the prior relationship (Bowlby, 1980; Freud, 1917/1957; Horowitz et al., 1993; Raphael, 1983; Raphael et al., 1993). By far, the most widely endorsed account of individual differences in grief outcome, however, attributes the successful recovery from loss to the degree that the bereaved individual had worked through the meanings and implications of the loss. Surprisingly, however, there is a paucity of empirical evidence to support of this "grief work" view. As the title aptly describes, in this paper I will attempt a critical review of a wide array of evidence pertaining to the assumed importance of grief work. I will first describe the grief work model as well as several recently proposed alternative approaches. Next I will review the available empirical evidence and in particular a series of studies recently conducted by my colleagues and I whose findings pose a strong challenge to the grief work model. Finally, I will selectively review both cultural and historic records that reveal the grief work model to be a primarily European-Western construction that arose in answer to the particular psychological needs of a 19th century industrial society.

The Traditional Grief Work Approach to Bereavement

Grief work has been described as a multidimensional process involving verbal, cognitive, and emotional components. The precise nature of these components and how they might interact have, however, not been well defined (Stroebe & Stroebe, 1993). One component typically emphasized in theories of clinical intervention with the bereaved is the *expression* of "grieving affects" (Raphael, 1983. p. 368). The *verbal disclosure* of grief-related thought and emotion is also typically associated with recovery (Bowlby, 1980; Parkes & Weiss, 1983; Shuchter & Zisook, 1993), as is the *review* and *experience* of the emotional meanings of the loss (Horowitz, Bonanno, & Holen, 1993; Osterwise et al., 1984). The salutary influence of these grief work components have long been thought to stem from their role in helping the bereaved sever their internal "attachment to the nonexistent object" (Freud, 1917/1950, p. 166).

The assumed benefit of reviewing and expressing the emotional meanings of a loss has generally been confined to negative emotion (Bowlby, 1980; Lazare, 1989; Osterwise et al., 1984;), in particular to the expression of anger (Bowlby, 1980; Belitsky & Jacobs, 1986; Cerney & Buskirk, 1991). The persistent avoidance of unpleasant feelings associated with a loss is assumed to be maladaptive, resulting from a defensive inhibition of the "natural release of affects related to the loss" (Raphael, Middleton, Martinek, & Misso, 1993). Bereaved individuals who "show no evidence of having begun grieving" have been described as suffering from "some form of personality pathology" and requiring "professional help" (Osterweis et al., 1984). Thus, the absence of grief-related emotion is assumed to predict either prolong grief (Bowlby, 1980; Freud, 1917/1957; Horowitz, 1989; Horowitz et al., 1993; Osterweis et al., 1984; Raphael, 1983; Raphael, Middleton, Martinek, & Misso, 1993) or, at best, to delay the inevitable onset of grief and somatic symptoms (Horowitz et al., 1993; Sanders, 1993; Osterweis et al., 1984). Similarly, the expression of positive emotion has also been commonly interpreted as diagnostic of a maladaptive denial of the loss, and as has similarly been assumed to contribute to chronic mourning (Bowlby, 1980; Horowitz et al., 1993) or delayed (Deutsch, 1937; Sanders, 1993).

Recent Alternative Psychological Approaches to Bereavement

Despite the widespread acceptance of the grief work view of bereavement (Stroebe & Stroebe, 1987), recent reviews of the literature on coping with bereavement have suggested that the prescriptive goal of working through grief-related emotions may owe its origins more to "clinical lore" than to systematic inquiry (Wortman & Silver, 1989; Wortman, Silver, & Kessler, 1993) and that clinical interventions based on such lore may actual exacerbate rather than ameliorate grief (Wortman & Silver, 1989). Consider, for example, that the majority of bereaved individuals have reported enduring difficulties in coming to terms with the meaning of their loss (Wortman & Silver, 1989; Shuchter & Zisook, 1993). Such a finding is not easily reconciled with an approach that emphasizes grief resolution as a normative end point. Because the grief work approach has been so widely accepted, few alternative approaches to bereavement have been considered. Recently, however, Stroebe and Stroebe (1987, 1993) suggested a reconceptualization of conjugal loss using the interactionist cognitive stress perspective (Lazarus, 1985; Lazarus & Folkman, 1984). Similarly, Dacher Keltner and I have proposed that the pain of a loss may be better understood using a social-functional account of emotional expression (Bonanno & Keltner, 1997). I will next describe these alternatives in more detail.

The interactionist stress perspective. When viewed under the lens of an interactionist stress perspective, events are "stressful" to the extent that they meet or exceed an individuals' perceived coping resources (Lazarus & Folkman, 1984). Coping mechanisms that are appraised as having successfully reduced stress can be considered adaptive (Lazarus, 1985). Importantly, an application of the stress reduction perspective to conjugal loss suggests a more flexible set of relationships between coping and outcome. Further, the stress perspective allows for a potentially adaptive role of emotional avoidance – essentially the opposite of that prescribed by the grief work approach. For instance, early levels of distress are consistently among the strongest predictors of later grief severity (Bonanno et al., 1995; Bornstein et al., 1973; Vachon et al., 1982; Wortman & Silver, 1989; Zisook & Shuchter, 1991). Individuals who manage to reduce their level of subjective distress in the initial stages of grief might be expected to experience the loss as less disruptive over the longer-term (Stroebe & Stroebe, 1987, 1993). Shifts in awareness to more benign content would lessen the emotional impact of the loss (Stroebe & Stroebe, 1987) and provide the time needed to integrate its more painful implications (Paulay, 1985). The capacity to regulate or "dose" feelings of grief would also help bereaved individuals to continue meeting ongoing responsibilities at work and with other important people in their lives (Shuchter & Zisook, 1993). Maintaining social contacts would likewise provide a buffer against the isolation and disconnectedness often characterizing severe grief reactions (Horowitz, Siegel et al., 1997).

A formal espousal of the stress reduction perspective in terms of specific intervention strategies and general guidelines for the care of the bereaved has not yet been developed. Nonetheless, several possible avenues for intervention may be considered. The stress reduction perspective emphasizes, for example, the importance of individual variation in subjective grief response (Stroebe & Stroebe, 1987). Thus, the absence of grief may be evaluated simply as a mild stress reaction rather than as a denial of symptoms. This view, in turn, suggests a more measured emphasis on emotional experience and expression. In contrast to the grief work model, the stress reduction approach would appear to suggest that therapists, counselors, loved ones, and family and friends encourage the bereaved to explore their emotions only to the extent that they might be naturally inclined to do so (Bonanno, 1995; Bonanno & Castonguay, 1994). Further, the stress reduction approach is not incompatible with the use of humor and benign distractions as a means of temporarily escaping the pain of the loss. Thus, those who care for the bereaved might be educated to balance their encounters so as to include a more normative mixture of emotional responses and activities. Bereaved individuals might be encouraged, for example, to focus on the meaning of the loss only at specified, planned time periods, to practice "letting go" of their pain for brief periods of time, to laugh, to watch in a funny movie, etc., as well as to focus on positive memories and experiences.

A social-functional account of emotional expression. In contrast to the cathartic role of emotional expression emphasized by grief work theorists, but compatible to the stress perspective, a social-functional account of emotion emphasizes its mediating role in an individual's adaptation to the social environment and to significant life events (Barrett & Campos, 1987; Bowlby, 1980; Darwin, 1872; Ekman, 1992). Overt emotional expression, for example, helps to inform and regulate internal emotional experience (Izard, 1990), informs others of current emotions, and evokes responses in others that shape social interactions in ways that directly influence personal well-being, relationship satisfaction, and adjustment to traumatic events (Keltner, 1995).

In general, intense negative emotion has been shown to result in immediate psychological and physical health consequences, e. g., increased visits to a doctor for health problems (Dua, 1993, 1994). The consistent experience and expression of negative emotion has been associated with increased stress and health problems (Watson, 1989; Watson & Clark, 1984; Watson & Pennebaker, 1989), with depression (Nolen-Hoeksema, 1987), with disrupted social and personal relationships (Lemerise & Dodge, 1993; Keltner, 1995; Keltner, Moffitt, & Stouthamer-Loeber, 1995; Levenson & Gottman, 1983), with pessimism and hopelessness (Keltner, Ellsworth, & Edwards, 1993), and with conflictual relations (Caspi, Elder, & Bem, 1987; Keltner, 1995; Lemerise & Dodge, 1993). During bereavement, early levels of distress tend to be one of the strongest predictors of subsequent grief severity (Bornstein, Clayton, Halikas, Maurice, & Robins, 1973; Vachon, Rogers, Lyall, Lancee, Sheldon, & Freeman, 1982; Wortman & Silver, 1989; Zisook & Shuchter, 1991). Thus, from a social-functional perspective, the intense or prolonged emphasis on negative affect during bereavement would likely increase psychological and physical distress and prolonged grief (Bonanno & Keltner, 1997).

By the same token, the tendency to experience and express positive emotion has been associated with increased personal well-being and goal directed activity (Schwarz, 1990; Taylor & Brown, 1988), and with more satisfying personal and social relationships (Keltner, 1995). The expression of positive emotion may also enhance social connectedness and support (Malatesta, 1990). Consistent with this interpretation, positive emotional expressions have been found to be most prevalent among individuals with higher scores on the socially-oriented personality characteristics of extraversion, agreeableness, and conscientiousness (Keltner, Bonanno et al., 1998). Thus, in the social-functional perspective, experiencing and expressing positive emotions may enhance coping and facilitate social support (Bonanno & Keltner, 1997).

Grief Work and the Empirical Evidence

The conceptual weak points in the grief work approach to bereavement, combined with the conceptual parsimony and potential clinical usefulness offered by applying the stress reduction and social-functional perspectives to bereavement, suggest an imperative need for empirical study of the role of emotion in the grief processes. Surprisingly, however, until recently few studies had been published which directly assessed the assumed importance of grief work and these have been inconclusive.

Initial studies. Mawson, Marks, Ramm, and Stern (1981), attempted to assess the possible salutary effect of a grief work by comparing a focused, "guided mourning" treatment group and a control treatment that emphasized avoiding thoughts about the loss and practicing of distraction techniques. Unfortunately, they used only a small sample ($n = 12$) of individuals who had lost a loved one on the average of three years earlier and whom they described as "morbidly grieved." Not surprisingly, Mawson et al. (1981) concluded that the expected positive influence of the guided mourning treatment was only "mod-est" and "not as potent as might have been hoped" (Mawson et al., 1981, p. 191).

Taking a more methodologically sound approach, M. Stroebe and Stroebe (1991) assessed the coping habits of a recently bereaved sample (4–7 months postloss) using a small set of self-report and interview questions pertaining to grief suppression and grief confrontation, avoidance of reminders, distraction, emotional control, and nondisclosure. They found that only a few of the items were linked to adjustment and only for the male but not the female partici-pants. Thus, Stroebe and Stroebe concluded that "the view 'Everyone needs to do grief work' is an oversimplification" (p. 481).

The San Francisco Study of Conjugal Bereavement. The inconclusive results of these studies are further clouded by their having been obtained using rela-tively idiosyncratic measures of emotion and coping processes. Given the con-ceptual ambiguities in the grief work construct, a better approach would be to use measures and methods with a previous empirical history (Bonanno, Znoj, Siddique, & Horowitz, 1998). This would offer the advantage of allowing for clear operational definitions and for comparisons with related stressor and coping behaviors. With this aim in mind, my colleagues and I have recently conducted a longitudinal study of the emotional component of grief work us-ing well-validated behavioral measures of emotional experience, expression, and avoidance (Bonanno & Keltner, 1997; Bonanno et al., 1995; Bonanno et al., 1998; Keltner, Bonanno et al., 1998). In this study, which I will refer to as the San Francisco Study, conjugally bereaved participants were recruited be-tween 3 and 6 months after the loss of their spouse and asked to complete a series of standardized paper-and-pencil measures and to participate in several interviews. One of the interviews was designed specifically to assess the extent that participants naturally engaged in emotional grief work in the social con-text of discussing their loss with another person. In this interview, participants were asked to "relate as openly as possible whatever comes to mind" regarding their prior relationship to the deceased spouse. Emotional processing of the loss was measured in terms of both the experience and expression of emotion, as well as physiological responsivity, while describing the lost relationship. To investigate the predictive relationship of these emotion variables to the course of bereavement, a structured clinical interview for grief-specific symptoms was conducted at approximately the same time and again at later follow-up dates. This design also allowed for the statistical separation of experienced and ex-pressed emotion from the general grief reaction.

We used this paradigm to assess grief-related emotion and emotional avoid-ance by comparing each participant's subjective level of emotion while they described their relationship to the deceased with their corresponding level of autonomic responsivity. A *verbal-autonomic response dissociation* was thus defined as occurring when the level of negative emotion participants reported was less than their corresponding level of cardiovascular responsivity. Verbal-autonomic response dissociation, operationalized this way, has been identified in a number of previous studies as an emotion-focused coping response linked to the reduced awareness of distress and repressive coping (Asendorpf & Scherer, 1983; Newton & Contrada, 1992; Weinberger & Davidson, 1994; Weinberger, Schwartz, & Davidson, 1979). We also reported both convergent and discriminate validity for the use of verbal-autonomic dissociation as a measure of reduced awareness of emotion (Bonanno et al., 1995).

In the first of the empirical reports from the San Francisco study, we found no support for the assumed necessity of emotional grief work (Bonanno et al., 1995; Bonanno et al., 1998). Rather, verbal-autonomic dissociation at the 6-month point in bereavement was linked to a mild grief course – low levels of grief symptoms through the 25 months measured in the study. Further, none of the participants in the sample evidenced the delayed elevations in grief often predicted by grief work theorists. Indeed, in direct contrast to the assumed importance of emotional grief work, the prolonged grief pattern was exhibited primarily by individuals who at 6 months had experienced heightened negative emotion relative to cardiovascular responsivity, or *emotional sensitization*.

What about the physical cost of emotional avoidance? The failure to consciously experience and express the emotional aspects of the loss has been commonly linked to a delayed elevation in somatic complaints (Horowitz et al., 1993; Sanders, 1983; Osterweis et al., 1984; Worden, 1991). These observations are not necessarily inconsistent with more general somatic theories in which emotional dissociation or inhibition is considered a form of "physiological work" that, when enacted over a period of time, is "cumulative" and extracts an eventual cost in the form of decreased physical health (Harber & Pennebaker, 1992; Pennebaker, 1989). We found some evidence for a physical cost of avoidance during bereavement in that emotional dissociation at 6 months was linked to concurrent elevations in the level of somatic symptoms. Importantly, however, by 14 months these individuals had relatively low levels of somatic symptoms and remained at low levels when assessed again at 25 months. Thus, individuals showing verbal-autonomic response dissociation at 6 months did *not* appear to evidence a cumulative or delayed physical cost.

The individual differences in coping suggested by the verbal-autonomic dissociation findings were explored further in a second study by investigating the grief course associated with two related trait dimensions, the repressor personality style (Weinberger, Schwartz, & Davidson, 1979) and dispositional self-deception (Paulhus, 1984, 1991). On self-report measures of trait anxiety, individuals categorized by questionnaire as "repressors" report the same low levels of anxiety as so-called "true low anxious" individuals. Repressors are distinguished from low anxious individuals, however, by their elevated scores on an *indirect* self-report measure of defensiveness (Weinberger, Schwartz, & Davidson, 1979). This psychometric distinction between repressors and low anxious individuals has been clearly supported in myriad empirical studies (see Bonanno, Siddique, Keltner, & Horowitz, 1998). The items used to assess a related dispositional measure of self-deceptive enhancement are similar to those used to measure repressors (Paulhus, 1991). Further, high self-deceivers appear to perform in a manner similar to repressors (Bonanno & Singer, 1993; Paulhus & Levitt, 1987; Paulhus & Reid, 1991).

According to the grief work perspective, repressors and self-deceivers would be expected to experience a more severe or protracted grief course. The stress reduction and social-functional perspectives, on the other hand, would allow a broader view of repressive, self-deceptive functioning, one that would include the possibility that such habits may serve an adaptive role in response to stress. Our examination of the grief course associated with these dispositions again clearly contradicted the assumed importance of grief work but supported the latter view (Bonanno et al., 1998). Both the repressor and self-deception dimensions were linked to lower levels of interviewer-rated grief across time. In addition, self-deception was also associated with less distress and better perceived health across time.

Finally, in an additional study from the San Francisco project (Bonanno & Keltner, 1997), we examined predictions from the grief work and social-functional accounts by directly coding overt facial expressions of emotional from the 6-month videotapes. We used a version (EMFACS) of the Facial Action Coding System (FACS, Ekman & Friesen, 1976, 1978) which focuses only on the visible emotion-relevant facial muscle movements that have been derived from previous theory and research (Ekman, 1984). Consistent with descriptions of emotion in the bereavement literature (Shuchter & Zisook, 1993), this method revealed a diverse range of both positive and negative emotional expressions during participants' discussion of their deceased spouses.

Again in contrast to the grief work assumption, but consistent with the social-functional account, facial expressions of negative emotion 6 months into bereavement showed moderate to high correlations with increased grief severity at 14 and 25 months postloss while positive facial expression at 6 months were moderately correlated with lessened grief severity at 14 and 25 months. Importantly, these relationships were still significant using part correlations which controlled for the shared variance of facial expressions with self-reported emotion and with initial (6 month) levels of grief. In other words, when the unique contribution of facial expressions of emotion at 6 months was established, independent of any possible overlap with self-reported emotion or initial grief response, they were still significant predictors of later grief and in the direction opposite of that predicted by the assumed importance of grief work. Further, the adaptive role of positive emotion in grief outcome was strengthened further by a related study using the same participants which showed that positive themes in the bereaved participant's narrative were also predictive of reduced grief at later dates (Maercker, Bonanno, Znoj, & Horowitz, 1998).

In sum, the confluence of findings from the San Francisco study argues strongly against the traditional grief work intervention strategy of emphasizing the experience and expression of the deeper emotional meanings of the loss. Further, the finding that positive emotional expression was linked to reduced grief argues against the traditional suspicion that positive emotion serves as a form of maladaptive denial (Bowlby, 1980; Deutsch, 1937; Horowitz et al., 1993; Sanders, 1993). On the other hand, the stress reduction and social-functional accounts of emotional expression were compatible with these data, thus suggesting an alternative explanatory frameworks from which to guide the care of the bereaved. Clearly, the treatment implications of the stress reduction and social-functional accounts warrant further consideration.

Limitations and implications of the evidence. Despite the strength of the evidence against the grief work approach, however, a measure of caution is warranted. There are several important limitations of the San Francisco study. First, the San Francisco data did not address the *verbal* expression of emotion, often emphasized by grief work theorists (Bowlby, 1980; Parkes & Weiss, 1983; Shuchter & Zisook, 1993). Pennebaker and his colleagues have found considerable evidence for the general health benefits of both verbal and written disclosure or "confession" of thoughts and emotions linked to traumatic events (Harber & Pennebaker, 1992; Pennebaker & Beall, 1986; Pennebaker & Susman, 1988). In the specific context of bereavement, Pennebaker and O'Heeron (1992) found that the more often bereaved individuals discussed the death of their spouse with friends, the less likely they were to report increased health problems.

Dacher Keltner and I (Bonanno & Keltner, 1997) have suggested, however, that perhaps those individuals who show less negative emotion are also the same individuals who are able to discuss their feelings about a loss. We reasoned that listening to a person speak about their pain is usually difficult for the listener. A number of investigators have noted, for instance, that the verbal communication of intense negative affect can produce strong discomfort on the part of "would-be listeners" (Harber & Pennebaker, 1992). In other words, intense and prolonged expression of negative emotions, such as anger or sadness, can drive away the very people to whom one is hoping to communicate one's pain (Coyne, 1976; Gottlieb, 1991; Harber & Pennebaker, 1992; Pennebaker, 1993). This may be particularly true for expressions of anger (Caspi, Elder, & Bem, 1987; Keltner, 1995; Lemerise & Dodge, 1993) which, somewhat ironically, is emotion whose expression during bereavement is most widely prescribed by grief work theorists (Bowlby, 1980; Belitsky & Jacobs, 1986; Cerney & Buskirk, 1991). On the other hand, Bowlby (1980) has noted that it may not be emotional expression *per se* that is adaptive – rather, recovery may be fostered – when emotional and cognitive components are integrated into a deeper understanding of the loss (Parkes & Weiss, 1983; Shuchter & Zisook, 1993).

Another important limitation is that the links between emotion-focused coping and grief course observed in the San Francisco studies were limited to the first three years of bereavement. Previous bereavement studies have shown that symptom levels change very slowly beyond the first year of the loss (Wortman & Silver, 1989). Thus, three years should serve as an adequate duration to assess the various consequences of a specified coping behavior. The three year duration of the study may be inadequate, however, to fully investigate the delayed grief assumption inherent in the grief work approach to loss. Proponents of the grief work view assume that the absence of intense emotion results ultimately in the delayed onset of grief or somatic symptoms (Horowitz et al., 1993; Sanders, 1993; Osterweis et al., 1984). We are, however, currently beginning further data collection on this same sample at the 5-year mark.

Additionally, it must be noted that each set of findings which comprise the San Francisco study were based on samples drawn from the same pool of conjugally bereaved individuals. One limitation of this approach is that the participants across studies were relatively homogeneous with regard to ethnic and socioeconomic variables. Second, these conclusions may be limited by the fact that this was a study of a specific type of loss, conjugal loss, at a specific point in the lifespan, midlife.

Finally, while the San Francisco study suggested profound implications for the use of the grief work and stress reduction perspectives as theoretical approaches to the care of the bereaved, these data were based solely on the observation of individual differences and did not involve direct treatment interventions. Further research using such direct manipulations is needed to examine more fully the grief work and stress reduction perspectives.

Death and Mourning from a Cultural and Historical Perspective

The limited empirical support for the grief work approach to bereavement begs the compelling question of why it had until just recently been so widely endorsed. A cultural and historical analysis can provide an interesting lens through which to view this question. Clearly, such an analysis commands vastly greater attention than can be allotted in this chapter. Yet even a cursory review of the cultural and historical record suggests that the assumed importance of "grief work" is far from universal and unimpeachable. Rather, grief work appears to be a primarily *European-Western* construction, differing dramatically from non-Western views on death and bereavement. Further, the grief work view appears to have arise only recently, seeing its genesis in the great rise of Western industrial capitalism and in the late 19th century's "modern" fascination with the experience and success of the individual (Stroebe, Gergen, Gergen, & Stroebe, 1992).

Death and Mourning in Non-Western Cultures

Certain features of the human experience of death and bereavement appear to be remarkably consistent across all cultures. Indeed, the capacity to experience grief at the loss of a loved one may actually be a defining feature of "culture." For example, archeological evidence for ritualized burial of the dead is often cited as a marker for the emergence of human consciousness and the origins of society (Leakey, 1994). Yet, cultures also evidence undeniable differences in their attitudes about death and in their beliefs about the appropriate expression of grief (Rosenblatt, 1993). This difference is readily apparent in comparisons across European-Western and non-Western cultures. While the Western/non-Western distinction is far from unambiguous, generally non-Western cultures evidence a clear departure from the European-Western emphasis on "grief work" in at least three basic ways:

1) Non-Western cultures to a far greater extent than European-Western cultures tend to share belief in a continuity between the living and the dead.

2) In contrast to the European-Western emphasis on the realistic "work" of mourning, non-Western cultures more readily associate bereavement with humor and fantasy.

3) Bereavement in non-Western cultures is less a private, individual affair and more an affirmation of the individual's belongingness to the larger community. While not all non-Western cultures show each of these features, their presence is sufficiently common to undermine any assumptions about the universality of the grief work view.

The continuity between the living and the dead. The belief that the dead are not lost but continue to thrive in another realm is colorfully illustrated in the folk tales and burial rituals of the Saramaka of Suriname (Price & Price, 1991). The Saramaka are an extraordinary people, descendants of African slaves who were brought to South America by the Dutch in the 17th century but rebelled and against remarkable odds and won their emancipation in 1762. The vast majority of present-day Saramakas continue to inhabit the traditional riverine villages deep in the rainforest, living much the same way as their ancestors had two centuries earlier.

The Saramakas' behavior and customs during bereavement are informed by a strong belief that the spirit of the deceased does not vanish at death but is transported to "the land of the dead" (Price & Price, 1991, p. 45) from where they hold power over the living and may portend the future. A grandmother speaks directly to the spirit of deceased and "admonishes her to release [the deceased] from her mourning, to allow her to cease crying." Another relative prays to the spirit of deceased, "begging [her] to leave her children and other kinsfolk unharmed and not take them with her in death" (p. 47). In another instance, "all who have anything to do with the funeral 'have their bellies tied' – a protection against the deceased's taking others with her" (p. 54).

Perhaps owing to their respect for this supernatural power, bereaved Saramaka are strongly encouraged, even forced, by friends and relatives to let go of their pain and to get on with the land of the living. As in many non-Western cultures, and in complete contrast to the grief work approach, individual weeping and mourning behavior are monitored and strongly discouraged almost immediately following the death. A relative is observed delivering one of the "customary speeches" at the doorstep of a makeshift "funeral house": "You must not kill yourself over this . . . you much get on with your life, forget your sorrow" (Price & Price, 1991, p. 43). Similarly, during the funeral ceremonies, any displays of mourning on the part of the bereaved are again met with a strong reproach and admonished with the familiar refrain to "remain with the living" (p. 56).

The view of death as "a journey to man's original home, not as an annihilation" has been ascribed to African societies in general (Opoku, 1989, p. 15). The contrast of this view with European-Western concepts of the "after life" has been aptly pointed out by Metuh (1982).

The terms "this life," "next life," "after life," "eternal life" are terms borrowed from European Christian philosophy which are foreign to the African system of thought. Life is one continuous stretch of existence and is not split up into the "this life" and "the next life." "The concept of time is cyclic, not lineal [*sic*]. What happens after death is not the terminal, definitive stages of man's life, it is only a phase in the continuing round of human existence" (Metuh, 1982, p. 153).

Belief in the continuity between the living and the dead is certainly not limited to African cultures. Like the Saramaka, the Hopi Indians of the south-west United States, believe that the dead continue to exist in a separate realm that should under no circumstances be bridged with the world of the living (Mandelbaum, 1959). Hopi funeral practices have been described as "small, private affairs, quickly over and best forgotten" (Mandelbaum, 1959, p. 201). Further, while the Hopi may "feel the pain of loss as deeply as do mourners in any society," they dissuade the overt expression of grief (Mandelbaum, 1959, p. 210). If mourning relatives feel the need to cry they are encouraged to do so alone, away from the village where they will not likely be observed by others (Brandt, 1954). After a funeral, the Hopi "try to forget the deceased and continue with life as usual" (Eggan, 1950, p. 58). They show no interest in recalling the memory of the deceased (Mandelbaum, 1959) and have been observed clearly and explicitly avoiding reminders of the deceased (Titiev, 1944).

The importance of humor and fantasy. The continuity between the souls of the living and the dead are richly evident in Mexican culture. The Mexican celebration of the Day of the Dead, however, also reveals the cultural importance of humor and benign fantasy. As Octavio Paz observed, "the Mexican is familiar with death, jokes about it, caresses it, sleeps with it, celebrates it; it is one of his favorite toys and his most steadfast love." (Paz, 1961, p. 58). Perhaps the best, if not the most well known, example of Mexican light heartedness toward death is their festive use of the *Calavera* or skeleton. Unlike the lugubrious use of skeletal imagery in European-Western art, for Mexicans the skeleton is benign, a smiling, dear old friend.

The rich European imagery of death – Dürer's engravings, Holbein's woodcuts of the *danse macabre* – is clearly meant to affright us and at the same time to compel us to repent of our sins. The symbolic representation of death, the skeleton, seems to say: "Remember that soon you shall be like I am, Meditate on the vanity of your life in the world. Your destruction, your putrefaction, is very close to you. It is right here, it touches you!" The Mexican skeleton, in striking contrast, is no spook. It is a policeman, a city dandy, a hired ranch hand, or a bartender. "It is neither more horrible nor more frightening than men," wrote Paul Westheim. "A *Calavera*, though a skeleton, poses no threat." (Gonzalez-Crussi, 1993, p. 80–81)

Each year, in November, during the Catholic holiday known as All Saints Day, Mexicans engage in festive and, what may seem upon first encounter, almost shockingly ebullient celebration – *El Día de los Muertos* or "the Day of the Dead." Skulls and skeletons are everywhere. In shop windows or dancing among the ubiquitous traditional *ofrendas*, makeshift altars bearing "sugar skulls painted with gaudy floral motifs among piles of candies, foodstuff, and images of saints" (Gonzalez-Crussi, 1993, p. 37) are designed to appease the souls of dead relatives for a visit.

The Mexican Day of the Dead is based on the popular belief that the souls of the dead are "licensed" to visit the living once a year, during the November rite, and join in the celebration with friends and relatives. Although the sincerity of the Day of the Dead ritual appears to have been diluted in recent years by an influx of tourism, the custom still thrives unchanged in the villages and rural areas. The Mexican belief in a continuity between the souls of the living and the dead is beautifully illustrated in a rural Mexican woman's reminiscence of her mother. Each year her mother would

> "set up the altar, diligently tidy up the house, making sure the table was set before the church bells started sounding. Then, on the afternoon of the second of November, she would go out to the street and actually talk to the invisible souls in these terms:
>
> Come in, blessed souls of my father, my mother, and my sisters. Please, come in. How did you do this year? Are you pleased with your living relatives? In the kitchen we have tamales, tostadas, pumpkin with honey, apples, oranges, sugarcane, chicken broth, a great deal of salt, and even a little tequila so you may drink. Are you happy with what we have? My sons worked very hard this year so we could offer you this feast, as usual. Tell me, how is Saint Joseph? Did you receive the Masses we ordered for him?
>
> The old woman would talk to the 'blessed souls' for hours. It is not difficult to see how her daughter, impressed by the vividness of this intercourse, would endeavor to preserve the tradition, She must have felt that her mother's soul would never rest in peace, unless her postdeath solace were secured by continuing a periodic dialog she took so much in earnest" (Gonzalez-Crussi, 1993, p. 70–71).

As compelling as this anecdote may be, it would be incorrect to assume that the obvious comfort Mexicans gain in evoking the souls of the dead is completely devoid in European-Western culture. Nonetheless, indelible cultural differences are still evidenced among expatriate Mexicans living in the United States (Corr, Nabe, & Corr, 1994). Mexican-Americans tend to spend more time viewing, even touching and kissing, the body of the deceased, and spend greater periods of time at burials and grave sites relative to other Americans (Kalish & Reynolds, 1981; Moore, 1980). Interestingly, Mexican-Americans also report that these differences in cultural practices result in frequent conflicts with professionals in the American funeral and cemetery industries (Kalish & Reynolds, 1981).

The use of humor and fantasy during bereavement is also a fascinating aspect of the Saramaka funeral rites. For as long as several weeks, the Saramaka bereaved, most of the village, and representatives from neighboring villages, are virtually transported in a festival of drumming, dancing, singing, feasting, and, most important, story telling. Observers report being "struck by the general conviviality and lack of interpersonal tension of the sort that usually obtained between many of the participants" (Price & Price, 1991, p. 57). What is most relevant for our comparison with the European-Western emphasis on grief work, however, is the transcendent nature of this period and the almost complete absence of reference to the deceased or to the private experience of mourning. Rather, the participants, usually thirty to forty relatives and neighbors, engage in a mutual exchange of tales through which

> "they in effect agree to transport themselves into a separate reality that they collectively create and maintain: *kóntu-kôndè* ('folktale-land,' an earlier time as well as a distant place), where animals speak, the social order is inverted, Saramaka customs have been only partially worked out, and the weak and clever tend to triumph over the strong and arrogant. For Saramakas, folktales are sharply distinguished from history; *kóntu*s are fictions with deep moral lessons for the present, not accounts of 'what really happened.' Sitting by torchlight or the light of the moon, the participants at a tale-telling wake come face to face with age-old-metaphysical problems and conundrums; by turns frightened by the antics of a villainous monster, doubled over with laughter at a lascivious song, or touched by a character's sentimental farewell, they experience an intellectually and emotionally rich evening of multimedia entertainment" (Price & Price, 1991, p. 1).

The tales mix the "ordinary with the extraordinary" (p. 21) and "concern central structural tensions in Saramaka life" (p. 23) but, showing little relationship in content to the actual funeral or death. Thus, the duration and larger-than-life nature of the tale-telling – the weeks in which "everyone present steps over the invisible barrier into folktale-land" (p. 3) – seem to place the death of a friend and village member in a larger context, above individual needs and experience, and on the level of larger moral issues.

A slightly different use of humor and fantasy tales during mourning has been observed in the Dahomy people of West Africa. After a Dahomy funeral,

> "throughout the night, and until an hour or two before dawn, there is drinking and dancing and singing. Tales are recounted dealing with themes of the broadest sexual innuendo, for the native [*sic*] view is that this is the time to *amuse the dead* [my italics], for to moralize to a dead person is both indelicate and senseless" (Herskovits, 1938, p. 166).

The infusion of humor and joyous music has long been observed as an integral part of early 20th century, African-American funerals in New Orleans. In the words of New Orleans jazz great Jelly Roll Morton, African-Americans "Rejoice at the death and cry at the birth" (Lomax, 1950, p. 16). Consider, for instance, this historic account:

> "Marching to the cemetery is a mournful and sad affair, but it's an important kind of mournfulness and an impressive kind of sadness . . . They marched with solemnity, with dignity, and gusto. The [secret society] banner was red-lined in silver and bore the words 'Young and True Friends' in huge letters of gold . . . The ceremonies at the grave were short and simple . . . but when the procession was half a block from the cemetery, en route home, the band burst into 'Just Stay a Little While,' and all the True Friends performed individual and various dances, and the sister [of the deceased], but lately unconscious with grief, was soon trucking with the rest of them" (Stearns, 1956).

The transforming influence of the processional music is aptly summed up a musician's account:

> "We'd march away from the cemetery by the snare drum only until we got about a block or two blocks from the cemetery. Then we'd go right on into ragtime – what people call today swing . . . We'd have immense crowds following. They would follow the funeral up to the cemetery just to get this ragtime music comin' back. Some of the women would have beer cans on their arm. They'd stop and get a half can of beer and drink that to freshen up and follow the band for miles – in the dust, in the dirt, in the street, on the sidewalk, and the Law was trying not to gang the throughfare, but just let them have their way. There wouldn't be any fight or anything like that; it would just be dancin' in the street. Even police horse [*sic*] – mounted police – their horse would prance. Music done them all the good in the world. That's the class of music we used on funerals" (Stearns, 1956).

It is important to note here that the association of humor and music during bereavement with doing "all the good in the world" contrasts sharply with the traditional grief work model. Yet, these anecdotes are not inconsistent with the stress reduction and social-functional approaches to bereavement, reviewed earlier, and wholly supported by the findings from the San Francisco study showing the salutary effects of expressing positive emotion during bereavement (Bonanno & Keltner, 1997).

Affirmation of community. In contrast to the European-Western emphasis on individual understanding and grief resolution, many Non-Western cultures de-emphasize the personal experiences of a bereaved individual and instead affirm his or her belongingness to the larger community. Indeed, non-Western and so-called preindustrial or primitive "healing" rites are almost always performed on a communal rather than individual basis and typically involve the sufferer's entire extended family or village (Ellenberger, 1970). These patterns show an obvious consistency with the general association of non-Western cultures with "collectivism" (Triandis, Bontempo et al., 1988). In non-Western collectivist societies, the relations and values of the family and community, rather than the individual, "are the primary sources of demands and rewards, and the primary arbiters of what is desirable, what is permissible, and what is unthinkable" (Ross & Nisbett, 1991, p. 181). In contrast, Western "individualist" cultures are characterized generally by an emphasis on personal goals, preferences, and interests and, unlike collectivist cultures, these tend to be "relatively free of the dictates of family, neighbors, or others to whom one might be linked in traditional role relations" (Ross & Nisbett, 1991, p. 181).

During mourning, when a Saramaka villager dies, the handling of the body, the funeral ritual, and the care of the bereaved are seen as the responsibility of the entire community (Price & Price, 1991). "Ritual specialists" are brought in to manage the funeral (p. 41). During the day of the burial, "rites of separation" (p. 56) are shared by entire community so that the deceased may leave for the land of the dead in a symbolic, "final separation, from the village itself" (p. 57).

The African view of death in general has been characterized by a proverb "owu antweri obaako mforo" ("the ladder of death is not climbed by only one person") (Opoku, 1989, p. 20). For Africans, death traditionally is "not an individual affair" (Opoku, 1989, p. 20), but "binds up relationships in society, revitalizing the living and underscoring their sense of community" (Dickson, 1984, p. 196). Death becomes an opportunity to "give concrete expression to community solidarity (Opoku, 1989, p. 20)." This same emphasis on communal rather than individual mourning has also been associated historically with African-Americans (Kalish & Reynolds, 1981; Marsella, 1980).

Similarly, the mourning rituals of both Mexicans and Mexican-Americans have been found to involve family, friends, and the larger community in an extended "protective network" (Kalish & Reynolds, 1981; Moore, 1980). A remarkably intricate practice of communal mourning is also evidenced by the Hmong people of Laos and southeastern Asia. For the Hmong, the successful mourning of the dead requires a richly detailed set of functions and roles that, by virtue of their complexity, necessarily involve large numbers of friends, relatives, and neighbors (Kastenbaum, 1995). Likewise for the Hopi Indians, ritual activities pertaining to the "maintenance of proper relations with the dead" became the responsibility of the particular societal "clan" to which the deceased belonged (Eggan, 1950, p. 110).

Historical Antecedents in Europe and the West

The continuity between the living and the dead, the use of humor and fantasy during bereavement, and the emphasis on communal mourning form a striking contrast with the European-Western view of mourning as an individual, private, and sober process of working through the realistic meanings of the loss. These cultural differences become even more compelling when viewed through a historical lens. Considerable scholarship is available to suggest quite clearly that European-Western beliefs about death and mourning were once much closer to the beliefs typically attributed to non-Western cultures. These earlier beliefs appeared to change relatively rapidly beginning around the 18th century. By the end of the 19th century, European-Western views of death began to resemble those typically associated with the "modern" grief work perspective.

The "tame death" of Medieval Europe. In his scholarly history of the Western concept of death, Ariès (1981) describes a remarkably consistent European attitude toward death "that remained almost unchanged for thousands of years." Ariès refers to this attitude as "the tame death" and marks its appearance most clearly around the 5th century A. D. and its disappearance at the end of the 18th century.

Not unlike the non-Western attitude we reviewed earlier, one of the features of the tame death of medieval Europe was a markedly reduced boundary between the natural and the supernatural. Historical and literary accounts from this time were replete with references to a veiled continuity between the living and the spirit world, including the spirits of the dead (Ellenberger, 1970). The death of individual, for example, was commonly preceded by presentiments, visions, or ghost-like warnings that bridged the gap between the two worlds. The dead were thought to walk among the living, but their presence was "perceptible only to those who are about to die" (Ariès, 1981, p. 7). The infliction of the great and horrible plagues that ravaged Europe during this era swelled the fears of those who imagined, understandably, that the boundary to the world of death was becoming increasingly permeable. Defoe's (1721/1960) gripping *Journal of the Plague Year* recounts, for instance, how readily natural events, such as a comet or shooting star, were taken to be signals about when and how death would approach. In calmer times, the assumed presence of the dead was part of a long-standing "naive and spontaneous acceptance of destiny and nature" (Ariès, 1981, p. 29).

Another feature of the medieval tame death that evokes comparisons with the non-Western view was an "unconcerned familiarity with the places and artifacts of burial" (Ariès, 1981, p. 29). Considerable evidence suggests that ancient European cultures experienced a profound fear of the dead. Not unlike the Saramaka, it was not uncommonly believed that the dead could "come back" and "bother the living" (Ariès, 1981, p. 29). To protect against "contamination" from the dead, burials were almost exclusively restricted to areas outside the village walls. This practice continued until about the 6th century A. D. but gave way to a new attitude of familiarity that Ariès (1981) describes as bordering on indifference.

The Medieval European attitude toward the cemetery grounds, in fact, to some extent is reminiscent of the non-Western practice of communal mourning and affirmation. Ariès (1981) notes that the roots of the word cemetery suggests multiple meanings including that of an asylum or place of refuge. The Medieval cemetery served as a meeting place and public square. Cemeteries were, "together with the church, the center of social life," a place were "all members of the parish could stroll, socialize, and assemble" (Ariès, 1981, p. 62–64). It is somewhat surprising, given contemporary attitudes, that Medieval cemeteries also served as residences for refugees. Furthermore, it was not uncommon for temporary residents to build dwellings and inhabit the burial ground on a permanent basis.

The age of the romantic death. By the time of the Enlightenment of the 18th century, however, beliefs associated with the spirit world began to fade (Ellenberger, 1970). Educated Europeans began to experience an increasing sense of control over, and distance from, the natural world. Significant advances were made toward the development of true scientific methods. The power of reason and rational thinking offered new solutions to long-standing social and political problems. The great mysteries of life appeared to be within the grasp of "critical intelligence" (Gay, 1969).

By the 19th century, in the context of the general European backlash against the prominence of science and reason, belief in the tame death appears to have given way to a *romanticist* perspective (Stroebe, Gergen, Gergen, & Stroebe, 1992) – the belief that love and the human soul reside in the "deep interior," beyond consciousness, at the center of one's being (Gergen, 1991). For a 19th century romanticist, love was ideally the highest of all human endeavors, marriage was a "communion of souls," and the family was "bonded in eternal love" (Stroebe et al., 1992, p. 1208). In a study of 19th century diary accounts of pertaining to grief or lost loved ones, for example, there was little evidence of the attempt to sever ties to the deceased but, rather, profound disclosures of undying attachment and dreams and thoughts about reunion, either in the afterlife or through a seance or spiritualist medium (Rosenblatt, 1983, cited in Stroebe et al., 1992).

Worldly ascetisicm and the 19th century rise of Western capitalism. The historical changes in the European-Western character of love and mourning through the end of the 19th century evidence a relatively unambiguous link to the rapid economic and social changes of the same era. Not surprisingly, these developments reveal an increasing movement in the West toward individual autonomy and awareness and away from communal belongingness and ritual (Weinstein & Platt, 1989).

Max Weber (1904/1976), for example, linked Western industrial growth to a "reversal of what we should call the natural relationship" (p. 53). He noted the gradual but dramatic shift away from the general communal goal of material security – having enough to satisfy the material needs of oneself, one's family, and the community – and toward the individual ideal embodied by *The Protestant Ethic and the Spirit of Capitalism*. By the late 19th century, romanticism has given way and individual prosperity and financial success had become the "ultimate purpose" in life (p. 53). As a new religious ideal, "the earning of money within the modern economic order is, so long as it is done legally, the result and the expression of virtue and proficiency in *a calling* . . . an obligation which the individual is supposed to feel and does feel toward the content of his professional activity" (p. 54, my italics).

This "worldly asceticism" that informed 19th century Western capitalism necessarily separated the individual from the security and unconscious identity of the greater community. Weber associated the Protestant influence on the capitalistic way of life with the growing "feeling of unprecedented inner loneliness of the single individual" (p. 104) and the removal of the self from the "magic" salvation of communal ritual and safety.

With these developments, we can see the direct conceptual underpinnings of the grief work concept. In the absence of transformative ritual and sense of connectedness to the community and the world of the spirit, the enduring psychological presence of the deceased must be refuted. In other words, the stage was set for the emergence of the idea that mourning necessarily involves a severing of "attachment to the nonexistent object" (Freud, 1917/1950, p. 166). Weber's discussion of Western religious development illuminates this very point.

That great historic process in the development of religions, the elimination of magic from the world which had begun with the old Hebrew prophets and, in conjunction with Hellenistic scientific thought, had repudiated all magical means to salvation as superstition and sin, came here to its logical conclusion. The genuine Puritan even rejected all signs of religious ceremony at the grave and buried his nearest and dearest without song or ritual in order that no superstition, no trust in the effects of magical and sacramental forces on salvation, should creep in (p. 105).

Thus, in the absence of transformative, communal ritual and the sense of continued, magical connection to the world of the spirit, there is isolation from and refutation of the memory of the deceased.

The birth of the psychoanalytic idea. Although Weber's analysis, and in particular the proposed direction of causation between cultural developments and economic trends, have not gone without criticisms (Giddens, 1976; Ross & Nisbett, 1991), his observations of the 19th century's divorce from unconscious communal ritual stand as valid and astute historic observations. Homans (1989) has recently evoked a similar argument in specific reference to the psychoanalytic movement and the emergence of the "modern" view of mourning. Homans' central thesis is that psychoanalysis and Freud's theory of mourning – essentially the foundation of the grief work assumption – arose in response to the West's loss of community and cultural meaning. Extending Weber's analysis, Homans views the psychological impact of industrialization as "diminishing the capacity of individuals to invest representative persons in their communities with the same quality of primitive and unconscious affect which, today, tends to be associated with the nuclear family" (p. 121). This resulted, near the end of the 19th century, in a kind of "mourning" for the "lost spontaneity and immediacy which the social formations and symbols of Western religious culture had built up and guaranteed" (p. 26). The major tenets of psychoanalysis, including Freud's (1917/1957) writings on the "work of mourning," were, thus, "a creative response to disillusionment and disenchantment, for in its farthest reaches analysis is nothing less than the injunction to give up many of the illusions or 'enchantments' which traditional culture had praised" (p. 27).

Conclusion

Combining these various sources of evidence, it is tempting to conclude that the "grief work" approach and the view that mourning must involve relinquishment of attachment to the deceased represent nothing more than a transitive construction of European-Western culture, one that had its genesis in the wake of the industrial revolution and the increasing isolation and loneliness wrought by modern, urban capitalism. A further and perhaps even more alluring conclusion might be that we can now see through and dismiss the grief work model of mourning as apocryphal only because of the contemporary social and political changes brought about by the recent shift towards a "post-industrial" society (the "third wave," "information age," etc.). As tempting as these conclusions might be, however, they are perhaps a bit too hasty. There is still a relative paucity of empirical evidence from which to evaluate any theory of mourning. In the same vein, it must be acknowledged that cultural and historical analyses, in a paper as short as the present article, can only tease the point. Somewhat like contemporary attempts to explain human behavior using the evolutionary theory and the idea of natural selection – attempts that are plagued by an explanatory plasticity or what Gould (1981) has called "just so stories" – arguments based on a few pages of cultural and historical speculation may easily be inverted or countered with perhaps equally strong citations. This seems to be the beginning of an exciting ferment in contemporary research and theory about bereavement. Perhaps more solid answers to these questions may soon be within reach.

References

Ariès, P. (1981). *The hour of our death*. New York: Knopf.

Barrett, K.C., & Campos, J.J. (1987). Perspectives on emotional development II: A functionalist approach to emotions. In J.D. Osofsky (Ed.), *Handbook of infant development* (2nd ed., pp. 555–578). New York: Wiley.

Belitsky, R., & Jacobs, S. (1986). Bereavement, attachment theory, and mental disorders. *Psychiatric Annals, 16*, 276–280.

Bonanno, G.A. (1995). Accessibility, reconstruction, and the treatment of functional memory problems. In A.D. Baddeley, B. Wilson, & F.N. Watts. (Eds.), *Handbook of memory disorders* (pp. 615–638). Chichester, England: Wiley.

Bonanno, G.A., & Castonguay, L.G. (1994). On balancing approaches to psychotherapy: Prescriptive patterns of attention, motivation, and personality. *Psychotherapy, 31*, 571–587

Bonanno, G.A., & Keltner, D. (1997). Facial expressions of emotion and the course of conjugal bereavement. *Journal of Abnormal Psychology, 106*, 123–137.

Bonanno, G.A., Keltner, D., Holen, A., & Horowitz, M.J. (1995). When avoiding unpleasant emotion might not be such a bad thing: Verbal-autonomic response dissociation and midlife conjugal bereavement. *Journal of Personality and Social Psychology, 46*, 975–989.

Bonanno, G.A., Siddique, H., Keltner, D., & Horowitz, M.J. (1998). *How do repressors and self-deceivers grieve the loss of a spouse?* Manuscript submitted for publication. Catholic University of America.

Bonanno, G.A., Znoj, H., Siddique, H., & Horowitz, M.J. (1998). Verbal-autonomic response dissociation and the course of midlife conjugal bereavement: A follow-up at 25 months. *Cognitive Therapy and Research* (in press).

Bornstein, P.E., Clayton, P.J., Halikas, J.A., Maurice, W.L., & Robins, E. (1973). The depression of widowhood after thirteen months. *British Journal of Psychiatry, 122*, 561–566.

Bowlby, J. (1980). *Loss: Sadness and depression (Attachment and loss, Vol. 3)*. New York: Basic Books.

Brandt, R.B. (1954). *Hopi ethics*. Chicago, IL: University of Chicago Press.

Caspi, A., Elder, G.H., Jr., & Bem, D.J. (1987). Moving against the world: Life-course patterns of explosive children. *Developmental Psychology, 23*, 308–313.

Cerney, M.W., & Buskirk, J.R. (1991). Anger: The hidden part of grief. *Bulletin of the Menninger Clinic. 55*, 228–237.

Corr, C.A., Nabe, C.M., & Corr, D.M. (1994). *Death and dying, life and living*. Pacific Grove, CA: Brooks/Cole.

Coyne, J.C. (1976). Toward an interactional description of depression. *Psychiatry, 39*, 28–39.

Darwin, C. (1872). *The expression of the emotions in man and animals*. New York: Philosophical Library.

Defoe, D. (1721/1960). *A journal of the plague year*. New York: New American Library.

Deutsch, H. (1937). Absence of grief. *Psychoanalytic Quarterly, 6*, 12–22.

Dickson, K.A. (1984). *Theology in Africa*. London: Darton, Longman, and Todd.

Deutsch, H. (1937). Absence of grief. *Psychoanalytic Quarterly, 6*, 12–22.

Doyle, P. (1980). *Grief counseling and sudden death: A manual and guide*. Springfield, IL: Charles C. Thomas.

Dua, J.K. (1993). The role of negative affect and positive affect in stress, depression, self-esteem, assertiveness, Type A behaviors, psychological health, and physical health. *Genetic, social, and general psychological monographs, 119*, 515–552.

Dua, J.K. (1994). Comparative predictive value of attributional style, negative affect, and positive affect in predicting self-reported physical health and psychological health. *Journal of Psychosomatic Research, 38*, 669–680.

Ekman, P. (1992). An argument for basic emotions. *Cognition and Emotion, 6*, 169–200.

Ekman, P., & Friesen, W.V. (1976). Measuring facial movement. *Journal of Environmental Psychology and Nonverbal Behavior. 1*, 56–75.

Ekman, P., & Friesen, W.V. (1978). *Facial action coding system: A technique for the measurement of facial movement*. Palo Alto, CA: Consulting Psychologists Press.

Eggan, F. (1950). *Social organization of Western pueblos*. Chicago, IL: University of Chicago Press.

Ellenberger, H.F. (1970). *The discovery of the unconscious: History and evolution of dynamic psychiatry*. New York: Basic Books.

Folkman, S., & Lazarus, R.S. (1990). Coping and emotion. In N. Stein, B. Leventhal, & T. Trabasso (Eds.), *Psychological and biological approaches to emotion* (pp. 313–322). Hillsdale, NJ: Erlbaum.

Freud, S. (1917/1957). Mourning and melancholia. In J. Strachey (Ed.), *The standard edition of the complete psychological works of Sigmund Freud, Vol. 14*, (pp. 152–170). London: Hogarth Press.

Gay, P. (1969). *The enlightenment: An interpretation*. New York: Norton.

Gergen, K.J. (1991). *The saturated self: Dilemmas of identity in contemporary life*. New York: Basic Books.

Giddens, A. (1976). *Introduction to Weber's "The protestant ethic and the spirit of capitalism."* London: Unwin.

Gonzalez-Crussi, F. (1993). *The day of the dead and other mortal reflections*. New York: Harcourt Brace.

Gould, S.J. (1981). *The mismeasure of man*. New York: W.W. Norton.

Gottlieb, B.H. (1991). The contingent nature of social support. In J. Eckenrode (Ed.), *Social context of stress*. New York: Plenum.

Harber, K.D., Pennebaker, J.W. (1992). Overcoming traumatic memories. In S.A. Christianson (Ed.), *The handbook of emotion and memory* (pp. 359–388). Hillsdale, NJ: Erlbaum.

Herskovits, M.J. (1938). *Dahomey*. New York: Augustin.

Holmes, T., & Rahe, R. (1967). The social readjustment scale. *Journal of Psychosomatic Research, 11*, 213–218.

Homans, P. (1989). *The ability to mourn: Disillusionment and the social origins of psychoanalysis*. Chicago: University of Chicago Press.

Horowitz, M.J. (1989). A model of mourning: Change in schemas of self and other. *Journal of the American Psychoanalytic Association, 38*, 297–324.

Horowitz, M.J., Bonanno, G.A., & Holen, A. (1993). Pathological grief: Diagnosis and explanations. *Psychosomatic Medicine, 55*, 260–273.

Horowitz, M.J., Siegel, B., Holen, A., Bonanno, G.A., Milbrath, C., & Stinson, C. H. (1997). Diagnostic criteria for complicated grief disorder. *American Journal of Psychiatry, 154*, 904–910.

Izard, C.E. (1990). Facial expressions and the regulation of emotions. *Journal of Personality and Social Psychology, 58*, 487–498.

Jacobs, S., Hansen, F., Kasl, S., Ostfeld, A., Berkman, L., & Kim, K. (1990). Anxiety disorders during acute bereavement: Risk and risk factors. *Journal of Clinical Psychiatry, 51*, 269–274.

Kalish, R.A., & Reynolds, D.K. (1981). *Death and ethnicity: A psychocultural study*. Farmingdale, NY: Baywood.

Kastenbaum, R.J. (1995). *Death, society, and human experience* (5th ed.). Boston: Allyn and Bacon.

Keltner, D. (1995). Facial expressions of emotion and personality. In C. Malatesta-Magai & S.H. McFadden (Eds.), *Handbook of emotion, aging, and the lifecourse*. New York: Academic Press.

Keltner, D., Bonanno, G.A., Caspi, A., Krueger, R.F., & Stouthamer-Loeber, M. (1998). *Personality and facial expressions of emotion*. Manuscript submitted for publication. University of Wisconsin-Madison.

Keltner, D., Ellsworth, P.C., & Edwards, K. (1993). Beyond simple pessimism: Effects of sadness and anger on social perception. *Journal of Personality and Social Psychology, 64*, 740–752.

Keltner, D., Moffitt, T., & Stouthamer-Loeber, M. (1995). Facial expressions of emotion and psychopathology in adolescent boys. *Journal of Abnormal Psychology, 104*, 644–652.

Lazare, A. (1989). Bereavement and unresolved grief. In A. Lazare (Ed.), *Outpatient psychiatry: Diagnosis and treatment* (2nd ed., pp. 381–397). Baltimore, MD: Williams & Wilkins.

Lazarus, R.S. (1985). The costs and benefits of denial. In A. Monat & R.S. Lazarus (Eds.), *Stress and coping* (2nd ed., pp. 154–173). New York: Columbia University Press.

Lazarus, R.S., & Folkman, S. (1984). *Stress, appraisal, and coping*. New York: Springer-Verlag.

Leakey, R.E. (1994). *The origins of humankind*. New York: Basic Books.

Lehman, D.R., Wortman, C.B., & Williams, A.F. (1987). Long-term effects of losing a spouse or child in a motor vehicle crash. *Journal of Personality and Social Psychology, 52*, 218–231.

Lemerise, E.A., & Dodge, K.A. (1993). The development of anger and hostile interactions. In M. Lewis & J.M. Haviland (Eds.), *Handbook of emotions* (pp. 537–546). New York: Guilford.

Levenson, R.W., & Gottman, J.M. (1983). Marital interaction: Physiological linkage and affective exchange. *Journal of Personality and Social Psychology, 45*, 587–597.

Lindemann, E. (1944). Symptomatology and management of acute grief. *American Journal of Psychiatry, 101*, 1141–148.

Lomax, A. (1950). *Mister Jelly Roll*. New York: Duell, Sloan, and Pearce.

Maercker, A., Bonanno, G.A., Znoj, H., & Horowitz, M.J. (1998). Prediction of complicated grief by positive and negative themes in narratives. *Journal of Clinical Psychology, 54*, 1–20.

Malatesta, C.Z. (1990). The role of emotions in the development and organization of personality. In R.A. Thompson (Ed.), *Nebraska Symposium on Motivation: Vol. 36. Socioemotional development* (pp. 1–56). Lincoln: University of Nebraska Press.

Mandelbaum, D.G. (1959). Social uses of funeral rites. In H. Feifel (Ed.), *The meaning of death*. (pp. 189–217). New York: McGraw-Hill.

Marsella, A.J. Depressive experience and disorder across cultures. In H.C. Triandis, & J.G. Draguns (Eds.), *Handbook of cross-cultural psychology: Psychopathology (Vol. 6)* (pp. 237–290). Boston, MA: Allyn & Bacon.

Mawson, D., Marks, I.M., Ramm, L., & Stern, L.S. (1981). Guided mourning for morbid grief: A controlled study. *British Journal of Psychiatry, 158*, 185–193.

Metuh, I.E. (1982). *God and man in African religion: A case study of the Igbo of Nigeria*. London: Chapman.

Moore, J. (1980). The death culture of Mexico and Mexican Americans. In R.A. Kalish (Ed.), *Death and dying: Views from many cultures* (pp. 72–91). Farmingdale, NY: Baywood.

Nolen-Hoeksema, S. (1987). Sex differences in unipolar depression: Evidence and theory. *Psychological Bulletin, 101*, 259–282.

Opoku, K.A. (1989). African perspectives on death and dying. In A. Berger, P. Badham, A.H. Kutscher, J. Berger, M. Perry, & J. Beloff (Eds.), *Perspectives on death and dying* (pp. 14–23). Philadelphia, PA: The Charles Press.

Osterweis, M., Solomon, F., & Green, F. (Eds.). (1984). *Bereavement: Reactions, consequences, and care*. Washington, DC: National Academy Press.

Paz, O. (1961). *The labyrinth of solitude – Life and thought in Mexico*. New York: Grove.

Parkes, C.M. (1970). The first year of bereavement. *Psychiatry, 33*, 442–467.

Parkes, C.M., & Weiss, R.S. (1983). *Recovery from bereavement*. New York: Basic Books.

Paulay, D. (1985). Slow death: One survivor's experience. In R.H. Moos (Ed.), *Coping with life crisis* (pp. 227–234). New York: Plenum.

Paulhus, D.L. (1984). Two-component models of socially desirable responding. *Journal of Personality and Social Psychology, 46*, 598–609.

Paulhus, D.L. (1991). *Assessing self-deception and impression management in self-reports: The Balanced Inventory of Desirable Responding, version 6*. Unpublished manual. University of British Columbia.

Paulhus, D.L., & Levitt, K. (1987). Desirable responding triggered by affect: Automatic egotism? *Journal of Personality and Social Psychology, 52*, 245–259.

Paulhus, D.L., & Reid, D.B. (1991). Enhancement and denial in social desirable responding. *Journal of Personality and Social Psychology, 60*, 307–317.

Pennebaker, J.W. (1989). Traumatic experience and psychosomatic disease. In L. Berkowitz (Ed.), *Advances in experimental social psychology* (Vol. 22, pp. 211–214). New York: Academic Press.

Pennebaker, J.W. (1993). Social mechanisms of constraint. In D.M. Wegner & J.W. Pennebaker (Eds.), *Handbook of mental control* (pp. 200–219). Englewood Cliffs, NJ: Prentice-Hall.

Pennebaker, J.W., & Beall, S.K. (1986). Confronting a traumatic event: Toward an understanding of inhibition and disease. *Journal of Abnormal Psychology, 95*, 274–281.

Pennebaker, J.W., Hughs, C.F., & O'Heeron, R.C. (1987). The psychophysiology of confession: Linking inhibitory and psychosomatic processes. *Journal of Personality and Social Psychology, 52*, 781–193.

Pennebaker, J.W., & O'Heeron, R.C. (1984). Confiding in others and illness rate among spouses of suicide and accidental-death victims. *Journal of Abnormal Psychology, 93*, 473–476.

Pennebaker, J.W., & Susman, J. (1988). Disclosure of trauma and psychosomatic processes. *Social Science and Medicine, 26*, 327–332.

Price, R., & Price, S. (1991). *Two evenings in Saramaka*. Chicago: University of Chicago Press.

Raphael, B. (1983). *The anatomy of bereavement*. New York: Basic Books.

Raphael, B., Middleton, W., Martinek, N., & Misso, V. (1993). Counseling and therapy of the bereaved. In M.S. Stroebe, W. Stroebe, & R.O. Hansson (Eds.), *Handbook of bereavement: Theory, research, and intervention* (pp. 427–456). Cambridge, England: Cambridge University Press.

Rosenblatt, P. (1983). *Bitter, bitter tears: Nineteenth century diarists and twentieth century grief theories*. Minneapolis: University of Minnesota Press.

Ross, L., & Nisbett, R.E. (1991). *The person and the situation*. New York: McGraw-Hill.

Sanders, C.M. (1993). Risk factors in bereavement outcome. In M.S. Stroebe, W. Stroebe, & R.O. Hansson (Eds.), *Handbook of bereavement: Theory, research, and intervention*, (pp. 255–270). Cambridge, England: Cambridge University Press.

Schwarz, N. (1990). Feelings as information: Information and motivational functions of affective states. In E.T. Higgins & R.M. Sorrentino (Eds.), *Handbook of motivation and cognition: Foundations of social behavior* (Vol. 2). (pp. 527–561). New York: Guilford.

Shuchter, S.R., & Zisook, S. (1993). The course of normal grief. In M.S. Stroebe, W. Stroebe, & R.O. Hansson (Eds.), *Handbook of bereavement: Theory, research, and intervention*, (pp. 23–43). Cambridge, England: Cambridge University Press.

Strearns, M. (1956). *The story of jazz*. Oxford: Oxford University Press.

Stroebe, M., Gergen, M.M., Gergen, K.J., & W. Stroebe (1992). Broken hearts or broken bonds: Love and death in the historical perspective. *American Psychologist, 47*, 1205–1212.

Stroebe, M., & Stroebe, W. (1991). Does "grief work" work? *Journal of Consulting and Clinical Psychology, 59*, 479–482.

Stroebe, W., & Stroebe, M. (1987). *Bereavement and health: The psychological and physical consequences of partner loss*. Cambridge, England: Cambridge University Press.

Stroebe, W., & Stroebe, M. (1993). Determinants of adjustment to bereavement in younger widows and widowers. In M.S. Stroebe, W. Stroebe, & R.O. Hansson (Eds.), *Handbook of bereavement: Theory, research, and intervention*, (pp. 208–226). Cambridge, England: Cambridge University Press.

Taylor, S.E., & Brown, J.D. (1988). Illusion and well-being: A social psychological perspective on mental health. *Psychological Bulletin, 103*, 193–210.

Titiev, M. (1944). "Old Oraibi." *Papers of the Peabody Museum, Harvard University, 22*.

Triandis, H.C., Bontempo, R., Villareal, M.J., Asai, M., & Lucca, N. (1988). Individualism and collectivism: Cross-cultural perspectives on self-ingroup relationships. *Journal of Personality and Social Psychology, 54,* 323–338.

Vachon, M.L.S., Rogers, J., Lyall, W.A.L., Lancee, W.J., Sheldon, A.R., & Freeman, S.J.J. (1982). Predictors and correlates of adaptation to conjugal bereavement. *American Journal of Psychiatry, 139,* 998–1002.

Watson, D. (1988). Intraindividual and interindividual analyses of positive and negative affect: Their relation to health complaints, perceived stress, and daily activities. *Journal of Personality and Social Psychology, 54,* 1020–1030.

Watson, D., & Clark, L.A. (1984). Negative affectivity: The disposition to experience averse emotional states. *Psychological Bulletin, 96,* 465–490.

Watson, D., & Pennebaker, J.W. (1989). Health complaints, stress, and distress: Exploring the central role of negative affectivity. *Psychological Review, 96,* 234–254.

Weber, M. (1904/1976). *The protestant ethic and the spirit of capitalism.* London: Unwin.

Weinberger, D.A., Schwartz, G.E., & Davidson, J.R. (1979). Low-anxious and repressive coping styles: Psychometric patterns of behavioral and physiological responses to stress. *Journal of Abnormal Psychology, 88,* 369–380.

Weinstein, F., & Platt, G.M. (1989). *The wish to be free: Society, psyche, and value change.* Berkeley, CA: University of California Press.

Worden, J.W. (1991). *Grief counseling and grief therapy: A handbook for the mental health practitioner.* New York: Springer-Verlag.

Wortman, C.B., & Silver, R.C. (1989). The myths of coping with loss. *Journal of Personality and Social Psychology, 57,* 349–357.

Wortman, C.B., Silver, R.C., & Kessler, R.C. (1993). The meaning of loss and adjustment to bereavement. In M.S. Stroebe, W. Stroebe, & R.O. Hansson (Eds.), *Handbook of bereavement: Theory, research, and intervention* (pp. 349–366). Cambridge, England: Cambridge University Press.

Zisook, S., & Shuchter, S.R. (1991). Depression through the first year after the death of a spouse. *American Journal of Psychiatry, 148,* 1346–1352.

The Roles of Meaning and Growth in the Recovery from Posttraumatic Stress Disorder*

Crystal L. Park

Posttraumatic stress disorder, an anxiety disorder that sometimes develops following exposure to an extreme psychological or physical stressor, is characterized by three major symptoms: the re-experiencing of the event or intrusive memories of it, emotional numbing or the avoidance of stimuli associated with the trauma, and increased autonomic arousal (American Psychiatric Association, 1994). The re-experiencing and intrusive memories can create intense anxiety and distress; avoidance symptoms are usually viewed as attempts to control or protect against the negative affect and arousal associated with the re-experiencing (Calhoun & Resick, 1993). These symptoms may be part of the natural recovery process following trauma (Greenberg, 1995); this process may also involve or lead to positive changes. The purpose of this chapter is to explore the potential links between PTSD symptomatology and stress-related growth.

Trauma and the Making of Meaning

Individuals vary widely in their responses to objectively similar experiences. Their responses depend, in large part, on the appraisals and subjective meanings they assign to the experience. Stress arises when people's interpretations of an event (their situational meaning) is discrepant with their beliefs about what should have happened and what they wanted to have happened (their global meaning). The perceived violation of these global beliefs (such as meaning, control, and self-worth) and goals can cause severe distress (Janoff-Bulman, 1992). Recovery for trauma survivors involves reducing the incongruence between their appraised meaning of a situation and their preexisting global meaning. This process has been referred to as "working through" (Epstein, 1993), "making meaning" (Park & Folkman, 1997), cognitive processing

* Many thanks to Jeanne Slattery for helpful comments on an earlier draft of this manuscript.

(McCann, Sakheim, & Abrahamson, 1988; McIntosh, Silver, & Wortman, 1993), account-making (Harvey, Orbuch, Chwalisz, & Garwood, 1991), working through to completion (Horowitz, 1982), or reworking (Andreason & Norris, 1977; Catlin & Epstein, 1992). Trauma survivors make meaning by changing either their interpretation of the situation or their global beliefs and goals to achieve integration of the appraised or reappraised meaning of the trauma into their global meaning system.

Following traumatic experiences, many survivors experience intrusions, during which thoughts and memories come unbidden into the person's mind. Alternating with intrusions are avoidance behaviors, characterized by the use of escape as a coping strategy in response to distressing intrusions. A number of theorists on cognitive processing have argued that these intrusions are not only symptomatic of disorder, but are actually a central part of recovery. In their view, survivors can revise the relevant meaning frameworks and complete the processing of the stressful information only by activating the distressing material and integrating it into their larger representations of global meaning (Creamer, Burgess, & Pattison, 1992; Horowitz, 1991). People modulate their exposure to these reminders through avoidance behaviors, but, over time they review and modify their representational schemas to bring their appraisals into accord with their global meaning system. This process is adaptive in allowing people to eventually accept a realistic view of the new situation. People continue to process the information until either their appraisals of the situation or their global beliefs and goals change, so that reality and their models of reality reach accord (McCann et al., 1988).

Horowitz (1991), for example, describes how situational and global meaning schemas change during the working through phase of grief. During bereavement, people may experience repetitive, disturbing thoughts of the loss that intrudes into consciousness. These intrusive thoughts represent efforts to process the new information, although the bereaved may purposely avoid reminders and try not to think about their loss. In time, this recursive process allows them to modify their representational schemas of their loss and the lost person, eventually coming to accept their changed reality. For example, a bereaved person may initially be angry about the death, but over time may come to see the death as a part of God's plan (change in situational meaning) or come to see the world as a less fair and predictable place (change in global meaning).

Working toward achieving comprehensive integration can help survivors of trauma revise and restore shattered beliefs, such as their sense of control and invulnerability within a structure of meaning about the trauma. Situational appraisals or meanings that provide a sense of understanding regarding why the trauma occurred, its long-term implications for the survivor's life, and perhaps even opportunities to bring added value or growth to his or her life can be particularly helpful (Harvey et al., 1991). Certainly, this process of integration does not occur for everyone, and may not occur spontaneously. Many survivors remain in chronic distress, while others seek therapy to aid in their recovery.

Cognitive Processing and Stress-Related Growth

What is Stress-Related Growth?

While the idea that people can experience stress-related growth has been around in popular lore for millennia, only recently has it begun to receive empirical attention (Tedeschi & Calhoun, 1995). Stress-related growth refers to the positive outcomes that people experience (or report experiencing) following stressful situations, either as a direct result of the event, or as learning that occurred through their efforts to cope with the stressor. People's reports of positive changes do not negate the negative impact and suffering that typically follow stressors, but seem, instead, to be an important part of the overall experience of coping with rather than succumbing to stressful and traumatic events. Literature to date has documented the fact that many individuals experience growth following a wide variety of stressors, including bone marrow transplant surgery (Curbow, Somerfield, Baker, Wingard, & Legro, 1993), cancer (Taylor, 1983), shipwreck (Joseph, Williams, & Yule, 1993), and bereavement (Calhoun & Tedeschi, 1989–1990). The types of positive changes people most commonly report following stressful events can be categorized into three general areas:

1) increased coping skills,

2) enhanced social relationships, and

3) deepened or renewed perspectives on life and philosophies of life (Schafer & Moos, 1992).

Increased coping skills include improved cognitive and problem-solving skills and emotional regulation. Survivors often report that they feel stronger and more aware of their own abilities to cope with adversity (Janoff-Bulman, 1992). Enhancement of social relationships involves the deepening of current relationship bonds with family and friends as well as the formation of new social support resources, such as the development of confidant relationships and expanded social networks. Deepened or renewed life perspectives and philosophies include cognitive and intellectual differentiation and increased self-understanding, compassion, altruism, and maturity. For many survivors, the confrontation with extreme stressors becomes a critical point for examining their basic life values, and survivors often reprioritize what they consider important in their lives. For example, survivors often report feeling as though they possess newfound wisdom and a rediscovered sense of appreciation for life, and a better sense of what is truly important (Janoff-Bulman, 1992).

Correlates of Stress-Related Growth

Personality Variables

What kinds of personal characteristics are most closely related to reports of growth following traumatic experiences? To date, a handful of personal characteristics have been identified as predictors or concurrent correlates of stress-related growth. Probably the most consistent finding in the literature is that people higher in the personality characteristics of optimism and hope – those who expect positive outcomes and who believe they have the ability to attain their goals – are more likely to report experiencing growth. This finding has been reported in studies of people experiencing various life stressors (e. g., Park, Cohen, & Murch, 1996; Tedeschi & Calhoun, 1996) as well as people experiencing particular stressors such as bone marrow transplants (Curbow et al., 1993), chronic fibromyalgia pain (Affleck & Tennen, 1996), and bereavement (Davis, Nolen-Hoeksema, & Larson, 1997).

Several studies have reported relationships between stress-related growth and other personal characteristics including spirituality or religiousness (e. g., Park et al., 1996), religious participation (Tedeschi & Calhoun, 1996) and extroversion (Tedeschi & Calhoun, 1996). Finally, women often report experiencing more stress-related growth than men (e. g., Park et al., 1996; Tedeschi & Calhoun, 1996), although not all studies have found a gender difference (e. g., Hettler & Cohen, 1997).

Coping Characteristics

Coping can be understood as responses to stressful experiences. Coping is often conceptualized as a transactional process between individuals and their environment, involving appraisals of whether the situation or event is a threat, a challenge, or a loss, and then appraisals of what can be done. Once an individual decides what can be done, coping strategies are implemented (Lazarus & Folkman, 1984). The particular approach that people take to deal with stressful or traumatic experiences will influence their likelihood of coping with stressors effectively.

Challenge appraisals, which involve interpreting situations as likely having successful outcomes, possibly even with some mastery or gain, have been theorized to lead to better coping as well as to experiences of more positive outcomes. To date, the relationship between challenge appraisals and growth has not been directly tested, although positive reinterpretation coping, (i. e., looking for the positives in a situation as a way of coping with it), has been found to be related to greater reports of stress-related growth (e. g., Maercker & Schützwohl, 1997; Park et al., 1996). Positive reinterpretation coping has consistently been related to better outcomes in terms of adjustment (Aldwin, 1994), and the use of positive reinterpretation as a way of coping may be an important key in determining who experiences growth, in that attempting to find the positive aspects of a situation and its implications for one's life as a way of coping (decreasing the aversiveness of a situation or its meaning) may be a prerequisite to actually recognizing the positive changes one has made as a result of the trauma.

Religious coping has also been found to be consistently related to growth (e. g., Hettler & Cohen, 1997; Park et al., 1996). In particular, certain types of religious coping seem to be strongly related to stress-related growth. A study of residents of Oklahoma City shortly after the Oklahoma City Bombing revealed that positive types of religious coping, including relying on one's personal relationship with God and religious social support, were strongly related to growth related to coping with the bombing. In a study of church members dealing with a variety of life events, the *only* predictors of stress-related growth were two types of religious coping, spiritually-based religious coping (receiving emotional reassurance and guidance from God) and good deeds coping (living a better, more religious life) (Hettler & Cohen, 1997).

Stress-Related Growth and Recovery from Traumatic Experiences

Theories of Stress-Related Growth and Recovery

A number of theorists have described how stress-related growth can be a part of trauma survivors' recovery. Many of these theories share the central assumption that distress is due, in part, to a shattered sense of safety and invulnerability; many survivors feel fearful and vulnerable. These theories postulate that the successful integration of the trauma into survivors' frameworks of global meaning in a way that restores feelings of security and invulnerability is essential to recovery. Survivors alter either their global beliefs and goals, or their appraised situational meaning of the trauma, to reduce the distress caused by a discrepancy between their situational and global meaning. One of the ways survivors make changes in situational meaning is by coming to view the situation in a more positive way (Park & Folkman, 1997). Experiencing stress-related growth can help with this integration by reducing the negative appraisal of the event, thereby facilitating assimilation of the event.

Two types of positive interpretations of the experience as growth seem to be particularly common and especially helpful to survivors. The first involves evaluations of the victimization in terms of important lessons learned and important life changes made in the survivor's own life. For example, survivors may identify challenging and potentially positive aspects of the situation, identifying as "growth" those changes they make in their global beliefs (e. g., coming to view life as fragile and precious), goals (e. g., replacing the goal of financial wealth with that of being closer to one's family), and behaviors (e. g., changing to a healthier lifestyle). The second type of growth entails understanding the traumatic experience as an impetus for the survivor to become an agent of change to help others, and through this altruistic behavior, come to discover new values and new sources of meaning. For example, people whose lives have been traumatized by drunken driving, rape, AIDS, or any number of other problems become involved in – or even create – organizations that affect change on personal, social, and political levels. While initially such involvement may be seen as attempts to help others and make some positive meaning out of tragedy, those involved in such activities, in turn, often report a deepened sense of meaning and purpose in their own lives (Janoff-Bulman, 1992).

Another important aspect of theories of growth in recovery involves attributions, or people's explanations of why the trauma occurred, particularly the search for uplifting meaning (see Park & Folkman, 1997, for a review). Meaning is often derived through making attributions involving purpose (Taylor, 1983). For example, a parent may come to understand a young person's death as a sign that the person had completed his or her mission in life and was rewarded, or as a necessary lesson to others, or as an alleviation of suffering. Negative attributions, such as viewing the trauma as some divine punishment, might also provide meaning, but such attributions preclude the survivors seeing themselves and the world in a positive way. More helpful for survivors, then, are attributions that have a positive impact on the trauma and their global meaning. These are explanations that involve positive re-evaluations of their traumatic experiences and of themselves from "broken" to "transformed," and perhaps, the transformation of unavoidable suffering into meaningful suffering. Trauma can be seen as the precursor of positive as well as negative changes. This is not to say that the trauma itself was a positive experience, but rather that it can be appraised as an important event, as a choice point at which the survivors can redirect their lives in a positive manner (Veronen & Kilpatrick, 1983a).

Stress-Related Growth: Coping Strategy or Actual Outcome?

The reports of positive outcomes and stress-related growth that arise from cognitive processing of the trauma are complex, and can be viewed in different ways. Some theorists and researchers have viewed reports of stress-related growth as a form of coping, while others have argued that reports of growth can be accurate accounts of positive changes that have actually taken place (For discussions of this issue, see Affleck & Tennen, 1993; Collins, Taylor, & Skokan, 1990; Park & Folkman, 1997).

As noted earlier, there are various ways to bring situational meaning and global meaning together, including either changing global meaning, situational meaning, or both. A major way survivors decrease the discrepancy between their global meaning and their appraisals of a particular traumatic encounter is to decrease the overall aversive qualities of the remembered experience. Awareness can be decreased through a number of cognitive strategies, including making downward social comparisons (focusing on ways that one is better off than others), selectively focusing on more congruent aspects of the situation, and searching for positives. This search for positives is a kind of positive reinterpretation coping that seeks to identify positive learning and positive changes that are taking place (or already have). In this context, stress-related growth can be understood as a way people cope with stressful experiences, an attempt to alleviate their distress.

On the other hand, stress-related growth can be regarded as an *outcome* of the coping process, and many people have reported different types of positive changes that appear to be at least somewhat veridical or "real." This distinction, similar to Affleck and Tennen's (1996) concept of "benefit reminding" versus "benefit finding," is critical to understanding the various meanings that stress-related growth may have for people who have experienced and who are coping with highly stressful situations or trauma. This distinction focuses on beliefs about or self-reports of benefits from adversity (positive changes that have occurred as a consequence of adversity) and the use of awareness or beliefs about positive change as a coping strategy during difficult times. Of course, coping processes and outcomes are closely related; positive reappraisal coping is highly likely to result in the identification, and actual formation, of positive aspects of change, and in order to remind oneself of benefits, one has already to have experienced some. While it is quite interesting to speculate on the theoretical differences between reports of growth as a way of coping and reports of growth as veridical reports of change, such distinctions are difficult to disentangle in a given person's reports of growth. However, the distinction between reports of growth as coping efforts and reports of growth as actual changes experienced may be useful for clinicians to keep in mind.

Empirical Research on Stress-Related Growth and Recovery from Trauma

General Relations Between Stress-Related Growth and Outcomes

Most of the studies that have examined the relationship between stress-related growth and measures of adjustment such as depression, anxiety, and life satisfaction report some evidence of positive relationships between growth and adjustment, although many studies report mixed results (Affleck & Tennen, 1996; see Park, in press, for a review). For example, in a study of women who were sexually abused as children, the degree of perceived benefit was associated with three of the five adult adjustment indicators included in the study. When compared with those who perceived no benefit, those who perceived a lot of benefit had higher self-esteem, more comfort depending on others, and less relationship anxiety. Perceiving benefits was not related to views of others or comfort with closeness.

A few studies failed to find any relationships between posttraumatic growth and outcomes. For example, no relationship was found between positive changes and psychological adjustment in a study of people who had lost a spouse or child in a car accident four to seven years previously (Lehman et al., 1993). However, the bereaved participants were worse off in terms of adjustment than a nonbereaved control group, which indicates that the bereaved participants may have still been coping with their loss. Their reports of positive changes may not only have reflected accurate positive changes they experienced, but also attempts to reappraise the situation positively. These very different meanings of perceived benefits (as coping strategy as well as of actual positive changes) may have weakened potential relationships between growth and adjustment.

Specific Relations with Trauma Severity and Intrusion and Avoidance Symptoms

Some studies have found that more intense experiences may produce greater opportunities for growth (Park et al., 1996; Tedeschi & Calhoun, 1996), probably by creating more perturbations in the survivor's meaning system. As noted before, intrusions of thoughts and emotions related to the trauma and avoidance of these are regarded as evidence of cognitive processing, and a number of studies have found that intrusions and avoidance are related to greater reports of stress-related growth (e. g., Park et al., 1996). For example, Creamer et al. (1992) studied office workers who had been exposed to a multiple shooting. They found that intrusions and avoidance mediated exposure to trauma and symptom development over time. In the study of survivors of the Oklahoma City Bombing, cited earlier, symptoms of intrusion and avoidance were related to higher concurrent use of positive religious coping strategies, which were related to increased reports of stress-related growth, supporting the theoretical relationships among these variables (Pargament et al., 1996). On the other hand, Maercker and Schützwohl (1997) found no direct relationships between intrusion and avoidance in a cross-sectional study of former political prisoners twenty-two years after their imprisonment. This could be because in the early posttrauma period, intrusions and avoidance serve as adaptive cognitive processes with which stress-related growth are related, but later on, when intrusions and avoidance are maladaptive, indicative of an individual's inability to make meaning, stress-related growth is no longer related to these processes.

Clinical Applications of Stress-Related Growth

Probably because "official" or empirical recognition of stress-related growth is so recent, very little has been written specifically relating empirical findings on stress-related growth to clinical work, in spite of its relevance and appropriateness. Fortunately, this lack of information is being addressed; for example, Lawrence Calhoun and Richard Tedeschi have written several articles on this topic specifically for practicing clinicians (e. g., Calhoun & Tedeschi, 1991), Karen Saakvitne and her colleagues have been working on a theory of posttraumatic personality change and psychotherapy called cognitive-experiential self-development theory (Saakvitne, 1996) and Lois Veronen and Dean Kilpatrick (1983) have written on the topic of encouraging stress-related growth in therapy with survivors of rape. Other clinical applications can be gleaned by a careful reading of many other works on psychotherapy.

Therapies based on cognitive processing theories posit that recovery from trauma requires survivors to process the trauma-related information until they can incorporate it into their preexisting inner models or until the preexistent schemas can be modified to accommodate the new information. This integration requires some form of extended exposure to the aversive thoughts (Calhoun & Resick, 1993; Lepore, Silver, Wortman, & Wayment, 1996). Talking about the traumatic experience with a supportive and empathic listener may help the survivor tolerate the aversive trauma-related thoughts for longer periods of time, facilitating integration and lessening the conditioned anxiety responses (Lepore et al., 1996). Through these discussions, newer and more adaptive meanings may be identified or created.

Interestingly, the importance of exposure to traumatic memories and incorporation of these has been expounded by therapists guided by very different theoretical orientations. For example, cognitive-behavioral therapists have emphasized the importance of helping the client assign new meanings to the trauma. While the occurrence and the aversive consequences of the traumatic experience cannot be denied or undone, assigning new meanings and identifying growth allows options for restoring purpose and control (Calhoun & Resick, 1993; Foa, Steketee, & Rothbaum, 1989). Existential psychotherapists such as Victor Frankl (1963) and Irvin Yalom (1983) have written about how meaning is created through the choices that people make in facing tragedy. By choosing to positively construe aspects of their experience in a positive way, they are able to find meaning in their suffering (Yalom, 1983).

Based on the limited information regarding experiences of stress-related growth in psychotherapy, the following guidelines may be useful to therapists attempting to incorporate these ideas into their work with clients who are dealing with severe stressors or trauma:

1) *Remain open to the idea of growth in psychotherapy.* As Calhoun and Tedeschi (1991) have noted, one of the most fundamental issues facing therapists treating a trauma survivor is whether growth is possible, and whether this growth might be related to other adaptive consequences of psychotherapy. While the evidence is still accumulating, the answer appears to be affirmative. It is critical that therapists think through their own beliefs regarding stress-related growth. It may also be critical for clients to challenge their own wholly negative beliefs about the relationship between trauma and growth.

2) *Understand how stress-related growth may arise.* In general, therapists should be familiar with the theories and empirical work regarding posttraumatic processes and recovery, and should keep an eye out for further writings on stress-related growth as work in this area becomes increasingly available. The possession of a solid theoretical understanding of how trauma affects the psychological functioning of the survivor will provide clinicians with a framework within which to examine opportunities for growth that may be inherent in the posttrauma recovery process (Saakvitne, 1996). Therapists should be especially aware that intrusion and avoidance are part of a natural healing process, and that through coping and continued processing, growth may also be a part of the healing.

3) *Develop a tolerance for unverifiable interpretations, illusions, and narrative.* The fact that so much of what clients report in the context of therapy is unverifiable interpretations may be frustrating to therapists who like to help clients identify "The Truth." In fact, much of what humans believe to be "true" about themselves, their relationships, and their futures is biased and distorted in many ways (See Taylor & Brown, 1988 and 1994, for reviews).

While helping clients to accurately perceive and negotiate reality is always a worthy goal of therapy, some therapists have argued that *what is truthful* may be less essential than *what is useful* for a particular client (Davison & Neale, 1994; Frank & Frank, 1991, p. 72). Perhaps clinicians who work with survivors of trauma may need to develop greater tolerance for the unverifiable, including the survivor's own identification of positive changes in their relationships, coping skills, and life philosophies (Calhoun & Tedeschi, 1991).

4) *Use the context of the therapy relationship in the service of possible growth.* As clients strive to understand and to create meaning from their traumatic experiences, they focus attention on themselves and their own inner processes. Through therapy, this attention becomes heightened and increases clients' access to their emotions, their insights, and their self-knowledge. The emphasis on the processes of constructing meaning and creating personal narratives allows the survivor's views of the traumatic events to become increasingly differentiated and elaborated, and eventually incorporated with other aspects of his or her self. As the therapeutic relationship deepens over time, the heightened trust and intimacy of the therapeutic relationship empower clients to explore the positive transformative effects of their trauma as well as the negative aspects.

5) *Respect clients' belief systems, personality characteristics, and coping styles.* Clients' belief systems, personality characteristics, and coping styles will predispose them toward particular types of appraisals and coping responses. These predispositions may limit a therapist's ability to suggest or facilitate growth (Calhoun & Tedeschi, 1991). It is important for therapists to set realistic expectations depending on clients' styles of coping, while also being open to helping them shift (or add) coping styles when possible. For example, clients who tend to make more challenge appraisals and to use active assertive coping and positive reappraisals may be more likely to perceive growth from their traumatic experiences, while clients with a less active coping style might rely more on coping strategies less strongly associated with growth and more oriented toward homeostasis.

The nature of the fundamental beliefs survivors use to construe the world will also strongly affect how they respond to trauma, whether they perceive growth, and how much growth they experience. For example, individuals whose pretrauma global beliefs are based on assumptions about the world that are directly open to empirical disconfirmation (e. g., personal invulnerability) may need to modify their global belief system in light of the victimization experience by, for example, becoming more aware of their own frailties, or by developing a more realistic notion of safety as well as realistic plans for how they might protect themselves in the future. On the other hand, clients whose world views are based on religious assumptions that are not amenable to empirical disconfirmation (e. g., God would never give me more than He knows I can handle) may be more easily able to assimilate the traumatic experience, perhaps even strengthening their preexisting beliefs (McIntosh, 1997). In the latter case, less growth may be expected simply because these clients' global meaning frameworks were less violated by the trauma.

6) *Be open to, focus on, and emphasize growth when you hear it.* Several therapists have offered very explicit practices they may utilize with particular traumas. Veronen and Kilpatrick (1983b) have given considerable attention to the issues of stress-related growth in working with survivors of rape. They advocate providing information about the political and social context in which rape occurs, offering general emotional support, gently confronting survivors about irrational self-blame, offering a conceptual framework to explain how rape-induced problems occur, and encouraging them to view their rape experiences in beneficial ways.

Their emphasis on rape as a choice point is central to their treatment. Once survivors cognitively appraise rape as a choice point from which they can go in positive as well as negative directions, they can be encouraged to identify ways in which they can take control of their lives rather than restrict or limit themselves. They note:

> As a part of treatment, a therapist might say something like this: "Now that you have been raped, you are at a crossroads. There are several things you can do. Some of these things restrict or limit your freedom. These include accepting subtle blame for the attack, limiting your physical movement (not going out at night, discontinuing a night course, never being alone), limiting yourself socially (not meeting new people, making yourself physically unattractive), and limiting your growth and positive potential. By doing other things, you can take control of your life. You can take an active role in the police investigation and court procedures of your case. You can set your own schedule. You can explore new avenues for personal growth. You can help other victims. You can overcome what has happened to you." (Veronen & Kilpatrick, 1983b, p. 351)

As part of grief-resolution therapy to treat clients with complicated mourning, Rando (1993) notes that a therapist can use the technique of "future-oriented identity reconstruction" (p. 293). This involves the therapist inquiring about ways that the mourner has grown and derived benefits from the experience of grieving, and whether he or she wishes to continue to grow along these lines.

These choices may be reinforced further by future-oriented therapy, which involves making projections into the future in order to crystallize the chosen values and ways of being (growth).

In addition to these specific therapeutic techniques for working with people experiencing a particular trauma, there are other, more general, approaches to helping clients to identify the growth they have experienced. For example, Yalom (1983) describes the types of meaning that therapists can help clients find in the midst of their suffering, and how this meaning can help clients endure. He noted that, in logotherapy, Frankl (1963) could be fairly direct in hinting and even explicitly suggesting the positive meanings clients might make from their suffering. Frankl typically suggested meanings that were related to one of three primary areas:

1) creativity (e. g., survivors can contribute unique works derived from the experience),

2) self-development (e. g., survivors can deepen relationships and increase their appreciation of them), and

3) attitudes towards suffering (e. g., survivors can try to set good examples, or even provide help for others who may be experiencing similar traumas).

Making suggestions or observations regarding growth may be quite useful for clients who have been working through their traumatic experiences. However, keeping an ear tuned towards expressions identifying growth does not mean that therapists should try to minimize the pain or the suffering of the survivors. On the contrary, therapists must remain vigilant to ensure that respect for the survivor's pain is conveyed. As Calhoun and Tedeschi (1991) have observed:

> What this approach does, however, is indicate that therapists working with survivors must be open to the possibility that participating in the client's construal of benefit is a helpful and useful component of good clinical care. Clinicians working with victims should think in terms of moving beyond the reestablishment of psychological equilibrium to engaging clients in a constructive reconsideration of fundamental aspects of their lives (p. 50).

Summary

Is stress-related growth an inevitable outcome for trauma survivors? Almost certainly, the answer is "no." Can survivors grow? Evidence is accumulating to suggest that many survivors can and do experience many positive changes in many domains of their lives through their recovery. It is important to note that while many people experience stress-related growth without treatment, other survivors may benefit greatly from psychotherapy that facilitates the normal healing process that, for some survivors, has somehow become blocked. While much remains to be learned about PTSD and recovery from traumatic experiences, the opportunities for growth are a promising avenue for therapists who want to help clients move beyond the trauma and create more positive, life-affirming posttraumatic adjustment.

References

Affleck, G., & Tennen, H. (1993). Cognitive adaptation to adversity: Insights from parents of medically fragile infants. In A.P. Turnbull, J.M. Patterson, S.K. Behr, D.L. Murphy, J.G. Marquis, & M.J. Blue-Banning (Eds.), *Cognitive coping, families, and disability* (pp. 135–150). Baltimore: Paul H. Brookes Publishing.

Affleck, G., & Tennen, H. (1996). Construing benefits from adversity: Adaptational significance and dispositional underpinnings. *Journal of Personality, 64,* 899–922.

Aldwin, C.M. (1994). *Stress, coping, and development: An integrative perspective.* New York: Guilford.

American Psychiatric Association (1994). *Diagnostic and Statistical Manual, Fourth Edition.* Washington, DC: Author.

Andreason, N.J.C., & Norris, A.S. (1977). Long-term adjustment and adaptation mechanisms in severely burned adults. In R.H. Moos (Ed.), *Coping with physical illness* (pp. 149–166). New York: Plenum.

Calhoun, K.S., & Resick, P.A. (1993). Posttraumatic stress disorder. In D.H. Barlow (Ed.), *Clinical handbook of psychological disorders* (2nd ed., pp. 49–98). New York: Guilford.

Calhoun, L.G., & Tedeschi, R.G. (1989–1990). Positive aspects of critical life problems: Recollections of grief. *Omega, 29,* 265–272.

Calhoun, L.G., & Tedeschi, R.G. (1991). Perceiving benefits in traumatic events: Some issues for practicing psychologists. *The Journal of Training and Practice in Professional Psychology, 5,* 45–52.

Catlin, G., & Epstein, S. (1992). Unforgettable experiences: The relation of life events to basic beliefs about self and world. *Social Cognition, 10,* 189–209.

Collins, R.L., Taylor, S.E., & Skokan, L.A. (1990). A better world or a shattered vision? Changes in life perspectives following victimization. *Social Cognition, 8,* 263–285.

Creamer, M., Burgess, P., & Pattison, P. (1992). Reaction to trauma: A cognitive processing model. *Journal of Abnormal Psychology, 101,* 452–459.

Curbow, B. Somerfield, M.R., Baker, F., Wingard, J.R., & Legro, M.W. (1993). Personal changes, dispositional optimism, and psychological adjustment to bone marrow transplantation. *Journal of Behavioral Medicine, 5,* 423–443.

Davis, C.G., Nolen-Hoeksema, S., & Larson, J. (under review). *Making sense of loss and growing from the experience: Two construals of meaning.* Unpublished manuscript.

Davison, G.C., & Neale, J.M. (1994). *Abnormal Psychology* (6th ed.). New York: Wiley.

Epstein, S. (1993). Bereavement from the perspective of cognitive-experiential self-theory. In M.S. Stroebe, W. Stroebe, & R.O. Hansson (Eds.), *Handbook of bereavement: Theory, research, and intervention* (pp. 112–125). New York: Cambridge University Press.

Foa, E.B., Steketee, G., Rothbaum, B.O. (1989). Behavioral/cognitive conceptualizations of posttraumatic stress disorder. *Behavior Therapy, 20,* 155–176.

Frank, J.D., & Frank, J.B. (1991). *Persuasion and healing: A comparative study of psychotherapy.* Baltimore: Johns Hopkins.

Frankl, V. (1963). *Man's search for meaning: An introduction to logotherapy.* New York: Pocket Books.

Greenberg, M. (1995). Cognitive processing of traumas: The role of intrusive thoughts and reappraisals. *Journal of Applied Social Psychology, 25,* 1262–1296.

Harvey, J.H., Orbuch, T.L., Chwalisz, K.D., & Garwood, G. (1991). Coping with sexual assault: The roles of account-making and confiding. *Journal of Traumatic Stress, 4,* 515–531.

Hettler, T., & Cohen, L.H. (1997). *Religious coping and stress-related growth in a sample of church-goers.* Unpublished manuscript.

Horowitz, M.J. (1982). Stress response syndromes and their treatment. In L. Goldberger & S. Breznitz (Eds.), *Handbook of stress* (pp. 711–732). New York: Free Press.

Horowitz, M. (1991). Person schemas. In M. Horowitz (Ed.), *Person schemas and maladaptive interpersonal patterns* (pp. 13–31). Chicago: University of Chicago Press.

Joseph, S., Williams, R., & Yule, W. (1993). Changes in outlook following disaster: The preliminary development of a measure to assess positive and negative responses. *Journal of Traumatic Stress, 6,* 271–279.

Janoff-Bulman, R. (1992). *Shattered assumptions: Towards a new psychology of trauma.* New York: Free Press.

Lazarus, R.S., & Folkman, S. (1984). *Stress, appraisal, and coping.* New York: Springer-Verlag.

Lehman, D., Davis, C., DeLongis, A., Wortman, C., Bluck, S., Mandel, D., & Ellard, J. (1993). Positive and negative life changes following bereavement and their relations to adjustment. *Journal of Social and Clinical Psychology, 12,* 90–112.

Lepore, S.J., Silver, R.C., Wortman, C.B., & Wayment, H.A. (1996). Social constraints, intrusive thoughts, and depressive symptoms among bereaved mothers. *Journal of Personality and Social Psychology, 70,* 271–282.

Maercker, A., & Schützwohl, M. (June, 1997). *Posttraumatic personal growth: Speculations and empirical findings.* Paper presented at the Fifth European Conference on Traumatic Stress, Maastricht.

McCann, I.L., Sakheim, D.K., & Abrahamson, D.J. (1988). Trauma and victimization: A model of psychological adaptation. *Counseling Psychologist, 16,* 531–594.

McIntosh, D.N. (1997). Religion-as-schema, with implications for the relation between religion and coping. In B. Spilka & D.N. McIntosh (Eds.), *The psychology of religion: Theoretical approaches* (pp. 171–183). Boulder, CO: Westview Press.

McIntosh, D.N., Silver, R., & Wortman, C.B. (1993). Religion's role in adjustment to a negative life event: Coping with the loss of a child. *Journal of Personality and Social Psychology, 65,* 812–821.

Pargament, K.I., Smith, B., Koenig, H. (1996). *Religious coping with the Oklahoma City Bombing: The Brief RCOPE.* Paper presented at Annual Convention of the American Psychological Association, Toronto, August.

Park, C.L., Cohen, L.H., & Murch, R. (1996). Assessment and prediction of stress-related growth. *Journal of Personality, 64,* 71–105.

Park, C.L., & Folkman, S. (1997). The role of meaning in the context of stress and coping. *General Review of Psychology, 1,* 115–144.

Rando, T.A. (1993). *Treatment of complicated mourning*. Champaign, IL: Research Press.

Saakvitne, K. (August, 1996). *Trauma and healing: A model of transformation and growth*. Paper presented at the Annual Meeting of the American Psychological Association, Toronto.

Schaefer, J.A., & Moos, R.H. (1992). Life crises and personal growth. In B. Carpenter (Ed.), *Personal coping: Theory, research, and application* (pp. 149–170). Westport, CT: Praeger.

Taylor, S.E. (1983). Adjustment to threatening events: A theory of cognitive adaption. *American Psychologist, 38,* 1161–1173.

Taylor, S.E., & Brown, J.D. (1988). Illusion and well-being: A social psychological perspective on mental health. *Psychological Bulletin, 103,* 193–210.

Taylor, S.E., & Brown, J.D. (1994). Positive illusion and well-being revisited: Separating fiction from fact. *Psychological Bulletin, 116,* 21–27.

Tedeschi, R.G., & Calhoun, L.G. (1995). *Trauma and transformation: Growth in the aftermath of suffering*. Thousand Oaks, CA: Sage.

Tedeschi, R.G., & Calhoun, L.G. (1996). The Posttraumatic Growth Inventory: Measuring the positive legacy of trauma. *Journal of Traumatic Stress, 9,* 455–471.

Veronen, L.J., & Kilpatrick, D.G. (1983a). Rape: A precursor of change. In E. Callahan & R. McCluskey (Eds.), *Life-span development psychology: Nonnormative life events* (pp. 167–191). New York: Academic Press.

Veronen, L.J., & Kilpatrick, D.G. (1983b). Stress management for rape victims. In D. Meichenbaum & M.E. Jaremko (Eds.), *Stress reduction and prevention* (pp. 341–374). New York: Plenum.

Yalom, I.D. (1983). *Existential psychotherapy*. New York: Basic Books.